LEO TOLSTOY

BY
DRAGAN MILIVOJEVIC

EAST EUROPEAN MONOGRAPHS, BOULDER

DISTRIBUTED BY COLUMBIA UNIVERSITY PRESS, NEW YORK

1998

EAST EUROPEAN MONOGRAPHS, NO. DXVIII

1002390085

T

Leo Tolstoy

CONTENTS

Title .... *Page*

Introduction .... *i*

Dragan Milivojevic
Tolstoy's Views on Buddhism 1

Vytas Dukas and Glenn A. Sandstrom
Taoistic Patterns in *War and Peace* 19

Dragan Milivojevic
Some Buddhist Inklings in Prince Andrei and Pierre Bezukhov
in *War and Peace* 33

Harry Hill Walsh
A Buddhist Leitmotif in Anna Karenina 41

Dragan Milivojevic
Tolstoy's Concept of Reason as Applied to Buddhism 49

Nathan T. Carr
Leo Tolstoy and Lao Tzu's *Tao-Te Ching*: Tolstoy as a Taoist Sage 61

Dragan Milivojevic
Some Similarities and Differences Between Tolstoy's Concepts
of Identity and Vocation and Their Parallels in Hinduism 77

A. Syrkin
The "Indian" in Tolstoy 85

Dragan Milivojevic, Translated by
Life and Teaching of Siddhartha Gautama called The Buddha,
that is, The Most Perfect One 115

Dragan Milivojevic, Translated by
Siddhartha, Called the Buddha, That is the Holy One...
His Life and His Teaching 141

Dragan Milivojevic, Translated by
Sunday Reading...*The Buddha* 157

Dragan Milivojevic, Translated by
Kunala's Eyes 163

Dragan Milivojevic, Translated by
It Is You 165

Dragan Milivojevic, Translated by
Mi-Ti...A Chinese Philosopher...The Teaching
of All-Embracing Love 169

Sources 181

INTRODUCTION

The aim of this book is to gather different aspects of Tolstoy's interest and involvement in Oriental religions: Buddhism, Hinduism, Taoism and the Chinese teaching of all-embracing love by Mi-Ti. This collection consists of two parts: articles dealing with the influence of and parallels between Oriental religions, and Tolstoy's concept of religion and philosophy formulated by him and conceived in an artistic way in his fiction and his popular summaries of Oriental religions, primarily Buddhism.

The first article in this collection by Dragan Milivojevic "Tolstoy's Views on Buddhism" presents a summary of Tolstoy's different and often contradictory statements and assessments of Buddhism and his comparison of Buddhism to Christianity. Influenced by Western scholars of Buddhism Tolstoy considered Buddhism to be a pessimistic and nihilistic teaching. His attraction to Buddhism was based on what he considered to be the absence of dogmas and the rational character of its message.

Vitas Dukas and Glenn A. Sandstrom in "Taoistic Pattern in *War and Peace*" bring up parallels and similarities between the characters of Platon Karataev and Kutuzov in *War and Peace* and an ideal Taoist sage. The authors find a broad overall range of analogies between *War and Peace* and Tao Te Ching.

Dragan Milivojevic in his article entitled "Some Buddhist Inklings in Prince Andrei and Pierre Bezukhov in *War and Peace*" describes the peak experiences of these two characters which result in the loss of ego and a merging with the universal spirit. They can be characterized in two different ways: as the externalization of the internal and the internalization of the external. These concepts are elucidated in Zen Buddhist mediation to which the experience of these two characters in *War and Peace* may be compared.

Harry Hill Walsh in "A Buddhist Leitmotif in *Anna Karenina*" elaborates on the candle image which is produced at four junctures leading up to Karenina's suicide. He presents different interpretations of this image by Tolstoy scholars and concludes by presenting his own. According to Walsh, Tolstoy was influenced by a false etymology of the word Nirvana as blowing out light, tantamount to blowing out life. In chapter 26 of *Anna Karenina*, Anna's foreboding of death is accompanied by the blowing out of a candle.

Dragan Milivojevic in "Tolstoy's Concept of Reason as Applied to Buddhism" discusses the term 'Reason' used in Tolstoy's rendition of Buddha's life and teaching. Religion, according to Tolstoy, should be based on two basic concepts – faith and reason. 'Reason' with a capital R is an all-embracing divine Reason and our human reasons are a part of the divine Reason. Buddha, in his emancipation from the fossilized and ritualistic hinduism, evolved his teaching of Buddhism by using his reason and by postulating a teaching and a religion based on its primacy.

Nathan T. Carr's article "Lao Tolstoy and Lao Tzu's Tao-Te-Ching: Tolstoy as a Taoist Sage" expands on Dukas' and Sandstrom's article "Taoistic Pattern in *War and Peace*" by comparing Tolstoy, himself, to a Taoist sage on the strength of his qualities of humility, non-violence and simplicity. Carr quotes Taoist commandments for a sage and finds that Tolstoy practiced them and lived up to them in his personal life: his opposition to violence, his love of mankind, his dislike of artificial life and his desire to live a simple life are well-known Taoist precepts.

Dragan Milivojevic in "Some Similarities and Differences Between Tolstoy's Concepts of Identity and Vocation and Their Parallels in Hinduism" analyzes these two concepts which were introduced by Gustafson who applies them to Tolstoy's understanding of Christianity. Identity can be located in one of the two conceptions of the self, "the animal self" or "the spiritual self." Vocation for Tolstoy means to do the will of God, it is selfless action which does not plan, calculate and deliberate. Tolstoy found an affinity to his views in Neo-Hinduism and its foremost representative Vivekananda and the teaching of 'bhakti' (loving devotion).

A. Syrkin in "The 'Indian' in Tolstoy" examines in great detail one aspect of Tolstoy's life which resembles the custom of old men in India to depart from their homes leaving their wives, children and possessions and to retreat to a secluded forest in order to meditate on the meaning of their lives. The author finds plentiful evidence in Tolstoy's private correspondence for his desire and plan to realize this idea. One of his inspirations was the example of Buddha who departed from his family to seek deliverance from the world full of suffering. As the years went by, Tolstoy's desire to leave him became ever stronger and was finally realized by his final departure undertaken shortly before his death.

Translated Writing of Tolstoy and his Editors
Tolstoy's and Bulanzhe's biography of Buddha's life "Life and Teaching of Siddartha Gautama Called The Buddha that is The Most Perfect One," is a popular narrative addressed to a large reading public. In the letter to the editor of the journal "The Life for Everybody," which accompanies this narrative, Tolstoy mentions that it is not intended to be a learned discourse on Buddhism but "...the very essence of the religious-moral teaching of Buddhism...in the full breadth of its meaning in a manner understandable and accessible to even the most unprepared reader." The narrative sums up the most important events in Buddha's life and it is characterized by Tolstoy's rational approach to religion which consists in the rejection of dogmas and rituals, and in the emphasis on the philosophical and ethical essence of religious teaching. Buddha in Tolstoy's narrative turns his back on Hinduism with its elaborate rituals and he becomes a founder of a new religion, Buddhism, based on the absence of meaningless traditions of worship and on a reliance on reason. In a way, this explanation mirrors Tolstoy's own rejection of the Russian Orthodox Church and his attempt to establish a syncretic system of religious and philosophical beliefs.

The other narrative of Buddha's life "Siddartha Called Buddha, that is The Holy One, His Life and Teaching" appeared six years after Tolstoy's death in Chertkov's edition. Tolstoy's close friend and collaborator repeats in greater detail events from Buddha's life from the previous Tolstoy and Bulanzhe account. The tone of the narrative is more lyrical and less polemical. It describes Buddha's childhood, youth and marriage and his first encounter with suffering in the shooting of a swan whom Buddha nourishes back to health. The narrative describes in lyrical detail Buddha's isolation in his father's palace from any encounter with unpleasant aspects of life such as sickness, old age and death. It ends before Buddha's outing where he would encounter sickness, old age and death.

Tolstoy's "Sunday Reading, the Buddha" presents in a succinct way Buddha's life from his miraculous birth to his natural death. It is a continuation of...Buddha...The Holy One...." It narrates Buddha's outing from his father's palace and his meeting with a sick man, an old man and a dead man. The realization that all of humanity is subject to the same fate of sickness, old age and death was an impetus for Buddha to preach his doctrine of salvation.

Tolstoy in "Kunala's Eyes" adapts a Buddhist legend about a prince whose eyes were gouged at the behest of his jealous stepmother. The gist of the story is that the ultimate truth about life and death can only be realized with the spiritual eye and without the help of our sense. The prince becomes enlightened and his sight is restored. The story conforms to Tolstoy's belief in the superiority of the spiritual self to the carnal self.

In "It is You," Tolstoy's adaptation of an Oriental legend, the principle of non-violence is expounded. In a dialogue between a wise man and a tyrant the wise man convinces the tyrant of the unity of mankind. The tyrant is about to execute one of his enemies but realizes that the person he is about to execute is actually himself. There is no difference between the two men in their essential humanity.

Tolstoy was attracted to the Chinese philosopher Mi-Ti (referred to as Mo-Tzu in English transcription) because of the similarity between Tolstoy's 'Love principle' and Mi-Ti's teaching of All-Embracing Love (Universal Love in English speaking publications). Mi-Ti argues that wars and dissensions in society can be eliminated following All-Embracing Love. The starting point for realizing the All-Embracing Love should be a family. From it, it will radiate further in all directions influencing all human relations: between a ruler and his subjects, fathers and sons, robbers and their victims, etc. The result will be an improvement of society leading to peace and order.

Tolstoy's choice of translated literature from different religious traditions conforms to his own ideas and predilections: rationality in religion, love as a basic ethical and religious principle, and the duality of human personality in spiritual and carnal selves whereby the primacy of the spiritual self is emphasized.

CHAPTER ONE

TOLSTOY'S VIEWS ON BUDDHISM
Dragan Milivojevic, University of Oklahoma

The aim of this article is to present some of the most significant Tolstoyan opinions and beliefs on Buddhism, to account for the sources of these beliefs and to make a critique of their adequacy in light of a full knowledge of Buddhist teaching.

Any attempt at summary or systematization of Tolstoy's views on Buddhism should define more narrowly their nature. Tolstoy's views and opinions on the Buddhist religion are not scholarly pronouncements based on long years of painstaking and minute research on which elaborate points of religious doctrine are either accepted or refuted. His initial impetus to read and study Buddhism as well as other religions was born out of an existential quest which often turned into polemics when certain aspects of religious teaching did not conform to what religion, in Tolstoy's opinion, should teach. Tolstoy had his own views on religion and his views and opinions on Buddhism and other religions are influenced by whether Buddhist teachings and doctrines corroborate his views. This does not mean that Tolstoy did not learn anything from Buddhism and that he did not include any Buddhist beliefs into the core of his creed. Tolstoy adopted the Buddhist concept of Karma in its totality. There is a curious dialectic in Tolstoy's approach to Buddhism whereby Tolstoy's own ideas are somewhat transformed and the product of this confrontation is a new synthesis of Tolstoyan and Buddhist beliefs. This dialectic of Tolstoy vs. Buddhism was not static since Tolstoy's views on religion in general and

Buddhism in particular changed throughout his life. The doubting Tolstoy in *Confession* of 1879 is different from Tolstoy in "What is Religion" in 1902.[1] Because of the nature of Tolstoy's dialectical thinking on religion and its evolution no internal consistency of his views on Buddhism could be found. On different occasions he both extolled and criticized different aspects of Buddhism.

Tolstoy's views on Buddhism also depended on the nature of Buddhist sources available to him as well as on the commentaries of Buddhist 19th century scholars whom he read and who influenced him. The 19th century was a period of discovery of the oriental religious heritage. The most prominent 19th century Buddhist scholars, among them Eugene Burnouf, Carl Koppen, Friedrich Max Müller, Hermann Oldenburg, and Rhys David, translated Buddhist manuscripts from Sanskrit and Pali originals. Tolstoy read their books in English, French and German and commented on them in his correspondence. He was also aware of Schopenhauer and his interest in Buddhism through his close friend Afanasij Afanasievich Fet, who was the Russian translator of Schopenhauer's *The World as Will and Idea* (*Die Welt as Wille und Vorstellung*) which appeared in the 1870's. Schopenhauer and all these scholars with the exception of Oldenburg and Rhys David considered Buddhism to be a pessimistic, life-denying religion and this is the view to which Tolstoy also subscribes.

Tolstoy's Four Fold Criteria as Applied to Buddhism

Tolstoy's religious quest centered on the religious universals, that is the common ethical and moral core in all religions. Huxley refers to a similar concept with his term "perennial philosophy," which he describes as "...primarily concerned with the one, divine reality substantial to the manifold world of things and lives and mind."[2] Huxley's definition of "perennial philosophy" is similar to Tolstoy's statement on true religion "according to my conviction there is only one true religion. This true religion of mankind has not yet been revealed com-

---

1. L. N. Tolstoy, *Polnoe sobranie sochinenij*, The Anniversary Edition, T, 39, pp. 3-26.
2. Aldous Huxley, *The Perennial Philosophy* (New York and London: Harper and Brothers, 1945), p. 8.

pletely, but it appears in fragmentary fashion in all needs."[3] Tolstoy's positive assessment of Buddhism and other religions depends on the extent to which they emphasize the perennial philosophy and his negative assessment on religions and the stages in their development depends on the extent to which these religions strayed from the common ground of perennial philosophy into idiosyncrasies of ritual, miracle and dogma. The universality of common religious ethics is Tolstoy's first requirement for an ideal religion. Tolstoy's second requirement finds the ritualistic, dogmatic and supernatural contrary to reason and he insists that religion be in full accord with the dictates of reason. The third Tolstoyan requirement for an ideal religion in addition to its universality and conformity to reason is its life-affirming and practical aspect. The fourth requirement is that the individual is responsible for his acts, the law of cause and effect, the karmic law which Tolstoy accepted from Buddhism. These four major requirements play an important role in Tolstoy's views on Buddhism.

Comments and Discussion of Buddhism in Tolstoy's Writing

Tolstoy already knew the story of Buddha's life as is demonstrated in his *Confession* (1879) where he invokes four sages – Socrates, Solomon, Schopenhauer and Sakya-Muni –as his spiritual mentors whom he asks for help in resolving his spiritual crisis. Tolstoy relates the story of Buddha's life, his encounters with an old man, a sick man and a dead man and he sums up Buddha's teaching in the following way: "To live with the consciousness of the inevitability of suffering, weakening, old age and death is impossible – one should free oneself from life, from any possibility of life."[4] If life is really so hopeless, then the only liberation, according to Tolstoy, is suicide. To live life without thinking about the future and its accompanying pains is impossible for Tolstoy. Before continuing with his life he insists on knowing the purpose and meaning of his existence. "I, just like Sakya-Muni, could not go on a hunt, when I knew that there was an old age, suffer-

---

3. Paul Birjukoff, *Tolstoi und der Orient* (Zurich und Leipzig: Rotapfel Verlag, 1925), p. 118.
4. L. N. Tolstoy, *Polnoe sobranie sochinenij*, T. 23, p. 26.

ing and death. My imagination was too vivid."[5] Tolstoy withdrew from Buddhism before this religion had any impact on him. Tolstoy, overawed by the enormity of its consequences, stopped at the first noble truth of Buddhism in which suffering, old age and death were proclaimed to permeate life. The first noble truth taken in isolation from the rest of Buddhist teaching is indeed not comforting although it is a statement of fact. Taken in isolation it does not indicate a way out of the human condition and this is how Tolstoy understands it. He conceives it as a pessimistic and life-denying teaching which he cannot accept unless he is ready to deprive himself of life. For Tolstoy the Christian message is the only life affirming message. To follow all other philosophers, east and west, is to end up with the same depressing conclusion.

In addition to *Confession*, sources for Tolstoy's assessment of Buddhism can also be found in scattered and brief statements he made in his diaries, essays and correspondence on the subject, in his treatise "Religion and Morality," written in 1893,[6] as well as in the life of Buddha prepared by his collaborator Bulanzhe and edited by himself,[7] his translation of Carus' story *Karma*,[8] his adaptation of "Eto Ty" ("This is Thyself")[9] from an anonymous German author and in his adaptation of the Buddhist legend "Kunala's Eyes."[10] There are, in addition, statements about Buddhism made by characters in his novels and a Buddhist view of the world appears in his later work, particularly "Master and Man" and *The Death of Ivan Il'ich*.

Tolstoy's life of the Buddha "The Life and Teaching of Siddartha Gautama called the Buddha, the Most Perfect One"[11] which he edited for Bulanzhe exemplifies the life and the activity of a religious founder in the context of Tolstoyan ideal religion. Siddartha, in this story, brought

5. L. N. Tolstoy, *Polnoe sobranie sochinenij*, T. 23, p. 20.
6. L. N. Tolstoy, "Religija i nravstvennost'," *Polnoe sobranie sochinenij*, T. 39, p. 8.
7. P. D. Bulanzhe, "Zhizn' i Uchenie Siddarty Gotamy, Prozvannogo Buddoi, t. e. Soversheneishim," *Zhizn'Dlia Vsekh*, no. 4 April 1910, pp. 75-84.
8. L. N. Tolstoy, *Polnoe sobranie sochinenij*, T. 31, pp. 47-56.
9. L. N. Tolstoy, *Polnoe sobranie sochinenij*, T. 34, pp. 138-140.
10. L. N. Tolstoy, "Glaza Kunaly," *Krug Chteniya*, No. 6, 1912, pp. 125-127.
11. P. D. Bulanzhe, "Zhizn' i Uchenie Siddarty Gotamy, Prozvannogo Buddoi, t. e. Soversheneishim," *Zhizn'Dlia Vsekh*, no. 4, April 1910.

up as a follower of Hinduism, turns away from this religion because of its meaningless, sacrificial ritual. He rebels against the narrow confines of the Hindu dogma and wants to establish a rational religion which conforms to common sense and reason. Tolstoy describes the true life to which the Buddha aimed as *razumnaia* ("reasonable") and quotes the Buddha's words to his disciples "Your reason and the truth which I have taught you will be your teachers after I depart."[12]

There are no supernatural agents or events, no miracles, in this version of the Buddha's life. The Buddha is a human being albeit an enlightened human being, who using his reason and his practical instructional skill points out the path for other human beings to tread. All the requirements of an ideal Tolstoyan religion are present here, the universality, the appeal to reason as a final arbiter of religious discrimination, and the life affirming and active pursuit of self-perfection on the part of the Buddha and his followers. While conforming to Tolstoyan requirements for an ideal religion this is an essentially true description of the Buddha according to the canons of early Buddhism.[13]

Contrary to his evaluation of Buddhism as a positive, life-affirming religion in the story of the Buddha's life in "Religion and Morality" (1893) Buddhism is regarded as the religion of extreme renunciation not only of all goods of life but of life itself. As Tolstoy puts it, "Buddhism considers that the world should disappear as it causes personal suffering."[14] In his pessimistic appraisal of Buddhism, Tolstoy follows Schopenhauer who defined Nirvana as a denial to live and who claimed, based on his understanding of early Buddhism, that suicide was far from being the denial of the will and represented its strong

---

12. P. Bulanzhe "Zhizn' i Uchenie Siddarty Gotamy, Prozvannogo Buddoi, t. e. Soversheneishim" *Zhizn'Dlia Vsekh* 3-v (1910), p. 81.
13. *Theravada* 'Doctrine of the Elders' is a name of the oldest form of Buddhist teachings handed to us in the Pali language. Theravada is the only one of the old schools of Buddhism that has survived among those which is called Hinayana. It is sometimes called Southern Buddhism or Pali Buddhism. This form of Buddhism was the first one to be discovered by Western orientalists. The Theravadins claimed that theirs was the authentic and original form of Buddha's teachings.
14. L. N. Tolstoy, "Religija i nravstvennost', "*Polnoe sobranie*, T. 39, p. 8.

affirmation.[15] Tolstoy's awareness and early enthusiasm for Schopenhauer's philosophy predates Tolstoy's interest in Buddhism and it is possible that Tolstoy's account of Buddhism as pessimistic is influenced and reinforced by his reading of Schopenhauer. Tolstoy's assessment of Buddhism as a pessimistic, life-denying religion is also reflected in the comments made by protagonists in his fictional works. In "The Kreutzer Sonata" Pozdnyshev talks about the futility of life, "But why live? If life has no aim, if life is given us for life's sake, there is no reason for living. And if it is so, then the Schopenhauers, the Hartmanns, and all the Buddhists as well, are quite right."[16] Anna Karenina's final reflection before her suicide is in the same spirit although she does not mention Schopenhauer or Buddhism: "Where did I leave off? On the thought that I couldn't conceive a position in which life would not be misery, that we are all created to be miserable, and that we all know it, and all invent means of deceiving each other, and when one sees the truth, what is one to do?"[17] A lady sitting in the same train compartment addressed her companion, "'That's what reason is given man for, to escape from what worries him....' The words seemed an answer to Anna's thoughts."[18]

The view that Buddhism is not only a pessimistic religion and philosophy but that it represents a complete annihilation of life is also present in Tolstoy's assessment of Buddhism. "I read Buddhist teaching. It is marvelous but it is only a teaching. The mistake is only to save one from life completely. Buddha is not saving himself but he is saving people. He forgot that if there were nobody to save, there would not be any life."[19] Tolstoy may have been led to the annihilatory view of Buddhism because of the popular belief among the 19th-century Buddhologists and Schopenhauer that the word Nirvana means 'blow-

15. Arthur Schopenhauer, *The World as Will and Representation*, ts. by E. F. J. Payne from the German *Die Welt als Wille und Vorstellung* (Indian Hills, CA: Falcon Wing Press, 1958, 1, p. 398. "The interest in Buddhism...was awakened in him (Tolstoy, D.M.) not without Schopenhauer's influence," S. Levitskij, "Tolstoy i Shopengauer," *Novyj Zhurnal*, Kn. 59, 1960, p. 210.

16. L. N. Tolstoy, *Polnoe sobranie sochinenij*, T. 27, p. 29.

17. L. N. Tolstoy, *Anna Karenina* (New York: The Modern Library, 1965), p. 796.

18. L. N. Tolstoy, *Anna Karenina*, p. 796.

19. L. N. Tolstoy, *Polnoe sobranie sochinenij*, T. 49, p. 121.

ing out life.' The metaphor of blowing out life as a Buddhist symbol for Nirvana, is present in *Anna Karenina* in the scene before her suicide when the light in her candlestick blows out as well as in a similar blowing out of light before old Prince Bolkonsky's death in *War and Peace*.[20]

The Perennial Philosophy in Buddhism

For Tolstoy early Buddhism and early Christianity are strikingly similar. When asked about the essential difference between early Buddhism and early Christianity, he says "There is none, in both there is a gospel of the God of love and a denial of a personal god."[21] Later, Mahayana Buddhism[22] in contrast to early Buddhism, developed elaborate devotional practices, in which the Buddha was given a divine status. For Tolstoy this transition from a religion of the mind to a religion of the heart and the imagination is tantamount to perversion and degeneration, a descent into the miraculous and the ceremonial and away from the conformity to reason. He remarks to his secretary, in 1908, "I read everything about Buddhism, what a strange teaching! And how it was perverted! Such an abstract teaching and suddenly there appeared the same creation of gods, the idol worship, the paradise and the hell.... Quite the same superstitions as in Christianity."[23]

The Unity of Life

Buddhist religion provides many examples illustrating the unity of life *Jatakas* stories of the previous incarnations of the Buddha from an animal to a human being and finally to an enlightened human being show the continuity and the unity of life in its different forms. Ine one of these stories the Buddha-to-be is a snake caught and tortured by village boys. The moral of the story is the reverence and respect for life, even the lowly animal forms of life have the potential for self-realization and enlightenment.

---

20. See Harry Hill Walsh, "A Buddhistic Leitmotif in Anna Karenina," *Canadian-American Slavic Studies*, 11, No. 4 (Winter, 1977), pp. 561-567.
21. V. F. Bulgakov "Knigi ob Indii v biblioteke L. N. Tolstogo" *Kratkie soobshcheniia Instituta Vostokovedenia*, V. 31, 1959, p. 46.
22. Mahayana. One of main traditions or schools of Buddhism: 'great' (maha), 'means of salvation' (yana). Late Buddhism in contrast is Hinayana (early Buddhism).
23. N. N. Gusev, *Dva Goda s Tolstym* (Moskva, 1912), p. 130.

Tolstoy's story *Eto ty*[24] is frequently repeated in the sixth chapter of the *Chandogya Upanishad* (1600 B.C.) as the teacher Uddalaka instructs his son in the nature of the supreme. The unity of life is also the cardinal principle of perennial philosophy. The ethical aspect of *Tat tvam asi* inspired Tolstoy's short story *Asarhadon, King of Assyria* (1903).[25] In this story the two warring kings Asarhadon and Lailie, one defeated and the other one victorious, exchange their personalities. Asarhadon is put in the place of Lailie who is about to be executed. The result of the exchange is Asarhadon's spiritual conversion; he realizes that "life is one in all and shows in himself or herself only a part of this all-pervasive life"[26] and "...you can only improve life in yourself by destroying the barriers that divide your life from others and by thinking of others as yourself and by loving them.[27]

The *Tat tvam asi* principle which is the source of Asarhadon, is of oneself. According to Tolstoy the culmination of the *Tat tvam asi* realization is love which he formulates as "...the only reasonable activity of man."[28]

The same idea of the unity of life is expressed in Tolstoy's story *What Men Live By*. The moral of the story is that man should not live by the self-centered concern and care for himself, but by his love for others. The authentic life is manifested in our concern and love for others.

In Tolstoy's story *Master and Man* Brekhunov, a self-centered, profit-oriented merchant realizes *Tat tvam asi* when he is lost in a blizzard with his servant. He realizes that he and his servant are one as he tries to revive his freezing servant with the warmth of this own body.

---

24. L. N. Tolstoy, *Polnoe sobranie sochinenij*, T. 34, pp. 138-140. Tolstoy translated this story from the German theosophical journal *Theosophischer Wegweiser* (1903, No. 5, pp. 163-166) written by an anonymous author under the title "Das bist du."
25. L. N. Tolstoy, "Assirijskij Tsar Asarhadon," *Polnoe sobranie sochinenij*, T. 34, pp. 126
26. Ibid., p. 129.
27. Ibid., p. 129.
28. L. N. Tolstoy, *Polnoe sobranie sochinenij*, p. 91.

The Karma Concept and the Individual Responsibility

Paul Carus' story *Karma*[29] made a big impression on Tolstoy, who translated it into Russian. The story states two propositions: the notion of individual moral accountability for acts and deeds committed and the notion that there is no happiness for an individual human being unless it is a part of universal human happiness, something which represents another variation on the *Tat tvam asi* theme. Karma is the law of cause and effect in Buddhism. Good deeds bring about good results and they influence our fate in the coming life and conversely evil, immoral actions are followed by bad consequences in the next life. This is how Tolstoy understands this concept in his preface to Carus' story "The truth, much slurred in these days, that evil can be avoided and good achieved by personal effort only and that there exists no other means of attaining this end...."[30] Karma in Sanskrit means "action" and in Buddhist interpretation "...denotes the wholesome and unwholesome volitions and their concomitant mental factors, causing rebirth and shaping the destiny of beings."[31] The Buddhist interpretation also includes mental factors such as wholesome or unwholesome thoughts.

Consequently, according to the ineluctable Karmic law evil doers in this story perish, while the individuals who perform good deeds find peace and happiness. The fate of each person in this story is determined by his actions and deeds.

The individuals in the story who do not realize the unity of life commit karmic evil in setting up their ego and its interests above the

29. Paul Carus, *Karma, a Story of Buddhist Ethics* (La Salle, Illinois: The Open Court Publishing Company, 1901). In this preface to the translation of this book Tolstoy gives his definition of the Buddhist term *karma* "Karma is a Buddhist belief that not only the character mold of each person but also all his fate in this life is a consequence of his or her actions in a previous life," L. N. Tolstoy, *Polnoe sobranie sochinenij*, T. 31, p. 47.
30. Paul Carus, *Karma*, p. 4.
31. A. I. Shifman, in his book *Lev Tolstoy i Vostok* (Moskva: Nauka, 1971), cites the reasons for Tolstoy's attraction to Buddhism: (1) the teaching of equality, (2) the denial of a personal god, (3) Buddhist ethics.

welfare of other human beings. Only those individuals who are able to set aside their selfish, egocentric impulses are able to find the truth. This is the moral of Karma.

Tolstoy's Sources of Buddhism

The prevailing opinion of European Buddhist scholars in the 19th century is that Buddhism is a life-denying, nihilistic religion. Their books, which Tolstoy read, exerted a strong influence on him as well as on his views, which parallel theirs. Schopenhauer, like Tolstoy, read their books and came to the same conclusion about the nihilistic nature of that religion. The first noble truth in Buddhism states that life is suffering because it entails sickness, old age and death. This statement alone can be interpreted as a depressing and a life-negating assessment of life. Nirvana, a basic concept in Buddhism, a goal of Buddhist aspiration and striving was understood to be an extinction of life by Schopenhauer and other Buddhologists. An understanding of life as something imbued with suffering was considered in their interpretation to be evil. Referring to a person who denies the will-to-live, Schopenhauer writes "He willingly gives up the existence that we know; what comes to him instead of it is in our eyes *nothing*, because our existence in reference to that one is *nothing*. The Buddhist faith calls that existence Nirvana, that is to say, extinction."[32] Schopenhauer and Tolstoy accepted the etymology of 'Nirvana' suggested by Colebrook as signifying "...extinct, as a fire which has gone out; set, as a luminary which has gone down..."[33]

Max Müller, a prominent 19th century orientalist and one of the chief sources of Tolstoy's knowledge on Buddhism, was mystified by Nirvana although he accepted Buddhist ethics. For him as for his predecessor Buddhist scholar Burnouf and St. Hilaire, Nirvana meant annihilation. Müller, relying on the same etymology of Nirvana accepted by Colebrook writes: "Every Sanskrit scholar knows that Nir-

---

32. Richard F. Gustafson in *Leo Tolstoy Resident and Stranger* (Princeton: Princeton University Press, 1986) does not treat Tolstoy's views on Oriental religions. Gustafson offers a detailed and insightful analysis of Tolstoy ideas on religion in general.
33. Nyanatiloka Bhikshu, *Buddhist Dictionary, Manual of Buddhist Transactions of the Royal Asiatic Society of Great Britain and Ireland* (1807), p. 566.

vana means originally the blowing out, the extinction of light, and not absorption. The human soul, when it arrives at its perfection, is blown out...."[34] and "True wisdom consists in perceiving the nothingness of all things, and in a desire to become nothing, to be blown out, to enter into the state of Nirvana."[35] Müller could conceive that all efforts at self-perfection which Buddhism preaches would result in "...trap bridge hurling man into abyss, at the very moment when he thought he had arrived at the stronghold of the Eternal."[36] Thus to Max Müller the very idea of nihilism appears as an impossibility.

The charge of Buddhism as being a nihilistic doctrine is also levied by Barthelemy Saint-Hilaire. He argues that even if Nirvana were to be an absorption in God, it would still be an annihilation: "I confess, moreover, that even in this mitigated form (as absorption), which it does not have, Nirvana would seem to be so close to nothingness that I should easily confuse the one with the other. Absorption in God — especially the God of Brahmanism — is the annihilation of the personality, that is to say, true nothingness for the individual soul...."[37]

The concept of Nirvana conceived as annihilation, death, and the renunciation of life, is presented in Tolstoy's fiction. Tolstoy describes death in his fiction (examples include the death of Prince Andrei in *War and Peace*, of Brekhunov in "Master and Man" and of Ivan Il'ich in *The Death of Ivan Il'ich*) as the loss of consciousness of self as an entity and as an immersion in some new mode of existence. The Tolstoyan concept of death resembles the Nirvana state of tranquility and purity. Tolstoy uses the word `awakening'[38] to describe the passage from life to death, the same term which is used in Buddhism to indicate the passage from 'samsara' (the everyday world of frustration and suffering) to 'nirvana.'

---

34. Friedrich Max Müller, *Selected Essays on Language, Mythology, and Religion* (London: Longman's, Green and Co., 1861), Vol. 2, p. 283.
35. Friedrich Max Müller, *Selected Essays*, Vol. 2, p. 219.
36. Friederich Max Müller, *Selected Essays*, Vol. 2, pp. 301-2.
37. Barthelemy Saint-Hilaire, *Le Bouddha et sa religion* (3rd ed., 1866), pp. 5-6.
38. "Yes, that was death. I died. I awoke. Yes, death is awakening!" Aylmer Maude, *The Short Work of Tolstoy* (New York, 1956), p. 577.

Not all 19th century orientalists believed as Tolstoy did in the anni- hilatory character of nirvana and in the pessimistic nature of Bud- dhism. Oldenburg and Rhys David, the orientalists whom Tolstoy read, and who did not influence his assessment of Buddhism, differed from the prevailing 19th century view on the subject. They insisted on the worldliness of nirvana.[39] Nirvana, in their opinion, is a state of sinlessness and painlessness realized in this life. As more Buddhist manuscripts became available and knowledge of Buddhism in its en- tirety became better known, the views of Tolstoy and the 19th century orientalists on the annihilatory understanding of nirvana and the pes- simistic character of Buddhism as a whole, turned out to be one sided. The etymology of the key Buddhist term nirvana as put forth by Colebrook and accepted by Schopenhauer and Tolstoy as an extinction of the will to live was superseded by a different and more appropriate and credible etymology in which nirvana in Sanskrit or nibbana in Pali is connected with the *nibbati* `to cool by blowing.' The cooling does not refer to cooling or freezing to death but "...to a state of greed, hatred and delusion, the three principle forms of evil in Buddhist thought."[40] A person thus cooled is 'healthy' and has attained salva- tion.

Pessimism as the philosophical doctrine asserts that the universe is fundamentally evil and malevolent. Buddhism is not philosophically pessimistic in that sense because it teaches that sorrow or evil is due to ignorance of the true nature of reality and a false conception of self.

Tolstoy considered nihilism and pessimism as negative qualities and he mistakenly attributed them to Buddhism like Schopenhauer and other 19th century European orientalists who did not have full access to all Buddhist schools and who based their opinions on a mis-

---

39. Unlike Müller and Burnouf, Oldenberg does not believe in the annihilatory charac- ter of Buddhism. "If anyone describes Buddhism as a religion of annihilation and seeks to develop it therefrom as from its specific germ, he has, in fact, succeeded in wholly missing the main drift of Buddha and the ancient order of his disciples." Hermann Oldenburg, *The Buddha, His Life, His Doctrine, His Order*, trans. by William Holy (London: William and Norgate, 1882), p. 260.
40. Trevor Ling, *A Dictionary of Buddhism, Indian and South-East Asian* (Calcutta: K. A. Bagchi, 1981), p. 150.

understanding of the notion of nirvana. He also contrasted in some of his statements and in his fiction the positive life-affirming message of Christianity to the negative life-denying message of Buddhism.

Rationality and Buddhism in Tolstoy's Interpretation

For Tolstoy "religion is the awareness of those truths which are common and comprehensible to all people in all situations at all times, and are as indisputable as 2x2=4... Religion is like geometry."[41] Awareness of the universal truths for Tolstoy is grounded not in blind faith but in faith coupled with reason and with reason as a final arbiter. As Tolstoy's biography of the Buddha suggests, early Buddhism is a religion where Buddhist truths are experientially validated and the Buddha's divinity is denied.

Paul Carus in *The Gospel of Buddha*, one of Tolstoy's favorite manuals of Buddhism and one he read intensively (it contains many marginal notes by Tolstoy) writes: "Now, Buddhism is a religion which knows of no supernatural revelation and proclaims doctrines that require no other argument than `come and see'."[42]

The first noble truth of Buddhism that life involves suffering is confirmed by the presence of old age, sickness and disease. The Buddha's authority in the early Buddhist scriptures is not based on his divinity but on his insight which can be always realized in human experience. Early Buddhism does not contain miracles, hardly any ritual and a minimum of dogma, and as such conforms to Tolstoy's ideal concept of religion. Later Buddhism, in which the Buddha's divinity was proclaimed and in which miracles, ritual and dogma abound, was considered by Tolstoy to be a debasement of the original doctrine.

This tendency to mythologize and mystify Buddhism can be observed directly in the interpretation of the life of the Buddha found in *Lalita Vistara*; each new edition of this book is more complex and miraculous, and Buddhist dogma becomes more elaborate and concrete through additions and commentaries which move away from the simple original abstractions.

---

41. L. N. Tolstoy, *Polnoe sobranie sochinenij*, T. 63, p. 339.
42. Paul Carus, *The Gospel of Buddha* (Chicago: The Open Court, 1902), p. 9.

This differentiation between an earlier pure form of Buddhism and a later debased form, often expressed in terms of a dichotomy between what the Buddha taught and the commentaries on his teaching or between Buddhism and the personal teaching of Buddha, exists in the writings of Burnouf, Saint Hilaire and Max Müller. Tolstoy's idea of freeing original early Buddhism from later "perversions" and misinterpretations is reflected in Max Müller's statement in a letter of July 26, 1895, to a Mr. Dharmapala: "You should endeavor to do for Buddhism what the more enlightened students of Christianity have long been doing in the different countries of Europe: You should free your religion from its latter excrescences, and bring it back to its earliest, simplest and purest form as taught by Buddha and his immediate disciples. If that is done, you will be surprised to see how little difference there is in essentials between the great religions of the world."[43] Müller's formulation is basically in agreement with Tolstoy's identification of a primitive Christianity and a primitive Buddhism, stripped of the alleged irrationality of rituals, miracles and dogma. Müller's and Tolstoy's high regard for early pure Buddhism and its wisdom and their disregard for later schools of Buddhism as being an adulteration of an earlier teaching is not justified within the historical framework of Buddhism. The contrast between the alleged rationality of earlier Buddhism and the alleged irrationality of later developments misses the point. The Buddhist tradition has always advocated a diversity of approaches to the Godhead depending on the psychological makeup of the believer. There was a way of knowledge and a way of devotion suitable to intellectual and emotional individuals respectively. Tolstoy obviously favors the former but this preference is due to his sober, rationalistic outlook and not to imperfections, ethical or philosophical, of later Buddhism where devotional and mystical elements predominate. Tolstoy criticized later schools of Buddhism as "...exalted Buddhism, which, with its monasteries and representations of Buddha, and its solemn rites, has changed into mystical Lamaism..." and

43. Friederich Max Müller, *Selected Essays*, Vol. 2, p. 350-51.

of Taoism "...with its sorcery and incantations."[44] It should be noted here that the term 'mystical' had for Tolstoy negative connotations as could be seen from the subtitle of *The Kingdom of God Within You*: "Christianity not as a mystical doctrine, but as a new understanding of life." Tolstoy's concept of 'rational' Buddhism has much in common with Oldenburg's who was cited in the bibliography of Tolstoy's biography of the Buddha. Oldenburg's interpretation of Buddhism was rationalistic; mysticism was foreign to him and he was criticized in his own time for his rationalistic presentation of Buddhism. This coincidence of views between Müller and Tolstoy on the degenerative development in Buddhism and Oldenburg and Tolstoy on the practice and rational character of early Buddhism does not imply the influence of the former on the latter since Tolstoy held similar views before reading these authors. Tolstoy's views were confirmed and reinforced through the reading of these writers.

Buddhism as a Positive Religion

In spite of Tolstoy's disagreement with the alleged nihilism and pessimism of Buddhist religion and with the mystical character of later schools of Buddhism, he found Buddhist ethics conforming to the perennial philosophy. These principles are condemnation of violence and war. Tolstoy believed that non-violence was practiced in Buddhist countries in contrast to Christian countries which inflicted violence on an Asian population and oppressed them. The history of Buddhist religion itself, one may add, shows more tolerance for divergent views and no outright persecution compared to the history of Christianity.

In "Kunala's Eyes," an adapted Buddhist legend, Kunala, an emperor's son, is blinded. Deprived of his eyes Kunala acquired a perfect, pure 'eye' of truth and higher reality. The abandonment of an ego-centered existence as a prerequisite for true happiness, occurs as a theme both in perennial philosophy and in Tolstoy's fiction (*The Death of Ivan Il'ich* and *Master and Man*). Tolstoy finds in Buddha's teaching the same ethical tenets he, himself, proclaimed in his essay "On

---

44. L. N. Tolstoy, "Chto takoe religija i v chom sushchestvo jejo," *Polnoe sobranie sochinenij*, T. 35, p. 166.

Life." "Buddha says that happiness consists in doing as much good to others as possible. Regardless of how strange this appears on superficial observation it is undoubtedly so; happiness is only possible by renouncing the aspiration toward personal, egoistic happiness."[45]

In summarizing Tolstoy's views on Buddhism several factors should be kept in mind. Tolstoy's early Christian upbringing and conditioning, his relatively late exposure to selective Buddhist writings, the polemical character of his statements on religions in general and Buddhism in particular as well as his own views on the essence of the ideal religion.

Orthodox Christianity was part of Tolstoy's heritage and his world view. He thought that it was superior to other world religions in its formulation and practice of eternal and universal ethical truths. In comparison with Buddhism with Christianity, he considered the latter to be more oriented towards "preaching the possibility and necessity of founding the Kingdom of God on earth."[46]

In the later period of his life in the late eighties and nineties as he evolved a concept of Christianity without supernatural elements he became more even-handed in comparing the merits of Buddhism with those of Christianity. He emphasized more the ethical principles of Buddhism and disregarded what he thought were the negative aspects of nirvana. On the metaphysical side, Tolstoy never reconciled the contradiction between the Christian concept of God and the self-regulating Karmic mechanism in Buddhism, preferring to ignore metaphysics in favor of common ethical grounds.

Tolstoy's first personal contact with Buddhism was a lesson in nonresistance to evil by a Buddhist lama who was his neighbor in the Kazan' hospital. He told Tolstoy the story of his life. During a sleigh ride in Siberia he was attacked by bandits. When asked by Tolstoy what he did then he answered, "I crossed my arms on my chest and I prayed to Buddha to forgive the lawbreakers." The evidence of Tolstoy's special interest in Buddhism came much later after his spiritual crisis

---

45. R. F. Christian, *Tolstoy's Letters* (New York: Charles Scribner's Sons, 1978), Vol. 2, p. 635.
46. A. I. Shifman, *Lev Tolstoy i Vostok* (Moskva: 1971), p. 115.

and his definite breakup with the Orthodox church in 1879. In 1886 Strahkov wrote to him about Burnouf's book *Le Lotus de la Bonne foi*. Several weeks later Strahkov refers to Koppen's *Die Religion des Buddha*, Barth's *Les religions de l'Inde*, Bergoine's *Vedes* and Müller's *Sacred Books of the East*.[47] Valuable as these books may have been as the sources for the study of Buddhism at that time they suffered from certain shortcomings. They often described Buddhism within the Christian framework of reference and they misinterpreted some key Buddhist terms such as nirvana. Their predilections and prejudices were reflected in Tolstoy's views on the subject, particularly on his understanding of nirvana and the ramifications of that concept on his evaluation of Buddhism in general. Tolstoy's intense involvement with Buddhism came at a stage of his life when his views on religion were already formed. Buddhism was for him a sounding board when his ideas and opinions could be confirmed and reinforced.

This dialectical interplay between his own ideas and those held and expounded by other philosophies, religions and people was polemical and the context of these polemics varied. This may explain differences and contradictions in his statements and assessment of Buddhism at different points in time. In *Confession*, Buddha is introduced as Sakia-Muni as a fourth "S" in addition to Solomon, Socrates and Schopenhauer, as a foil to his idea of salvation through Christianity. In his essay "Religion and Morality" Tolstoy's polemics is directed against Buddhism and other religions within the context of his belief in the primacy of Christianity. A corrective to this view came later when Buddhism and Christianity were both identified as a gospel of the God of love. His views, then, evolved in the direction of identifying an essential ethical identity shared by both religions.

---

47. Carl Koppen, *Die Religion des Buddha* (Berlin: Schneider, 1957-59), Vol. 1; Auguste Barth, *Les religions de l'Inde* (Paris: Sandoz et Fischbacher, 1879); Abel Bergoigne, *Le religions vedique* (Paris: E. Bouillon, 1895); Eugene Burnouf, *Le Lotus de la Bonne Foi* (Paris: 1850); Friedrich Max Müller, *The Sacred Books of the East*, continued series starting with 1875, "The Religions of China, (1) Confucianism, (2) Taoism, (3) Buddhism and Christianity," in *Nineteenth Century*, vol. 48 (1900).

CHAPTER TWO

TAOISTIC PATTERNS IN *WAR AND PEACE*
Vytas Dukas, San Diego State College
Glenn A. Sandstrom, San Diego State College

It is well known that Tolstoj responded warmly to Taoism from the time that he was first introduced to the *Tao Te Ching* of Lao-Tzu in 1878[1] and that Taoist ideas were important in the ideology and attitude of the older Tolstoj.[2] Although this direct influence came late, this ready acceptance is almost predictable in retrospect, for Tolstoj had long been employing patterns of thought surprisingly parallel to those of Lao-Tzu. Especially in the case of *War and Peace*, something very much like a vision of the Tao underlies the psychology, characterization, and ethic of the novel. This kind of analogy should not be carried too far – ignoring as it does such other lines of thought as Stoicism, Christianity, etc., which directly acted on Tolstoj earlier. Still, a demonstration of parallels can show a good deal about the movement of Tolstoj's mind in the sixties and also illuminate some aspects of the

---

1. The first recorded contact of Tolstoj with Taoism is a letter to N.N. Straxov of 3 January 1878; Tolstoj asks "From where did you take the words of Lao-Tzu?" See L. N. Tolstoj "Letters 1873-1879," Polnoe Sobranie Sochinenij (90 TT.; M., L., 1928-1958), LXII, 369. This edition is referred to as PSS in this article. It is strange that Tolstoj did not encounter the Julien translation much earlier, since it appeared in 1842, just prior to Tolstoj's enrollment in the reputable school of Oriental Languages at Kazan'; of course, he was not a student of Chinese. At any rate, there is no evidence of earlier contact, and Tolstoj's reply to Straxov, with its inquiry about the source of Lao-Tzu's ideas, indicates that the matter was new to him.
2. The point is well documented in Derek Bodde, *Tolstoy and China* (Princeton, N.J., 1950), and in PSS, XXV, 883-885; XLIX, 62; LV, 467; LXXXV, 37; etc.

novel by offering a new frame of reference.[3] Here we would like to consider, in the light of Lao-Tzu's Taoism, the characterization of Platon Karataev, Pierre, and Nikolaj; the character and military theories of Kutuzov; and the total world view of *War and Peace*.

Platon Karataev often voices the stoic truths of the Russian peasant and the pieties of primitive Christianity, but in basic ways he is strongly suggestive of the Taoist sage, who gains power from quiescence, durability from acceptance. His deft undoing of his leg wrappings,[4] which nudges Pierre toward a new life, is in line with Lao-Tzu's doctrine of economy – doing nothing superfluous. From that point, Platon expresses and dramatizes a way of life much like the Taoist Way. His peasant aphorisms, like "Don't fret, friend – suffer an hour, live for an age" (*WP*, XII, 3, p. 1073; *SS*, VII,54), fit in with Lao-Tzu's "he who is satisfied with his lot is rich...; he who dies and does not perish, has longevity."[5] When Platon says, "Where there's law there's injustice" (*WP*, 1074; *SS*, VII, 55),[6] he is close to Lao-Tzu's denunciation of moral rules: "If we could renounce our benevolence and discard our righteousness, the people would again become filial and kindly" (Ch. 19). Platon's view is that "things happen not as we plan but as God judges" ; Lao-Tzu says that "the Tao produces all things, nourishes them, brings them to their full growth, completes them, matures them, maintains them, and overspreads them" (Ch. 51). (The assumed interchangeability of "God" and "the Tao" may be questioned, of course; the treatment of Pierre, below, will clarify the issue.) Like the happy people of Lao-Tzu, "who think their [coarse] food sweet" (Ch. 80),

---

3. Diary entry of 15 March 1884, L. N. Tolstoj, Sobranie Sochinenij (20 TT.; M. 1960-1965), XIX, 311. This edition is cited as SS in this article. For a survey of previous philosophical approaches, see R. F. Christian, *Tolstoy's* War and Peace (Oxford, 1962), 87-94.

4. Leo Tolstoy, *War and Peace*, tr. by Louise and Aylmer Maude (N.Y., 1942), Bk. XII, Ch. 3, p. 1072; and SS, VII, 54. References in text to this edition are given in this article as WP, followed by book, chapter, and page number in that order. Book and chapter numbers are dropped where obvious.

5. *Tao Te Ching*, in *The Texts of Taoism*, ed. and tr. by James Legge (N.Y., 1959), Ch. 33. All references in text will be to this edition, with chapter numbers indicated.

6. Tolstoj's word *sud* suggests jurisdictional clutter and bureaucratic process more broadly than does the translation "law."

Platon (along with Pierre) feels that potatoes are "grand" (*važneju žčie*; *WP*, 1074; *SS*, VII, 55).[7] When Platon is described as speaking his simple truths without thought (*WP*, 1077; *SS*, VII, 58), we might think of Lao-Tzu's injunction: "Sincere words are not fine; fine words are not sincere....Those who know the Tao are not extensively learned; the extensively learned do not know it." (Ch. 81.) Platon is like the Taoist "ignorant man."

Tolstoj categorizes this unique peasant as "the personification of everything Russian" (*WP*, 1076; *SS*, VII, 58), but Platon is also close to the Taoist ideal of appearance and action. He shares literally the metaphors of Lao-Tzu: he is a "round" man, supple rather than muscular, with soft eyes and a voice "almost feminine." The total picture is forcefully reminiscent of key passages in the *Tao Te Ching*, especially these: "The softest thing is the world dashes against and overcomes the hardest" (Ch. 43), and, from Ch. 28:

> Who knows his manhood's strength
> Yet still his female feebleness maintains
> As to one channel flow the many drains,
> All come to him, yea, all beneath the sky.
> Thus he the constant excellence retains;
> The simple child again, free from all stains.
> (Ch. 28.)

Platon's warm but almost impersonal attachment to people puts him closer to Taoism than to Christianity. Pierre feels "that in spite of Karataev's affectionate tenderness for him (by which he gave Pierre's spiritual life its due) he would not have grieved for a moment at parting from him" (*WP*, 1078; *SS*, VII, 60). This rather puzzling attitude is typical of Epictetus and other Stoics but also fits in with the Taoist outlook. Partings and bereavements are part of the inscrutable flow of

---

7. The Russian *važnejuščě*, as applied to potatoes here, is an unusual use of the present active participle. The word itself is generally reserved for important persons; this, and the literal meaning "the potatoes are making themselves important"—combine a whimsical quality with a suggestive naturalistic connotation.

the Tao; grieving at such vicissitudes is a rebellion of the ego, a placing of one's own desires above the universal course of things – and one must be "always without desire" (Ch. 1). Besides being self-aggrandizing, grief is an emotional waste in the face of the all-powerful. In this and other ways, Platon lives by the triad of values proclaimed by Lao-Tzu's wise man: "But I have three precious things which I prize and hold fast. The first is gentleness; the second is economy; and the third is shrinking from taking precedence of others." (Ch. 67).

Like Lao-Tzu's sage, Platon is "skillful at saving men,' but the man he saves, Pierre, comes closer than he to an expression of Taoist truths. More fluid intellectually, less deeply rooted in dogmas of sin and retribution, and grounded in philosophical ideas, Pierre defines a God much like the Tao and an ethic similar to the Taoist *te*. We notice that when Platon tells the tale of the merchant who suffers in innocence and finds surcease in death, Pierre's soul is "rejoiced" not by the theology of the story but by "its mysterious significance: by the rapturous joy that lit up Karataev's face as he told it, and the mystic significance of that joy" (*WP*, XIV, 3, pp. 1178-1180; *SS*, VII, 179).

Pierre moves toward his climactic insight in a rapid series of responses. At nadir after his imprisonment – "as if the mainspring of his life, on which everything depended and which made everything appear alive, had suddenly been wrenched out and everything had collapsed into a heap of meaningless rubbish.... He felt that it was not in his power to regain faith in the meaning of life." (*WP*, XII, 3, p. 1072; *SS*, VII, 53) – he is driven toward restoration more by an intuitive recognition of Platon's harmonious life than by any specific communication. After watching Platon's economical actions, listening to a few automatic apothegms, and enjoying Platon's snores, Pierre "felt that the world had been shattered was once more stirring in his soul with a new beauty and on new and unshakable foundations" (*WP*, 1076; *SS* VII, 57). His later experience only guides him toward a codification of this simple and almost immediate apprehension. During his four weeks of imprisonment, he comes to see the moral anatomy of Platon's life: "Every word and action of his was the manifestation of an activity unknown to him, which was his life. But his life, as he regarded it, had no meaning as a separate thing. It had meaning only as part of a whole of which he was always conscious. His words and actions flowed from him as evenly, inevitably, and spontaneously as fragrance exhales from a flower. He could not understand the value or significance of any word or deed taken separately." (*WP*, 1078; *SS*, VII, 60.) What Pierre takes from this is much like the Taoist ethic, the *te*. Lao-Tzu's sage puts "his own person last" (Ch. 7) and senses that all is one within "the enduring and unchanging Tao" (Ch. 1); he diminishes his doing "till he arrives at doing nothing [on purpose]," and at that point "there is nothing which he does not do." (Ch. 37). Pierre sees that the individual's spontaneous acquiescence to the enveloping spontaneous mover – the opposite of "striving" – is the source of happiness. The implications of a summarizing passage – "The absence of suffering, the satisfaction of one's needs, and...freedom in the choice of one's occupation, that is, of one's way of life, now seemed to Pierre to be indubitably man's highest happiness" (*WP*, XIII, 3, p. 1123; *SS* VII, 113) – parallel a basic idea from the *Tao Te Ching*: "He who overcomes others is strong; he who overcomes himself is mighty. He who is satisfied with his lot is rich; he who goes on acting with energy has a firm will." (Ch. 33) The somewhat confusing stress on "satisfaction of needs" squares with the regimen of the Taoist sage, who "seeks to satisfy the craving of the belly, and not the insatiable longing of the eyes" (Ch. 12). Likewise Tolstoj's injected comment on Pierre, who "forgot that a superfluity of the comforts of life destroys all joy in satisfying one's needs," might remind one of Lao-Tzu's "He whose desires are few gets them; he whose desires are many goes astray" (Ch. 22). Intrinsic to the sense of the whole is a wholeness of self, or a consciousness of the whole within self. Thus, when Pierre almost falters again before the horrors of war, he suddenly feels "that the fatal force which had crushed him during the executions.... again controlled his existence...but he felt that in proportion to the efforts of that fatal force to crush him, there grew and strengthened in his soul a power of life independent of it" (*WP*, 1129; *SS*, VII, 122). The process behind this internal discovery of man's vital nature is exceptionally similar in two works:

Pierre glanced up at the sky and the twinkling stars in its faraway depths. "And all that is me, all that is within me, and it is all I!" thought

Pierre, "And they caught all that and put it into a shed[8] boarded up
with planks!" (*WP*, XIII, 3, p. 1130; *SS*, VII, 123.)

Without going outside his door, one understands all that takes place
under the sky; without looking out from the window, one sees the Tao
of Heaven. The further one goes out [from himself] the less he knows.
(Ch. 47.)

Although Pierre's reaction to Platon's death is at first a shockshield
of indifference engendered by crisis, it comes to resemble a Taoist
doctrine that at death one is re-absorbed into the total flow. Within
Pierre's comprehension that Platon is gone there obtrudes a vision of
his own immersion in water – "so that it closed over his head." Apparently his intuition is striving to make personal and immanent the fluid
truth of life as cryptically limned out just before this by the vision of
the old tutor holding out a globe covered with drops: "And all these
drops moved and changed places, sometimes several of them merging
into one, sometimes one dividing into many. Each drop tried to spread
out and occupy as much space as possible, but others striving to do the
same compressed it, sometimes destroyed it, and sometimes merged
with it." (*WP*, XIV, 3, pp. 1181-1182; *SS*, VII, 182-183.) The dream-
metaphor parallels the omnipresent water imagery of Taoism and the
view of Lao-Tzu that "Men come forth and live; they enter [again] and
die" (Ch. 50).[9] Pierre's dream-lesson about Platon is in line with this
Taoist view: "There now, Karataev has spread out and disappeared."

The metaphysical level of Pierre's thought is as similar to Taoism
as the ethical. Pierre, while retaining the conventional name "God,"
arrives at a view of deity much like Lao-Tzu's delineation of the absolute Tao: not transcendent, not quite pantheistic, but both palpably and
indefinably immanent in all movement and life. His most succinct formulation states, "Life is everything. Life is God.[10] Everything changes

---

8. Tolstoj's word *balagan*, meaning a tent or market-stand, gives a stronger sense of
flimsiness and tawdriness in contrast to Pierre's strength and dignity.

9. A striking parallel is seen in Bk. XVIII of *Chuang-Tzu;* see Legge, *The Texts of
Taoism*, 441-450.

10. The monosyllabic pungency and alliterative quality of the Russian—"_izn' est'
bog."—suggest Lao-Tzu's elemental simplicity more than does the English.

and moves and that movement is God. And while there is life there is joy in consciousness of the divine. To love life is to love God. Harder and more blessed than all else is to love this life in one's sufferings, in innocent sufferings." (*WP*, XIV, 3, p. 1181; *SS*, VII, 181.) Comprehending this "ever-palpable God" that is found "here and everywhere" Pierre "naturally threw away the telescope through which he had till now gazed over men's heads, and gladly regarded the ever-changing, eternally great, unfathomable, and infinite life around him" (*WP*, XV, 5, p. 1227; *SS*, VII, 234). This religion of experience and life reflects the entire burden of Lao-Tzu and most particularly the following passages:

All pervading is the Great Tao! It may be found on the left hand and on the right (Ch. 34.)

All things depend on [the Tao] for their production, which it gives to them, not one refusing obedience to it....All things return to their root and disappear and do not know that it is it which presides over their doing so. (Ch. 34.)

Thus it is that the Tao produces all things....It produces them and makes no claim on the possession of them.....it brings them to maturity and exercises no control over them; – this is called its mysterious operation. (Ch. 51.)

Both Pierre and Lao-Tzu stress the known supremacy and the completely unknowable operation of divine motion; "the law of the Tao [and also of Pierre's God] is its being what it is" (Ch. 25). And Lao-Tzu's comment that the Tao "might appear to have been before God" (Ch. 4), if read as an expression of the primacy of a natural God over a rationalized God of organized belief, parallels Pierre's awareness that Karataev's God was "greater, more infinite, and unfathomable than the Architect of the Universe recognized by the Freemasons" (*WP*, XV, 5, p. 1226; *SS*, VII, 234). Chapter 14 of the *Tao Te Ching*, in which the Tao is described as inaccessible to sight, hearing, or touch, offers a full analysis of the unfathomability which Pierre stresses here.

After Pierre is freed, he finds no need to probe the metaphysical questions further; the issue is whether he can retain the stabilizing ethic generated by the metaphysics. The ethic itself operates like the *te* of Taoism: "As soon as it [the Tao] proceeds to action, it has a name.

When it once has that name, [men] can know to rest in it. When they
know to rest in it, they can be free from all risk of failure and error."
(Ch. 32.) Pierre is fully tested only when he leaves the isolation of his
ambulant prison and can "proceed to action" again. In his first inter-
personal challenges he displays cheerful tolerance and an ability to
inject himself into others' experiences: he "knew how to listen." The
old princess, previously hostile to him, feels now as though "he seemed
to be trying to understand the most intimate places of her heart";[11]
Pierre satisfies his benevolent urges by "drawing out the human qualities of the embittered, hard, and (in her own way) proud princess."
(*WP*, 1227-1228; *SS*, vii, 235-236.) Pierre's "recognition of the possibility of everyone thinking, feeling, and seeing things each from his
own point of view" is similar to the insight of the Taoist sage, who
"has no inviolable mind of his own; he makes the mind of the people
his mind" (Ch. 49). In more mundane affairs Pierre "no longer felt
either doubt or perplexity.....There was now within him a judge who
by some rule unknown to him decided what should or should not be
done." (*WP*, 1230; *SS*, VII, 238-239) In essential ways, these ideas
correlate with both the practical psychology and the ethic of Lao-Tzu:
"It is the way of the Tao to act without thinking of acting; to conduct
affairs without feeling the trouble of them; to taste without discerning
any flavor; to consider what is small as great, and a few as many; and
to recompense injury with kindness." And at this same time, like "the
master of the Tao," Pierre "anticipates things that are difficult while
they are easy, and does things that would become great while they are
small" (Ch. 63).

Pierre balances precariously in a state of truth as long as he can
remain (in Lao-Tzu's terminology) "without desire" (Ch. 37), but he
finds his vision weakened by the now-restored world of love, struggle,
and complexity. Even though Nataša can sense and share the significance of Pierre's prison-march experience, she diminishes his freedom by giving him "a judge of his every word and action" – a finite
and less indubitable judge (*WP*, 1237; *SS*, VII, 247). Also, Pierre can-

---

11. For Tolstoj's word _izni_, "of her life" would be a better translation and more
indicative of Pierre's new sense of total process than is "of her heart."

not rein in his intellect to the Taoist ideal of being "simple and ignorant" (Ch. 65); he must pursue scientific pursuits and political ratiocinations. Perhaps superfluity is unavoidable for the politically conscious Pierre, since a type of wisdom that was probably not viable even in "a little state with a small population" (Ch. 80) cannot provide remedies for the gigantic diseases of the Russian autocracy. Because of these emotional, intellectual, and political forces of deviation, Pierre must compromise the simplicity and passivity of his ideal: Nataša must be desired, science must be taken into account; the state must be brought back to antique truths and yet moved forward in the world through devious processes. Despite the fact that Platon "would not have approved" (*WP*, First Epilogue, 4, p. 1307; *SS*, VII, 328) of Pierre's choices, something much like the Tao still stands as a firm foothold for Pierre in the midst of harassing reality and as a solid if unattainable ideal, on the basis of which necessary compromises are made.

Thus, the Tao-like truths imparted by Platon are truly focal for the career of Pierre. Looking backward over events antecedent to the prison march, we see dissipation, reformism, Freemasonry, and ameliorative terrorism as logically coherent way-stations en route to these truths. The epilogic events indicate not the failure of Platon's simple truths, but the inability of the modern world – Tolstoj was too much the realist to evade the fact – to contain and apply them in their pure form.

The other fictional characters of *War and Peace* – with Andrej a most important exception – can be most clearly given their moral evaluation by applying the standards of the enlightened Pierre. Nataša at first is an ebullient and arrogant "Cossack," doubly driven by social superficialities and an unmanageable excess of the life force; guilt, deprivation, and closeness to death cleans her of superfluities and redirect her vitality toward a state of finite motherhood (vide the Tao as infinite mother). Her now-domesticated spontaneity, her envelopment in Pierre's thought, and her ability to purge Pierre's ideas of the superfluous (*WP*, First Epilogue, 3, pp. 1284-1285; *SS*, VII, 302) are measures of her rapport with Pierre's truths. Princess Mar'ja changes in no dramatic way as the book progresses, since she is never tempted by ego, society, or the intellect; she stays consistently just off the path of the satisfying insight of earth, at the end still searching too vigorously for perfection – still deluded by transcendence (*WP,* First Epilogue, 2, p. 1281; *SS,* VII, 297). The headstrong and worldly Nikolaj travels through romanticism and practicality to come as close as his wife to the Tao – "Only when he had understood the peasants' tastes and aspirations...and felt akin to them did he begin boldly to manage his serfs, that is, to perform toward them the duties demanded of him." Even less clearly than Pierre can Nikolaj define his standard, "but the standard was quite firm and definite in his own mind" (*WP*, First Epilogue, 2, pp. 1271-1272; *SS,* VII, 286-287). Mar'ja's pietism balances his pragmatic simplicity just as Nataša's acceptant, maternal earthiness balances Pierre's flights toward complexity, and we can see the relevance of Tolstoj's tentative title for the novel, *All's Well That Ends Well.* Of course, the unsympathetic figures – Boris, Èlen, Prince Vasilij and his sons – are premeditators, desirers, caught in the toils of *yu-wei* (positive action), who never see or find the way.

Following the lead of his sister, Andrej moves throughout the book toward a metaphysic and ethic sharply different from Taoistic naturalism. A taut and intense man, destined to die rather than survive, Andrej develops a rigid and transcendental answer to the questions of suffering and death. The Christian lesson of Mar'ja – "love...for those who hate us, love of our enemies" (*WP,* X, 37, p. 908; *SS,* VI 292) – inevitably grows into an identification of love with God and in turn into an eschatology of love" to die means that I, a particle of love, shall return to the general and eternal source" (*WP*, XII, 4, p. 1089-1090; *SS,* VII, 74-75). Andrej thus represents the Christian side of Tolstoj, who, after his confrontation with Oriental thought, endeavored to synthesize and reconcile the thought of East and West. The challenge is suggested by a diary entry of 1884: "I must compose for myself a Circle of Reading: Epictetus, Marcus Aurelius, Lao-Tzu, Buddha, Pascal, the Gospels."[12] In *War and Peace* the main thrust is still toward earth and immediacy rather than toward heaven and eternity.

The effects of the *te* will be seen not only "in the person" but also "in the state, and in the kingdom," says Lao-Tzu (Ch. 54). Andrej, while of less importance than Pierre as a philosophical thermometer

---

12. Diary entry of 15 March 1884, *SS,* XIX, 311.

for other characters, is crucial as a medium for ideas concerning war and government that again parallel Taoistic doctrines. Very early in his military career Andrej perceives that events in battle take place by chance despite the pretensions of Bagration (*WP*, II, 13, p. 193; *SS*, IV, 245). Later he channels to the reader a portrait of Kutuzov, who "understands that there is something stronger and more important than his own will – the inevitable course of events," who can see events and grasp their significance, and who "has the wisdom to avoid meddling" (*WP*, X, 16, p. 831; *SS*, VI, 199). Despite Tolstoj's designation of him as the complete Russian, Kutuzov, by his acquiescence, his unmilitary sloppiness, his rapport with the all-important spirit of the army, and his avoidance of battle, strongly suggests the warrior-ideal of Lao-Tzu:

> He who in [Tao's] wars has skill
> Assumes no martial port;
> He who fights with most good will
> To rage makes no resort.
> He who vanquishes yet still
> Keeps from his foes apart;
> He whose hests men most fulfil
> Yet humbly plies his art.
> Thus we say, "he ne'er contends,
> And therein is his might."
> Thus we say, "Men's wills he bends,
> That they with him unite."
> Thus we say, "Like Heaven's his ends,
> No sage of old more bright."
> (Ch. 68.)

Tolstoj chose to have his sage-general follow the dictate of making "the mind of the people his mind" (Ch. 49) rather than that of bending men's wills. Other passages in the *Tao Te Ching* add weight to the analogy. For example, Kutuzov's preference for defensive war is like that of the Taoist. Compare his "We can only lose by taking the offensive. Patience and time are my warriors" (*WP*, XIII, 4, p. 1135; *SS*, VII, 129) with this from Lao-Tzu: "A master of the art of war has said, `I do not dare to be the host [to commence the war]; I prefer to be the guest [to act on the defensive]. I do not dare to advance an inch; I prefer to retire a foot.'" (Ch. 69.) Kutuzov could have patterned his post-Borodino strategy on Lao-Tzu: "A skillful (commander) strikes a decisive blow, and stops. He does not dare (by continuing his operations) to assert and complete his mastery. He will strike the blow, but will be on his guard against being vain or boastful or arrogant in consequence of it. He strikes it as a master of necessity; he strikes it, but not from a wish for mastery." (Ch. 30.) As the French retreat, Kutuzov attempts to re-strain his army "from useless attacks, maneuvers, and encounters with the perishing enemy" (*WP*, 1138; *SS*, VII, 131).

Even in the discursive sections of the novel, the analogy with Tao-ism can serve a purpose. Despite the elaborate intellectual superstruc-ture, it is a simple wisdom like that of Lao-Tzu – the wisdom of Platon and Pierre – that contains the key to Tolstoj's sweeping decisions of man and history. That is, if we dig back to the core of the intellectual-ity, we arrive against cryptic formulations like those of Lao-Tzu. A brief consideration of one pervasive, complex issue – namely, deter-minism and free will – will suffice to illustrate the tight relationship between intellectual structure and intuitive foundation. In various ways Tolstoj asserts that the cause of historical events is hundreds of thou-sands of individual wills – the idea is a basic weapon in what was called his "war against Napoleon." But he denies freedom to those individual wills by dissolving them in mass movements, the "collec-tive will," and by eventually limiting freedom to a "consciousness of freedom" (*soznanie svobody; WP*, Second Epilogue, 1338; *SS*, VII, 364). For this paradox of all-determining wills without volition, a resolution might be suggested by the Taoistic analogue. The peasants with their determinant wills are intimately in touch with the "force uncomprehended" by Platon, just as sages are in touch with the Tao that is the Mother of all and the stream of history; freedom is the abil-ity to become coincident with this sensed flow. Lao-Tzu never directly confronts the issue of freedom, but the Taoist "will" is apparently based on a type of double vision that would clarify Tolstoj's thornier syllo-gisms. Tolstoj says that "man in connection with the general life of humanity appears subject to laws which determine that life. But the same man apart from that connection appears to be free." (*WP,* 1338; *SS,* VII, 364). He adds later, "Reason gives expression to the laws of inevitability. Consciousness gives expression to the essence of freedom...Freedom is the content. Inevitability is the form." (*WP,* 1347; *SS,* VII, 376.) Lao-Tzu would seem to say: if we violate the Tao by articulating it and seeing it as form, we become rational and see determinism; if we merely live the Tao we find freedom in our own consciousness. Or, to state the matter differently, if we act purposefully we commit ourselves to the external and feel compulsion; when we act with no intent (*wu-wei*) we live, in a sense, freely. Again, Tolstoj's comment that we cannot comprehend free will within space and time (*WP,* 1345; *SS,* VII, 372) could be answered by the possibility of living in the Tao, which is like "the emptiness of a vessel" (Ch. 4) – that is, spaceless and timeless. Thus, although we must try to extrapolate some unwritten implications of Taoism, we find, at the end, a correlation both of answers and of unanswered questions. Tolstoj's final comment that "it is similarly necessary to renounce a freedom that does not exist, and to recognize a dependence of which we are not conscious" (*WP,* 1351; *SS,* VII, 381) is, typically, compatible with Taoism.

Despite a divergence of mood in the outer, expository circles of the novel, there is a broad overall range of analogies between *War and Peace* and the *Tao Te Ching.* The fact that these analogies link such diverse elements as Platon and history, Pierre and the question of free will, suggests a unity not always clear from other perspectives. More important, these analogies reveal a good deal about the drift of Tolstoj's mind. At the time of *War and Peace,* drawing from Rousseau, the Gospels, Marcus Aurelius and Epictetus, Hegel, De Maistre, and numerous other sources, Tolstoj had moved toward an intellectual stance much like that of Lao-Tzu. In *Anna Karenina* we find a sense of naturalistic acquiescence and a critique of egocentric attachment that are compatible with Taoism. Thus, there was a readiness for the actual encounter with Taoist materials in the late seventies. Tolstoy's "post-conversion" thought remains eclectic and becomes increasingly dogmatic regarding morality, but Taoism took hold and persisted as a steady, central vein within the complex structure. In 1884 Tolstoj wrote, "I attribute my good moral condition to the reading of Confucius and, mainly, to

Lao-Tzu."[13] And in the same month he noted, "Remarkable indeed is Confucius' Doctrine of the Mean. In it, as with Lao-Tzu, a fulfillment of natural law is what constitutes wisdom, strength, and life. And this law fulfills itself silently, with its meaning unrevealed. It is the Tao, which unfolds itself evenly, imperceptibly, and without trace, and yet has powerful effects.'"[14] An interesting comment by Maksim Gor'kij indicates the enthusiasm of Tolstoj for Taoism in 1901-1902: "he is expounding the teaching of Lao-Tzu, and it seems to me that he is some kind of unusual man orchestra, having the capability to play at once on several instruments – on a brass horn, on a drum, on a harmonica, and on a flute.[15] By 1909, Tolstoj's thought apparently had come to a tighter focus on Christian and Oriental wisdom, for another observer describes the old master as follows: "The first hour he spoke about his understanding of religion....He spoke of the powers which are founded on the people, about the awakening of religious consciousness; he said that the intelligentsia is good for nothing in its low state of decadence; he advised sternly – all this with cold eyes – not to read books except the Gospels, the Veda, Confucius, Lao-Tzu."[16] Thus through a half-century we move from Platon, the ignorant man who symbolizes the wisdom and strength of the people, to a doctrine of anti-intellectualism and faith in the "powers" of the ordinary Russian. The concepts of Taoism, as analogy and influence, help explain this thread of coherence that connects Tolstoj the artist and Tolstoj the prophet.[17]

---

13. Ibid.

14. Diary entry of 23 March 1884, PSS, LIV, p. 436, n. 150; cited in Bodde, *Tolstoy and China*, 21.

15. L. N. Tolstoj v Vospominanijax Sovremennikov Red. S. N. Golubova and others, M., 1960), II, 445.

16. Ibid., 375.

17. The authors would like to express their appreciation to the San Diego State College Foundation, whose support made the research for this article possible.

CHAPTER THREE

SOME BUDDHIST INKLINGS IN PRINCE ANDREI AND PIERRE BEZUKHOV IN *WAR AND PEACE*
Dragan Milivojevic

To try to mould Tolstoy's ideas and thoughts, which are expressed through his main characters, Prince Andrei and Pierre Bezukhov, in terms of a single philosophical or religious system, be it Christianity, Buddhism, Hinduism or Schopenhauer's philosophy, would be futile. That is not to say that such influences are absent but they are so intimately and tightly interwoven in Tolstoy's narrative in *War and Peace* in an artistic structure that they cannot be perceived as extraneous. To say that Tolstoy's characters in War and Peace, Prince Andrei and Pierre Bezukhov, in their search for truth experience some Buddhist-like inklings and intimations does not mean that they embraced Buddhist philosophy and espouse Buddhist beliefs. The similarities can be interpreted as purely coincidental or they can be attributed to some universal religious and mystical experiences not unique and specific for Buddhism. And yet they exist and the purpose of this article is to compare Prince Andrei's and Pierre's peak mystical experiences to those of Buddhist sages and meditators. The two key concepts of Buddhist philosophy are considered in relation to Prince Andrei's and Pierre's insights. These concepts are the externalization of the internal and the internalization of the external.

The externalization of the internal in the context of Zen Buddhist philosophy is manifested by the loss of ego consciousness when a person encounters an 'external' object. Loosing our ego consciousness opens our insight into the metaphysical ground of Being-a person becomes identified and submerged into an object. Suppose that a person is looking at a beautiful flower and is so entranced with its beauty that a sense of separation between a person as a subject and a flower as an object is lost. There is only an awareness and there is no consciousness of oneself or of the flower. The internalization of the external is the reverse. In it the external world (Nature) becomes internalized and a part of our consciousness. What has been thought to be 'external' to oneself is really 'internal.' Here again the difference between the perceiving mind and the perceived object is abolished as the external world is internalized.

An anecdote from Buddhist history illustrates this point. Two monks were arguing about why a flag was flapping in the wind. One said that it was the flag itself which caused its own flapping while the other said the wind was the cause. A senior monk told them that neither the flag nor the wind were the causes. It was their minds which were flapping.[1] It is, however, an enlightened mind with a capital 'M' which is able to realize that. The flag flapping in the wind is no longer an event which occurs in the external world; it is a part of one's own landscape. The altered unitary state of consciousness resulting from the externalization of the interior and the internalization of the exterior differs from the ordinary state of consciousness where the exterior, nature (the world) is opposed to the interior, the mind. The ordinary state of consciousness is deceptive and misleading as Prince Andrei's experience shows and his experience of an altered and elevated consciousness resulting from the externalization of the internal is superior as it is accompanied by a state of blissful peace.

Prince Andrei is persistently and agonizingly searching for that experience which will lead him to the truth and he is endowed with the

---

1. While the Sixth Patriarch was there, the wind began to flap the flag. There were two monks there, who started an argument about it. One of them remarked, 'Look! The flag is moving'. The other retorted: 'No! It is the wind that is moving'. They argued back and forth endlessly, without being able to reach the truth. Abruptly Hui Neng cut short the fruitless argument by saying: 'It is not that the wind is moving, it is not that the flat is moving. O honorable Brethern, it is in reality your minds that are moving!' The two monks stood aghast." Toshihiko Izutsu *Toward a Philosophy of Zen Buddhism* (Boulder-Prajna Press, 1982), 211. The concepts 'The Externalization of the Internal' and 'The Internalization of the External' are used in Izutsu's book.

spiritual and moral qualities which will make that search easier and more attainable. He is intelligent, courageous, independent and perceptive. He sees through the bravado and the conceit of Napoleon; he has no romantic illusions about the war and its spurious glories, and he is also able to see what is wrong in his father's life. Nevertheless, the truth in its entirety eludes him. It only comes in bits and pieces in his reflective moments or when his conscious thinking is temporarily suspended. On the eve of the Borodino battle, faced with the possibility of dying, he makes a summary of his life, of his ambitions and goals. The confession is honest and courageous. With his sharp intelligence and perception, he cuts through the layers of his illusions and deceits:

"His whole life seemed to him like a magic lantern, which he had been looking at through the glass and by artificial light. Now he saw suddenly, without the glass, in the clear light of day, these badly daubed pictures. Yes, yes, there they are: there are the cheating forms that excited torments and ecstasies for me."[2]

This account of his life is devastating in its meaninglessness. The 'cheating forms' are his previous deceptions and illusions. Andrei's realization does not leave him anything to seize upon in an attempt to impart meaningful direction for the rest of his life. It succeeds, though, in clearing the ground, in separating the wheat from the chaff and doing away with illusions. Andrei can now start with a clean slate if he only knew where to go. This negative way of eliminating wrong views as the beginning of wisdom, that is of right thinking, is recommended as an initial but an important step in Buddhism. Andrei's vision is still not unitary or integrated; it is dualistic, separating wrong desires and ambitions from an unqualified and unspecified goodness.

"The ignorant discriminate and try to adjust themselves to external conditions, and are constantly perturbed in mind; unrealities are imagined and discriminated while realities are unseen and ignored,"[3] This quotation from Lankavatara Sutra appropriately describes Andrei's state of mind before his realization of the emptiness and unsubstantiality of his worldly pursuits. His realization may be summed in another quota-

2. Leo Tolstoy, *War and Peace*, Polnoe Sobranie Sochinenij, 11, 201.
3. Dwight Goddard, *A Buddhist Bible* (Boston: Beacon Press, 1966), 298.

tion form the same source: "All that is seen in the world is devoid of effort and action because all things in the world are like a dream, or like an image miraculously projected."[4] Andrei has been pursuing a dream which he considered real but which he realized was unreal.

It was after the battle of Austerlitz when Andrei awoke from his faint that another insight came to him.

"Above him there was nothing but the sky-the lofty sky, not clear yet immeasurably lofty, with grey clouds gliding slowly across it. 'How quiet, peaceful and solemn, not at all as it was when I ran', thought Prince Andrei...how differently do these clouds glide across that lofty infinite sky! How was it that I did not see that lofty sky before? And how happy am I to have found it at last! Yes! All is vanity, all falsehood, except that infinite sky. There is nothing, nothing but that. But even it does not exist, there is nothing but quiet and peace."[5]

This second insight repeats the theme of illusion exemplified in the words 'vanity' and 'falsehood' but adds to it a counterpoint in the image of the infinite, lofty sky which, in turn, stands for quietness, repose and peace. While the previous experience was purely negative and as such conducive to nihilism and meaninglessness, this one has a positive aspect which cancels doubt and negativism. In a world replete with 'cheating forms' there is hope in the image of the ever present infinity of the sky which by its vastness contrasts with the pettiness and self-centeredness of human affairs. For Andrei this experience after his fall is like the first day of his life; his discursive intellect has not yet emerged to dissect reality into different compartments, of 'this' and 'that'. This vision, unlike the previous one, is non-dualistic and unitary because it focuses on a single image of the sky and excludes everything else and because it cancels the opposition between Andrei, the observer and the sky which is being observed. Andrei's ego is expanded and absorbed in the infinity of sky and it is encompassed by it. The Internal, Andrei's consciousness, is externalized.

The third insight is related during Pierre's captivity:

"The huge endless bivouac that had previously resounded with the cracking of camp-fires and the voices of many men had grown quiet,

---

4. Ibid, 278.
5. Leo Tolstoy, *War and Peace*, Polnoe Sobranie, 11, 201.

the red camp-fires were growing paler and dying down. High up in the lit sky hung the fall moon. Forests and fields beyond the camp, unseen before, were now visible in the distance. And farther still, beyond those forests and fields, the bright, oscillating, limitless distance lured one to itself. Pierre glanced up at the sky and the twinkling stars in its far-away depths. `And this is me, and all that is within me, and it is all I!' thought Pierre. `And they caught all that and put it into a shed boarded up with planks!' He smiled, and went and lay down to sleep beside his companions."[6]

Pierre's ego has extended so far into infinity that it has become infinity itself and thereby ceased to be an ego. It resembles an all absorbing circle whose center is pulled away as its borders recede into space. It is neither here nor there as it is everywhere. Pierre experiences the divine essence: "God is a sphere of which the center is everywhere and the circumference is nowhere."[7] Such an abstract entity cannot be confined in "...a shed boarded up with planks," in a coffin; it cannot be annihilated. Although both Andrei's and Pierre's experience of themselves and the sky result in the same intimation of what life is all about, there are differences in the way their experience is related to the natural and material world around them. In Andrei's example we observe the externalization of the internal and in Pierre's example we see the opposite process of the internalization of the external. Pierre says: "And this is me, and that is within me, and it is all I." The `I" which Pierre refers to is not an ordinary physical `I' of flesh and bone, it is an `I' which contains everything-the whole universe. Andrei's ego is absorbed by the sky and through it by silence and peace. Pierre, on the other hand, internalizes the world around him until the sky, the stars, the fields and the forests become a part of him. In both cases, there is a loss of the everyday, intentional, planning and scheming consciousness and an intimation of higher and superior knowledge. In the everyday state of consciousness, we stay apart from the world around us, judging, planning, evaluating and scheming and in this state of

---

6. Leo Tolstoy, *War and Peace*, Polnoe Sobranie, 12, 106.
7. Georges Poulet, *The Metamorphosis of the Circle*, trans. by Carley Dawson and Elliot Coleman, (Baltimore: Johns Hopkins University Press, 1966), 99.

dualism it is impossible for us to achieve the state of unification and oneness which is characteristic of both states of consciousness-the externalization of the internal and the internalization of the external. The prior behaviour and experiences of both Andrei and Pierre confirm the unsatisfactorinnes of their everyday consciousness.

The fourth insight is again Pierre's and it is from the twenty-second chapter of Book VIII which contains a description of Pierre's feelings as he drives home in his sled after telling and assuring Natasha that she is worthy of love. He is in a euphoric mood anticipating their future life together.

"It was clear and frosty. Above the dirty ill-lit streets, above the black roofs, stretched the dark starry sky. Only looking up at the sky did Pierre cease to feel how sordid and humiliating were all mundane things compared to the heights to which his soul had just been raised. At the entrance to the Arbat Square an immense expanse of dark starry sky presented itself to his eyes. Almost in the center of it, above the Perchistenka Boulevard, surrounded and sprinkled on all sides by stars but distinguished from them all by its nearness to the earth, with its white light, and its long uplifted tail, shone the enormous and brilliant comet of the year 1812-the comet which was said to portend all kinds of woes and the end of the world. In Pierre, however, that comet, with its long luminous tail aroused no feeling of fear. On the contrary, he gazed joyfully, his eyes moist with tears, at this bright comet which, having travelled in its orbit with inconceivable velocity through immeasurable space, seemed suddenly-like an arrow piercing the earth-to remain fixed in a chosen spot, vigorously holding in its tail erect, shining, and displaying its white light and countless other scintillating stars. It seemed to Pierre that this comet fully responded to what was passing in his own softened and uplifted soul, now blossoming into a new life."[8]

In this image it appears that the whole universe is descending on Pierre and becoming part of his consciousness. The external world is symbolized and concentrated in the image of the comet which like an arrow is aimed at the earth and about to pierce it. Pierre's soul, his

---

8. Leo Tolstoy, *War and Peace*, Polnoe Sobranie, 10, 375.

consciousness, had just been raised to new heights to meet and absorb the starry firmament and his soul offers no resistance to the outside but fully responds to the comet. The comet has become a part of his internal world. Its uplifted tail corresponds to Pierre's uplifted soul. "It is as if a man had widely cast his net and were drawing it in."[9] The process of "drawing in" is comparable to Pierre's state of consciousness during his captivity when his consciousness expanded to infinity and was subsequently absorbed by it. The essence of these two insights is the same, an altered state of consciousness, the internalization of the external.

Two states of mind or two states of consciousness are described in the lives of Prince Andrei and Pierre. One is ordinary consciousness where they face the world as subjects facing objects, opposing their consciousness to the external world. This ordinary, everyday dualistic consciousness, separating the thinking, feeling, planning and scheming subject from the world outside, is unsatisfactory because it is subjective and partial as it views the world from a particular individual view. Prince Andrei acknowledges its shortcomings as he refers to his life "as a magic lantern" and Pierre in his spiritual meanderings cannot make sense of the human folly exemplified in the battle of Borodino and the death of Karataev through the prism of his ordinary consciousness. Totality of consciousness is achieved by expansion of the mind or by drawing the universe into the mind; the distinction between a subject and an object is obliterated by either expanding the subject to embrace the object, the sky in Prince Andrei's insight, or internalizing the object to become a part of the subject, the sky and the twinkling stars in Pierre's first insight and the descending comet in his second insight. According to Buddhist philosophy, what remains in this state of egoless and objectless perception is pure awareness, an impartial and total perception of the world. The painters in the Japanese Buddhist tradition who paint bamboos are advised by long contemplation of the bamboo trees to "become bamboos" that is to sink their senses so deeply in the object perceived that they merge with it. Only in this merger is total and impartial perception of the true nature of the bam-

---

9. George Steiner, *Tolstoy or Dostoevsky*, (New York: Vintage Books, 1959), 271.

boo possible, a perception which is rendered immediately and hurriedly on the canvas. An authority on Japanese Zen Buddhism sums up the Zen view of reality:

"(1) The initial stage, corresponding to the world-experience of an ordinary man, at which the knower and the known are sharply distinguished from one another as two separate entities, and at which a mountain, for example, is seen by the perceiving 'I' as an objective thing called 'mountain'.

(2) The middle stage,... explained as a state of absolute unification, a spiritual state prior to subject-object bifurcation. At this stage the so-called 'external' world is deprived of its ontological solidity. Here the very expression 'I see a mountain' is strictly a false statement, for there is neither the 'I' which sees nor the mountain which is seen. If there is anything here it is the absolutely undivided awareness of Something eternally illuminating itself as the whole universe."

(3) The final stage, a stage of infinite freedom and tranquility, at which the undivided Something divides itself into subject and object in the very midst of the original oneness, the latter being still kept intact in spite of the apparent subject-object bifurcation.[10]

Prince Andrei's and Pierre's experiences of ordinary consciousness and pure awareness correspond to stages one and two while stage three is reached in Pierre's vision of the comet. The developmental stages of the growth of human consciousness as outlined in Japanese branch of Zen Buddhism and the insights of Prince Andrei and Pierre show striking resemblance. Through his artistic creativity and his inspirational insight, Tolstoy independently rendered the same stages of consciousness described in Buddhist Philosophy.

---

10. Toshihiko Izutsu, *Toward a Philosophy of Zen Buddhism*, (Boulder Prajna Press, 1982), 209.

CHAPTER FOUR

A BUDDISTIC LEITMOTIF IN ANNA KARENINA
Harry Hill Walsh

The most cursory reading of *Anna Karenina* reveals it to be a sort of *Erziehungsroman* developing in two directions. Along one axis the title character is brought by stages to utter disillusionment with her worldly milieu and to eventual suicide. Along the other axis Tolstoi's *alter ego* Konstantin Levin arrives finally at a tentative faith in an unknowable God, whose immanent manifestations appear to lie in pastoral harmony and the extended family. In bringing these two main subplots to resolution Tolstoi uncharacteristically resorts to the hackneyed literary symbolism of darkness and light. Thus is Levin transfixed by lightning flashes at the culmination of his interior monologue of the transcendental nature of God at the novel's end. And thus is the death of Anna at the end of Part 7 likened to the blowing out of a candle. The incremental repetition of the motif of light and darkness is so conspicuous as to force the reader to recognize its function as the objective correlative of life and death. The point of departure for the present study is the suspicion that the candle image has a specific connotation separate from the overall motif of light and darkness.

The candle image is produced at four junctures in the chapters leading up to Karenina's suicide at the end of Part Seven. In Chapter 26, after it first occurs to her that she might kill herself in order to elicit remorse in her lover Vronskii, we find this passage: "'Death! she thought. And such a terror came over her that for a long time she did not know where she was, and her trembling hands were unable to find matches and light a candle to replace the one that had burned down and gone out."¹ In Chapter 27, following Vronskii's departure for the countryside, Anna recalls the experiences of the previous night: "'He's left? It's finished?' Anna asked herself, standing at the window. And in answer to this question the recollections of the darkness when the candle had gone out and of the terrible dream, all merging together, filled her heart with cold terror." In the final chapter of Part 7 Anna overhears a fellow railway passenger express the sentiment that people are endowed with reason in order that they might be delivered from distress. Hearing this Anna thinks to herself: "Reason is given to one for deliverance; therefore, one should be delivered. Why shouldn't I blow out the candle when there is nothing more to look at, when everything is so repulsive to the sight?" And finally, after she has thrown herself under the wheels of the train, Tolstoi writes: "And the candle, by whose light she had been reading the book filled with anxieties, lies, grief, and evil, flared up with a light brighter than ever before, illuminated for her all that had previously been in darkness, crackled, began to grow dim and went out forever."

The candle image was not gone unnoticed by Tolstoi scholars. Konstantin Leont'ev dismisses its appearance in the novel as "nothing more than an exquisite allegory" (*krasivoe inoskazanie, bol'she nichego*).² Boris Eikhenbaum sees the origin of the candle theme in Tolstoi's attraction to the philosophy of Schopenhauer, without, it must be said, making a convincing case for his argument.³ And Elizabeth Stenbock-Fermor devotes an entire chapter of her recent monograph on the structure of *Anna Karenina* to the candle image.⁴ Stenbock-Fermor rejects as unconvincing Eikhenbaum's hypothesis about Schopenhauer's influence, emphasizing instead the functional importance of the motif as one of the "vaults" on which rests the doctrinal content of the work. The present author hopes to demonstrate below the correctness of Eikhenbaum's hypothesis.

---

1. All translations of passages from *Anna Karenina* are by the author and are taken from the jubilee edition of Tolstoi's works, *Polnoe sobranie Sochinenii*, 90 vols. (Moscow: Khud. Lit., 1928-58).

2. K. Leont'ev, *O romanakh gr. L. N. Tolstago* (Moscow: V. M. Sablin, 1911), p. 65

3. B. Eikhenbaum, *Lev Tolstoi. Semidesiatye gody* (Leningrad: Khud lit., 1974), pp. 185-186.

4. E. Stenbock-Fermor, *The Architecture of Anna Karenina; A History of Its Writing, Structure and Message* (Lisse: de Ridder, 1975), pp. 41-51.

The history and details of Tolstoi's attraction to Schopenhauer's theories has been told elsewhere and need not be repeated here.[5] Let it suffice to say that there is abundant proof that Schopenhauer's works exerted a strong and abiding influence on Tolstoi's writings from 1868 to Tolstoi's death. There are numerous instances of probable Schopenhauerian themes in *Anna Karenina*.

Eikhenbaum has argued convincingly, on syntactic as well as contextual grounds, that the novel's epigraph ("Vengeance is mine; I will repay") was inspired by passages from *The World As Will and Representation*, and that Levin's figure of eighty thousand prostitutes for the city of London is taken from Schopenhauer's essay on women in *Parerga und Paralipomena*. Also one might add that Levin's reflections on the instinctive, as opposed to rational, modes of behavior characteristic of women recall in often strikingly similar passages the misogyny of Schopenhauer, who reserved the quality of *Wissen*, or rational knowledge, for the male sex, leaving women to grope for knowledge through Gefühl alone (a distinction Tolstoi would continue to make as late as 1887 in *On Life*). In the epithalamic paean devoted to the Levins' conjugal bliss Tolstoi on two occasions associates Kitty with the symbol of a bird building its nest in response to blind instinctive urges.

In Part 5 of the novel we find Levin repelled at the condition of his dying brother, while Kitty "thought, felt, and acted quite differently. At the sight of the sick man she felt pity. And in her woman's heart this pity did not at all create the feeling of horror and aversion which it had created in her husband but aroused a need for action." This is highly reminiscent of the notion of functional adaptation by sex embraced by Schopenhauer, who suggested in *Parerga und Paralipomena* that women, because of their weaker powers of reasoning, manifest "mehr Mitleid und daher mehr Menschenliebe und Teilnahme an unglückliche als die Männer."[6]

Sigrid McLaughlin has shown that the outcome of the Vronskii-Karenina affair is predictable in its main outlines in terms of Schopenhauer's metaphysics of sexual love, as presented in the second

5. See Sigrid McLaughlin, "Some Aspects of Tolstoy's Intellectual Development: Tolstoy and Schopenhauer," *California Slavic Studies*, 5 (1970), 187-248.
6. A. Schopenhauer, *Sämtliche Werke*, 5 vols. (Stuttgart: Cotta Verlag, 1965), V, 722.

and subsequent editions of *The World As Will and Representation*."[7]
Thus, in the light of the numerous coincidences with Schopenhauerian
themes found in *Anna Karenina*, it would not seem unreasonable to
examine Schopenhauer's work for some clue as to the inspiration for
the candle image, which so transparently bears the mark of symbolic
function.

Schopenhauer did as much as any of his contemporaries to spread
the doctrines of Buddhism in the West, where the systematic study of
that religion begins only in the 1840s with the writings of such scholars as Hodgson, Burnouf, and Spence Hardy.[8] In this capacity, it now
seems likely, Schopenhauer supplied his quondam Russian disciple –
either directly through his writings or indirectly through Afanasii Fet –
with the image of the candle not, as Stenbock-Fermor contends, as the
symbol of life, but as the oxymoronic symbol of a particular kind of
existence equatable to death – that denoted as *samsara* in Buddhist
texts and characterized by unreasoning personal desire. George Gibian
has noted this use of the symbol, and writes of it as follows:

"To speak of intellectual understanding in terms of a light is one of
the oldest, traditional similes. Yet Tolstoj is not using the image in this
manner. Anna's bright light does not stand for clear understanding –
far from it....Anna's bright light is the light of her disappointment, re-
sentment, desire to avenge herself, to make Vronskij pay for imagined
slights, to make him feel sorry for Anna and to repent. It is the same
distorting light by which she now judges everyone whom she encounters to be hateful, repulsive, unhappy. Its dazzling brightness blinds
instead of revealing. Its clarity is one of special selection, distortion."[9]

A Buddhistic-Schopenhauerian interpretation of the candle image
would certainly offer some explanation for some of the questions arising from its use in the novel. One could thus understand the candle as
representing Schopenhauer's *Wille zum Leben*, which Tolstoi equated

7. McLaughlin, *loc. cit.*, pp. 207-11.
8. For Schopenhauer's links with Indic thought, see C. A. Muses, *East-West Fire: Schopenhauer's Optimism and the Lankavatara Sutra* (Indian Hills, Colo.: Falcon's Wing Press, 1955) and D. W. Dauer, *Schopenhauer As a Transmitter of Buddhist Ideas* (Berne: Lang, 1969).
9. G. Gibian "Two Kinds of Human Understanding and the Narrator's Voice in *Anna Karenina*," in *Orbis Scriptus. Dmitrij Tschizewskij zum 70. Geburtstag* (München: W. Fink Verlag, 1966), p. 317.

with Kant's *Ding an sich*, the noumenal source of all perceived phenomena, and held to lie "with all its force and clarity in the soul of
everyone, even of the most savage individual."[10] For Schopenhauer, in
line with *hinayana* Buddhist practice, maintained that suicide, far from
being the denial of the will, represents its strong affirmation. The suicide, he observes, wills life, and is dissatisfied only with its immediate
conditions.[11]

In this regard Stenbock-Fermor points out what may be a significant revision in the section of the novel dealing with Anna's suicide.
As printed in the April, 1877, number of *Russkii vestnik* the text reads:
"And the candle, by whose light she had been reading the book filled
with anxieties, grief, deceits, and evil, crackled, began to grow dim,
flared up, and everything went out." In revising the novel for publication as a book Tolstoi removed the word "everything," so that only the
candle is extinguished. Stenbock-Fermor links this change to Levins'
inquiry in Part 1 as to whether anything of human consciousness remains after the destruction of the senses. While such an interpretation
may have merit, I would suggest an alternative motivation for the
change, namely, the Buddhistic doctrine that holds death to be, in
Schopenhauer's words, "a sleep in which individuality is forgotten;
everything else awakens again, or rather has remained awake."[12]
Stenbock-Fermor's perceptive observation that the light of the candle
in Anna's railway carriage in Part 1 may be linked to the temptation
offered by Vronskii and to her own eagerness to "live" also provides a
connection between the candle and *samsara*, for the candle again represents immortality. A Buddhistic explanation may also shed light on
the servant Kornei's prophecy that Anna is destined to die in childbirth. Since she in fact does not die in childbirth, it seems possible that
Tolstoi has in mind metempsychotic rebirth.[13] The fact that transmigration of the soul was on Tolstoi's mind at the time of writing *Anna
Karenina* is shown by his attribution of such a belief to Dolly

---

10. Tolstoi, XV, 246.
11. Schopenhauer, *The World As Will and Representation*, tr. E. F. J. Payne from the
German *Die Welt als Wille und Vorstellung* (Indian Hills, Colo.: Falcon's Wing Press,
1958), I, 398.
12. *Ibid.*, I, 278.
13. The prophecy is found in book 4, chapter 3 of *Anna Karenina*.

Oblonskaia.[14]

The opposite of samsara in Buddhist belief is nirvana, regarded as the state of release from worldly cravings. It is interesting to note in this regard Tolstoi's letter to Fet in April, 1876, wherein he speaks against the world of samsara and practices of the Orthodox religion, and numbers himself and Fet among those privileged few who are able to peer into the world of nirvana while yet bound to the world of samsara.

In addition to the doctrinal and epistolary evidence linking the candle image to Schopenhauer's influence, there is a strong etymological clue. In the second and later editions of *The World As Will and Representation* appears the chapter entitled "On Death and Its Relations to the Indestructibility of Our Inner Nature," which concludes with Schopenhauer's eschatology in brief.

Dying is the moment of that liberation from the one-sidedness of an individuality which does not constitute the innermost kernel of our true being, but is rather to be thought of as a kind of aberration thereof. The true original freedom again enters at this moment which...can be regarded as a *restitutio in integrum*. The peace and composure on the countenance of most dead persons seem to have their origin in this. As a rule the death of very good persons is peaceful and gentle, but to die willingly, to die gladly, to die cheerfully, is the prerogative of the resigned, of him who gives up the existence that we know; what comes to him instead of it is in our eyes, *nothing*, because our existence in reference to that one is *nothing*. The Buddhist faith calls that existence *Nirvana*, that is to say, extinction [erloschen].

It is noteworthy that Schopenhauer chooses to think of nirvana as *erloschen* rather than the etymology most commonly accepted in modern Indic lexicography, namely as the adjectival form derived from the Sanskrit root *van* "desire," with a negative prefix.[15] His understanding

---

14. The passage occurs in part 3, chapter 8: "She professed her own strange religion of metempsychosis, in which she staunchly believed, with little regard for the dogmas of the church." This makes seem all the more curious R. P. Blackmur's statement "Stiva and Dolly are too near the actual manner of things, are too wholly undifferentiated from the course of society and of individuals, ever to feel the need or the pang of rebirth." (*Eleven Essays in the European Novel* [New York: Harcourt, Brace, 1964], p. 4.
15. See, for instance, F. Edgerton, *Buddhist Hybrid Sanskrit Grammar and Dictionary*, 2 vols. (New Haven: Yale Univ. Press, 1953). The root *van* is derived from Proto-European *uen* in A. Walde and J. Pokorny, *Vergleichendes Wörterbuch der indogermanischen Sprachen*, 3 vols. (Berlin and Leipzig: 1927-32).

of the term becomes clear from a footnote he attaches to this section, wherein he provides the reader with several suggested etymologies, beginning with the following: "According to Colebrooke (*Transactions of the Royal Asiatic Society*, Vol. I, p. 566), it comes from *va* 'to blow' [*wehen*] like the wind, with the prefixed negative *nir*, hence it signifies a lull or calm, but as an adjective 'extinguished' [*erloschen*]."

The work of Henry Thomas Colebrooke, cited by Schopenhauer, was published as a separate volume in 1858 under the title *Essays on the Religion and Philosophy of the Hindus*. A copy of this work, which is cited in four places in the second and subsequent editions of *The World as Will and Representation*, was found in Tolstoi's library after his death.[16] In Tolstoi's notebooks for January, 1873, i.e., two months before he began the preliminary work on *Anna Karenina*, we find this work listed with the name of its author, spelled there "Colbrouk" (the indices of Tolstoi's complete works in Russian render the name in Roman script as H. T. Calebrooke in Volume 48 and as H. G. Calenbrooke in Volume 90). In his work Colebrooke understands nirvana as expressing "a state of final release from the world." His version of the etymology, alluded to above, reads in full as follows: "The term which the Bauddhas, as well as the Jainas, more particularly affect...is nirvana, profound calm. In its ordinary acceptation, as an adjective, it signifies *extinct, as a fire which has gone out; set, as a luminary which has gone down....*Its etymology is from *va*, to blow as wind, with the proposition *nir* used in a negative sense [Italics mine]."[17]

This etymology for nirvana was probably reinforced in Tolstoi's mind by his reading of Max Müller, whom Tolstoi mentions to Nikolai Strakhov in a letter dated 30 November 1875.[18] The work Tolstoi was reading appears to have been a French translation of Müller's *Essays on the Science of Religion*, which was being read in connection with another work by Eugene Burnouf, an authority on Buddhism and other

---

16. V. F. Bulgakov, "Knigi ob Indii v biblioteke L. N. Tolstogo," *Kratkie soobshcheniia Instituta vostokovedeniia*, 31 (1959), 51; cited in A. I. Shifman, *Lev Tolstoi i Vostok* (Moscow: Izdat. vostochnoi lit., 1960).

17. H. T. Colebrooke, "On the Religion and Philosophy of the Hindus," *Transactions of the Royal Asiatic Society of Great Britain and Ireland*, I (1827), 566.

18. Tolstoi, LXII, 228. Tolstoi was apparently reading the same work by Müller in 1877. See in this regard *Literaturnoe nasledstvo*, 60, No. 2 (19??), 120.

Eastern religions. Müller, in common with most Indologists of the nine-teenth century, accepted the same false etymology embraced by Colebrooke. He gives it in the work in question as follows: "What was the original meaning of Nirvana may perhaps best be seen from the etymology of this technical term. Every Sanskrit scholar knows that Nirvana means originally the blowing out, the extinction of light....The human soul, when it arrives at its perfection, is blown out, if we use the phraseology of the Buddhists, like a lamp."[19] There would thus appear to be compelling evidence to suggest that Tolstoi was very interested in the doctrines of Buddhism during the period of his writing of *Anna Karenina*, that his use of the candle image was probably inspired by Colebrooke's false etymology of nirvana, and that Eikhenbaum's attribution of the use of this motif to the influence of Schopenhauer is in all likelihood a sound assumption.

This is not to imply that Tolstoi was ever at any stage of his life a confirmed or consistent Buddhist. It is a matter of record that he repudiated the pessimistic conclusions of Buddhism in his *Confession*, begun at the end of the 1870s. But it does seem obvious that Buddhist thought pervades his own thinking during the writing of *Anna Karenina* and serves as a propaedeutic doctrine anticipating in many details what would eventually become Tolstoism. It may not be amiss here to note also that the images of the train and the candle and the doctrines of Buddhism and of Schopenhauer are brought together in Chapter 11 of *The Kreutzer Sonata*, where Pozdnyshev, finding the lamp in his train carriage unpleasant, covers it before launching into a discussion of the futility of life, in which he says: "But why live? If life has no aim, if life is given us for life's sake, there is no reason for living. And if it is so, then the Schopenhauers, the Hartmanns, and all the Buddhists as well, are quite right."[20]

University of Houston

---

19. F. Max Müller, *Essays on the Science of Religion* (Oxford: Oxford Univ. Press, 1867), p. 279.

20. Eduard Hartman (1842-1906), German philosopher and imitator of Schopenhauer.

CHAPTER FIVE

TOLSTOY'S CONCEPT OF REASON
AS APPLIED TO BUDDHISM
Dragan Milivojevic, University of Oklahoma

Tolstoy's interest in Buddhism and other Oriental religions came after 1880. By that time his views on Christianity in particular and religion in general were already set, and his extensive reading of Hindu, Taoist and Buddhist literature did not in any way change his world view. On the contrary, his reading of Oriental religions was motivated by an attempt to find parallels to his own religious views which were based on his understanding of Christianity. In order to keep Tolstoy's comments regarding Buddhism in their proper perspective, one should bear in mind that his point of reference remained firmly anchored in his interpretation of Christianity.

Tolstoy maintained that when Christianity and other world religions became institutionalized, their respective churches suppressed the dynamism, spontaneity and revolutionary nature which had originally characterized these religions. It was only the heretics, the dissidents, who kept the original flame burning. Ossification and degeneration of the original teachings were brought about by accretions and additions, through commentaries and explanations based on misunderstanding, ignorance or plain distortion. Although the founders of Christianity and Buddhism – Jesus and Gautama (the historical Buddha)[1] – shocked people out of their complacency through the profundity of their teach-

---

1. *The* Buddha (with the definite article) denotes the historical Buddha – Gautama Siddhartha who was born around 563 B.C. and died around 483 B.C.

ing, the church and church fathers allowed these teachings to be compromised by human indolence and weakness. As an example of such a compromise Tolstoy points out that the church ignored the commandment "Thou shall not kill" when training army chaplains.

Going back to primitive Christianity as the most genuine and trustworthy source of that religion, Tolstoy attributes to it a union of two basic concepts – faith and reason. According to Tolstoy, the two concepts are inseparable: faith without reason is blind faith; reason without faith is intellectually sterile. As an example, Tolstoy brings up the doctrine of the Trinity. Reason tells us that 3=1 is absurd and false, hence the concept of the three aspects of the Trinity must be rejected. For similar reasons, the doctrine of immaculate conception, the belief in the resurrection, and the mystery of the communion should also be rejected. However, pure logic, Tolstoy argues, although useful and practical in everyday life and often an antidote to blind faith, cannot bring us closer to any metaphysical certainty.

razum, the Russian word for reason, has a wide variety of senses and uses.[2] Tolstoy was neither a systematic philosopher nor a learned

---

2. According to Marcus Wheeler, the English translation of *razum* is "reason, mind, intellect" *(The Oxford Russian-English Dictionary, vol. 2* [Oxford, The Clarendon Press, 1972] 675). It is defined by A. P. Yevgen'eva as "an ability to evaluate a situation with common sense and sensibility, a capacity to weigh all circumstances and to be guided by them in one's behavior in contrast to behavior dictated by feelings" *(Slovar 'Sinonimov Russkogo Iazyka* [Nauka, 1970] 352). Closer to Tolstoy's meaning of reason is Belinskij's definition. Belinskij used the term *razum* frequently in his literary critical writings. His definition of *razum* appears to be rather close to the concept of intuitive reason in Tolstoy: *"Razum* embraces the infinite sphere of that which cannot be experienced *(Sverkhopytnogo)* and that which is beyond the grasp of the senses. It makes the inexplicable clear, the vague obvious, and it defines that which is inaccurate" (Vissarion Grigor'evich Belinskij, *Polnoe Sobranie Sochinenij,* vol. 4 [Moskva, 1953-1959] 48). *Razum* also has religious connotations: In Belinskij, *"Razum* was for him a matter of concern, less a subject of a philosophical effort than a matter of the heart, almost a matter of faith...." (Rolf Lettman, *Die Abstrakta, Um 'und, Razum' bei Belinskij* [Munchen: Semasiologische Untersuchungen, Verlag Otto Sagner, 1971] 133). "But, following St. Paul (cf. Romans 1:18), the church has no less strenuously maintained the capacity that human reason still has, in reflecting on the data of experience, to arrive at a belief in a creating God, as well as at a discernment of the basic moral obligations that are imposed on every man" (Alan Richardson, *A Dictionary of Christian Theology* [Norwich: SCM Press, 1969, 382). Cf. Tolstoy's concept of reason.

theologian, and thus we cannot expect to find in his writings the consistency and logical cogency we expect of philosophers and theologians. Tolstoy was driven to define *razum* not as an object of a dispassionate inquiry, but, struggling to find the meaning of his own life, he could not always afford to be scientific and consistent. In any case, what is important is not what *razum* means, but, rather, what meaning he attached to it, especially since he uses it throughout his biography of the Buddha.

Faith and reason are closely related although quite different concepts. For Tolstoy, there are two different modes of knowing: knowledge by way of faith *(znanie very)* and knowledge by way of reason *(znanie razuma)*. The former, according to Tolstoy, is the certainty of knowledge which we have of the things which our reason cannot conceive; it is a self-contained certainty not subject to reason, an intuitive knowledge. *znanie razuma,* knowledge by way of reason, on the other hand, derives from previous knowledge; it is a deductive knowledge. This relationship is based on the distinction between *Razum* – Reason with a capital *R,* an all-embracing divine Reason, the Logos of St. John and its derived reflection in human beings – and *razum,* reason with a small *r,* human reason. Intelligence, the intellectual and cognitive aspect of the latter, cannot be isolated from its origin in the former. At the same time, although human reason is employed in science, it cannot provide insight and answers to the ultimate truths, anymore than the part can define the whole. Human reason in its totality (including its cognitive aspects), however, because it is grounded in divine Reason, can aspire to identify itself with the latter and thereby reach perfect knowledge. Tolstoy maintains that this aspiration cannot be fully realized because divine Reason is not accessible to human reason. It is obvious that Tolstoy's interpretation of the meaning of reason is not a narrowly rationalist one but one which is informed by theological hermeneutics originating in the framework of Christian doctrine. Faith and Reason (both divine Reason and human reason) are not antagonistic concepts as they are in rationalist philosophy. They are rather like yin/yang in the Taoist philosophy – entities which are not autonomous and which obtain their full meaning only as a part of an indivisible binary opposition. To pursue the Taoist analogy one step further, in the same way as the opposition of yin/yang does not center on itself but is a part of larger entity – the Tao, the combination of faith and reason in its close unity, points a way to moral perfection. Tolstoy insists on the necessity of having faith based on and tempered by reason. When irrational elements enter a religion, he argues, the religion will become overwhelmed by superstition. Faith must make that first intuitive leap into the unknown where reason is incapable of going in order to find the certainties which are inaccessible to reason. But the knowledge retrieved by faith must accord with reason. Tolstoy believed that reason was given to us by God to guide us, and he regarded it as important as faith. Reason cannot conceive intuitive certainties but it can confirm or reject them. Tolstoy's notion of reason goes back to St. John, whose gospel Tolstoy rewrote to conform to his own views on Christianity, replacing the opening words "In the beginning was the Word..." with "The foundation and the principle of everything is the understanding of life."[3] In that way, Logos-Word was replaced by *Razum* (Reason) can be sought in Saint Thomas's *Summa Theologica* where Saint Thomas explains different ways in which God speaks to human beings: through an action on the senses and imagination; through a direct influence on intelligence (reason); and through a special light.[4] It is the second way which resembles very closely the Tolstoyan term *Razum* (Reason) brought about by an inner revelation.

In a catechism addressed to the common people based on his altered version of St. John's gospel, Tolstoy gives several definitions of divine Reason *(Razum):*

"The essence of everything existing is Reason" (John 1:3); "The self-knowing and the self-creating force without a beginning and without cause" (John 1:1-2); "Having existence in itself" (John 8:26); "All-encompassing, all-knowing and all-creating, Reason understands everything, has everything in it and is understood only by itself" (John 1:4); "Everything is in Reason and Reason is in everything, as there is no Reason, except one" (John 1:10); "Reason can be seen as life ac-

---

3. L. N. Tolstoi, *Polnoe Sobranie Sochinenij,* vol. 24 (Moskva: Gosudarstvennoe Izdatel'stvo Khudozhestvennoi Literatury, 1957) 25.

4. Saint Thomas, *The Summa Theologica Quinas,* trans. by the fathers of the English Dominican Province, vol. 14 (London, 1935) 37, question 173, art. 1.

cording to the laws of love and freedom: as love and freedom are the image of Reason created by them for it. No one has seen God, except in the form of Life according to the laws of love and freedom" (John 1:18); "Reason is light without shade, hidden from human beings" (John 3:9).[5]

Of all the statements and writings by Tolstoy on Buddhism, "The Life and Teaching of Siddartha Gautama, Called the Buddha, the Most Perfect One"[6] summarizes most faithfully both his application of the term *Razum* to the context of Buddhist teachings as well as his interpretation of that religion. Tolstoy's search for a rational religion centered on Southern (Theravada) Buddhism, the oldest branch of Buddhism, dating back to at least the third century B.C.[7] Tolstoy's knowledge of Buddhism came from French, German and English translations of the original Pali and Sanskrit sources. The teaching of Theravada appealed to him with its atheism,[8] its description of the Buddha as a human being rather than a divine being, its absence of dogma and ritual, and its emphasis on personal effort and responsibility. In the words of Murti, "Religion is the consciousness of Supermundane Presence immanent in things.... Early Buddhism (Theravada) was not a religion in this sense...there was no element of worship, no religious fervour, no devotion to a transcendent being. No cosmic function was

---

5. Protoie'rej T. I. Boutkevitch, *Obzor Rousskikh Sekt i Ikh Tolkov s Izlozheniem Ikh Proiskhozhdenia, Rasprostranenia i Verouchenia, i s Oprovereniem Poslednevo,* 2nd ed., vol. 12 (Petrograd: Tolstovstvo, 1915) 539.

6. P. Bulanzhe, "Zhizn' i Uchenie Siddarty Gotamy, Prozvannogo Buddoi, t.e. Soversheneishim," *Zhizn'Dl'a Vsekh 3-4* (1910). This biography of the Buddha was edited by Tolstoy. The author of this article translated the biography.

7. The 'Doctrine of the Elders' who formed the first Buddhist Council...until recently this school was known in the West by its generic name of Hinayana, which means small or lesser vehicle (of salvation), but this term of reproach, coined by the Mahayanists, has now been dropped" (Christmas Humphreys, A *Popular Dictionary of Buddhism* [London: The Buddhist Society, 1984] 197.

8. When Tolstoy was asked "What is the essential difference between Buddhism and Christianity?" he replied, "Real Christianity? None, in both there is a sermon of the god of love and denial of a personal god" (V. F. Bulgakov, "Knigi ob Indii u Biblioteke L. N. Tolstogo," *Kratkie Soobshchenia Instituta Vostokovedenia,* vol. 31 [Moskva: ido-vo Akademii Nauk SSSR, 1959] 46).

assigned to Buddha, he was just an exalted person and no more."[9]
More than anything else Tolstoy believed that the life of the Buddha
and his teaching demonstrated Tolstoy's own concept and understanding of Reason.

Tolstoy's life of the Buddha starts with the well-known facts of the
Buddha's life: his birth in a princely family, his isolation from all the
ugly aspects of life, his outing away from the palace and confrontation
with three events (sickness, old age and death), his period of asceticism, his enlightenment and his preaching. In this chain of events in
the Buddha's life, Tolstoy sees Reason as the single most important
motivation behind the Buddha's actions. Siddhartha[10] was raised a
Hindu and taught by Brahmans that everyone should fulfill all obligations prescribed by their caste, including that of being a soldier and
going to war.

Siddhartha, however, was skeptical about Brahmanic teaching:
"Siddhartha's healthy mind could not accept on faith that which his
Reason could examine."[11] Siddhartha's example mirrors Tolstoy's rejection of the teaching of the Russian Orthodox Church, and his quest
to use Reason within the framework of Russian Christianity as an antidote to blind faith. In both cases, a venerable religious tradition had
to give way to the rule of Reason, and in Siddhartha's case the use of
Reason, according to Tolstoy, led to deeper religious insights and the
birth of a new religion.

In Tolstoy's interpretation, the rejection of extreme asceticism was
also based on Reason. Siddhartha, as Tolstoy describes him, understood that by exhausting his body he also "consciously extinguished
the only light which illuminated everything in the world – namely Reason. Siddhartha understood that while he was alive, he could not reject
this light, his Reason, that he could only believe in Reason, and that
only Reason could put him on the right path."[12] In Tolstoy's biography
of the Buddha, *Razum* (Reason) appears as the crucial factor in the
Buddha's spiritual quest. This interpretation is Tolstoy's and is not shared

---

9. T.R.V. Murti, *Buddhism* (London: George Allen, Unwin, 1980) 6.
10. Siddhartha was Buddha's name before his enlightenment.
11. Bulanzhe 118.
12. Bulanzhe 82.

by historical evidence. Tolstoy used the common Russian term and endowed it with religious connotations as *Razum* while using the word in its common meaning as *razum*. His identification of reason with light goes back to St. John's metaphor of light as Reason.

There are, however, limits to the use of reason, and questions such as the nature of God and the soul are beyond its scope. The Buddha refused to answer such questions, his silence indicating that they were logically unanswerable. Tolstoy cites the story where the Buddha compares a metaphysician to a foolish man wounded by an arrow who, before accepting treatment, insists on knowing what sort of arrow struck him, whence it came, who aimed it, etc. Obviously the wounded man would have died before receiving satisfactory answers to his questions. The moral of the story is that metaphysical inquiries are unnecessary and can even prove harmful to spiritual life. Buddha's "inexpressibles" (questions for which reason cannot provide an answer)[13] are different from Tolstoy's. The question of the nature of God never came up as an inexpressible in Theravada Buddhism because the religion did not have a supramundane concept of divinity. Tolstoy emphasizes the moral of the story by adding, "Therefore, do not attempt to penetrate matters which reason cannot comprehend and concentrate on matters which it can comprehend."[14] This pragmatic attitude is common to both Theravada Buddhism and Tolstoy's concept of Christianity. We find it in Tolstoy's story "The Kingdom of God is Within You" where he argues that the search for spiritual perfection should be inner-directed and that looking for answers elsewhere is pointless. The Buddha explicitly stated that suffering and liberation from suffering were the object of his teachings, not metaphysics. In response to a person who kept asking metaphysical questions which belong to the

---

13. Tolstoy's "inexpressibles": 1) Why do I live? 2) What is the origin of all life? 3) What is the purpose of all life? 4) Where does the fundamental difference between the good and the bad lie? 5) How should I live and what is death? (Tolstoi, vol. 48-49, 187). Buddha's "inexpressibles": 1) Whether the world is eternal, or not, or both 2) Whether the world is finite (in space) or infinite, or both, or neither 3) Whether the Tathagata exists after death, or does not, or both, or neither 4) Is the soul identical with the body or different from it? (Murti 381).

14. Bulanzhe 81.

domain of "inexpressibles," the Buddha's statement was intended to divert the questioner's attention from metaphysics to the realm of concrete reality. We can see that the Buddha and Tolstoy shared an emphasis on the here and now.

Tolstoy opposes reason not to faith, its conventional binary opposition, but to the passions, the instinctive, unconscious aspect of human behavior. Tolstoy believes that a vital task for human beings in the pursuit of spiritual perfection is to strengthen and enlighten reason, and to extinguish the passions. He describes the true life to which the Buddha aimed as *razumnaia* ("reasonable"), and alleges that Buddha's words to his disciples invoked reason. "Your reason and the truth which I have taught you will be your teachers after I depart."[15] Reason, according to Tolstoy, is "the most powerful weapon in the cognition of life."[16] Tolstoy's Buddha argues that Reason is the only light in life which illuminates our path, and Tolstoy describes it as one of the virtues which attracted people to the Buddha, and as "the most precious thing in a human being."[17] He believes that Siddhartha's reason could not reconcile itself "to the existence of a god who created injustice and evil in the world."[18] Tolstoy sees in the Buddha's invocation to Ananda, his personal servant and a chief disciple, an appeal to reason which is identified with Truth: "Be an island unto yourself, Ananda! Be a refuge to yourself; do not take to yourself any other refuge. See Truth as an island, see Truth as a refuge. Do not seek refuge in anyone but yourself."[19]

---

15. Bulanzhe 81.

16. Bulanzhe 82.

17. Bulanzhe 82.

18. Bulanzhe 120.

19. Christmas Humphreys, *The Wisdom of Buddhism* (London: Curzon Press, 1979) 93. Cf. the Buddha's last words, "The Dhamma, and the Rules for the Sangha which I have expounded and laid down for you, let them, after I am gone, by your Teacher" (Humphreys, *The Wisdom 94*). *Razum* corresponds here to the Buddhis term *dhamma* in Pali. The term *dhamma* is widely used in Buddhist literature and it has broad connotations: "dhamma: lit. bearer. Constitution (or nature of a thing), norm, law *(jus)*, doctrine; justice, righteousness; quality; thing, object of mind; phenomenon" (Nyanaponika, *Buddhist Dictionary* [Kanaly: Buddhist Publication Society, 1980] 55). The Russian term *razum* is more specific than the Buddhist term *dhamma*.

In Tolstoy's version of the Buddha's life, faith does not play a significant role in Siddhartha's spiritual transformation. The relationship between faith and Reason, which Tolstoy argues was indivisible, appears to be dominated by Reason. At each of the crossroads in Siddhartha's progress towards spiritual perfection, it is reason which shows the way, as in his decision to abandon Brahmanic teaching and, later, extreme asceticism. Even Siddhartha's transformation into the Buddha through the process of awakening to the true meaning of life is described by Tolstoy as the triumph of Reason; and the true life is described by Tolstoy as the rational life. The Buddha, according to Tolstoy, reached it through the contemplation of two modes of existence: one causing both happiness and suffering because it is based on the carnal, perishable, and acquisitive aspects of life; and the other based on *mudrost poznania* ("cognitive wisdom"), which leads to true peace of mind and the realization of a rational life appropriate to human beings as "rational creatures."[20]

Enlightenment in Buddhism, in contrast to Tolstoy's interpretation of "cognitive wisdom," is considered to be a transcendence of "the barriers of thought to the non-duality which lies beyond the One and the Many, and all other binary opposites."[21] The dualism of faith and reason postulated by Tolstoy, even if it were complementary rather than oppositional, would still be a hindrance in the realization of Buddhist enlightenment.

When Tolstoy describes the function of reason as a deductive process he elaborates on the logical premises of this deduction. If the premise of the logical impossibility concerning the doctrine of the Trinity is an example (3=1, 1=3), then faith (defined as "a firm belief in something for which there is no proof"[22]) could have overcome the logical inconsistency. Tolstoy's refutation of the doctrine of the Trinity is not founded on a mystical notion of Reason or faith but on common sense logic without an intervening act of faith.

---

20. Bulanzhe 121.
21. Humphreys, *A Popular Dictionary* 74.
22. *Webster's Seventh New Collegiate Dictionary* (Springfield, Mass.: G. & C. Merriam Co., 1965) 299.

In *V Chom Moja Vera* ("What Is My Faith?") Tolstoy gives a novel definition of faith, ascribing to it an ethical rather than metaphysical character. Following St. James (11:14-19), Tolstoy defines faith as a springboard of actions, with good works as its tangible manifestation. A faith which does not result in good works is not a true faith. In such an interpretation faith and reason are still connected. The tangible manifestation of faith are good works in which reason is embodied. The relationship between faith and reason is not on a metaphysical level, but on an ethical one.

Faith has to be justified experientially through reason to be correct. Here Tolstoy finds a striking parallel to the role faith plays in early Buddhism. To enter on the Buddhist path of enlightenment as shown in the formulation of the four noble truths[23] requires only faith in the four noble truths and in the Buddha who proclaimed them. Since each of the four noble truths is anchored in experience, they can be confirmed experientially. For example, the first truth, that life is suffering, can be corroborated by the facts of old age, disease, and death. The second one, that the cause of suffering is rooted in desire, can also be tested through individual experience.

This tendency to avoid metaphysics and theology and concentrate on the everyday human problems of suffering and rational life are common to early Buddhism and Tolstoy's understanding of primitive Christianity. As Tolstoy saw it, both Christianity and Buddhism (with the development of the Mahayana branch)[24] became institutionalized and static; the devotional aspect of religion replaced the dynamics of reason. The rational kernel of these religions was later perverted and overwhelmed by superstition. He told his secretary on April 7, 1908, "I read everything about Buddhism. What a strange teaching! And how it

---

23. (1) There can be no existence without suffering.
(2) The cause of suffering is egoistic desire.
(3) The elimination of desire brings the cessation of suffering.
(4) The way to the elimination of desire is the Noble Eightfold Path.
24. Mahayana: The School of the Great Vehicle of Salvation, also called the Northern School. The teaching of Mahayana is more distinctly religious, making its appeal to the heart and intuition rather than to the intellect.

was perverted! Such an abstract teaching and suddenly there appeared the same creation of gods, the idol worship, the paradise and the hell.... Quite the same superstitions as in Christianity."[25]

Tolstoy's interpretation of the Buddha's teaching and Buddhism was influenced by his own views on religion in general and Christianity in particular. For Tolstoy, "religion is the awareness of those truths which are common and comprehensible to all people in all situations at all times, and are as indisputable as 2x2=4.... Religion is like geometry."[26] It centers around his key concept of *Razum,* which he felt to be the dynamic, guiding force in both early Christianity and early Buddhism. The closest concept in Buddhism to Tolstoy's *Razum* is *prajna* – knowledge, wisdom or insight. Part of the noble eightfold path,[27] *prajna* comprises right understanding and right aspiration and is at the same level as morality and mediation. It is not the supreme factor in the realization of enlightenment in early Buddhism, but "It is the attainment of *prajna* that imparts a unity and singleness of purpose to several acts of morality."[28] This interpretation is very similar to Tolstoy's concept of *Razum* as a metaphysical underpinning of faith manifested in acts of morality.

It is morality (tempered by reason) which is the core of Tolstoy's religion. Tolstoy formulated the four noble truths of the Buddha as: (1) the awakening of the heart; (2) purification of thoughts; (3) liberation from ill will; and (4) awakening in oneself love not only for human beings but everything alive: "True liberation is only realized in love."[29] His interpretation of the fourth noble truth of Buddhism, however, has more in common with the pronouncements in Jesus' "Sermon on the Mount" than with the overall import of the fourth noble truth – the eightfold path – although it resembles the concept of morality which comprises part of the eightfold path. Closer to Tolstoy's principle of

25. N. N. Gusev, *Dva Goda s L. N. Tolstym* (Moskva, 1912) 130.

26. Tolstoi, vol. 63, 339.

27. (1)*faith8-FoldPath* right understanding}} wisdom right thought} (2)*morality* right speech; right bodily action; right livelihood (3)*mediation* right effort; right mindfulness; right concentration (Trevor Ling, *Dictionary of Buddhism*: Indian and South-East Asian [Calcutta: K. P. Bagchi, 1981] 90).

28. Murti 31.

29. Tolstoi, vol. 41, 99.

love is the Buddhist *metta* or *maitri*, described as "a detached and impersonal benevolence raised to the highest possible pitch of intensity."[30]

The saying that one's philosophy is mainly due to one's temperament applies very well to Tolstoy. His whole life was spent in the search for philosophical and religious certainties in an attempt to reconcile his desire to understand with his desire to believe. The synthesis of these two elements, reason and faith, did not crystallize in practice; Reason took the upper hand, as is demonstrated in Tolstoy's version of the Buddha's life.

St. Anselme's maxim *Credo ut intelligam* ("I believe in order to reason") was reversed by Tolstoy as *Intelligo ut credam* ("I reason in order to believe"). For St. Anselme faith illuminated reason; for Tolstoy only reason could enlighten faith. His affinity for and interpretation of early Buddhism rested on this assumption.

---

30. Bhikshu Sangharakshita, *A Survey of Buddhism* (Boulder: Shambhala, 1980) 145.

CHAPTER SIX

LEO TOLSTOY AND LAO TZU'S *TAO-TE CHING:* TOLSTOY AS A TAOIST SAGE
Nathan T. Carr

Leo Tolstoy, in the last decades of his life, underwent a marked transformation from the man he had once been. He began this period with pious devotion to the Orthodox Church. He fasted, prayed, confessed and studied the Gospels. Emulating the devout peasants, who were not troubled by the doubts which had haunted him for years, he did his best to live by blind faith.[1]

Within a few years, however, Tolstoy began to question the teachings of the Church. By 1879, the year in which he began to write *Confession* (which chronicled the internal conflict which led him away from the Orthodox Church), he felt that "From the third century to the present, the Church has been nothing but lies, cruelty and deceit." He therefore decided that he must, beginning with Gospels, reexamine religion and consider what was true and what was false.[2]

This search for the truth in religion was to last the rest of his life. Eventually, it even led to his excommunications from the Russian Orthodox Church. In his pursuit of true religion, Tolstoy found valuable guidance in the writings of the Chinese philosophers Confucius and Lao Tzu. In fact, in 1884 he ascribed his "....good moral condition to reading Confucius, and *especially Lao-Tzu*," (italics mine). He wrote in the same place that he needed to compile a cycle of reading for himself, which would include Epictetus, Marcus Aurelius, Lao-Tzu,

---

1. Henri Troyat, *Tolstoy,* trans. by Nancy Amphoux (Doubleday & Co., Inc.: Garden City, New York, 1967), pp. 396-397.
2. Troyat, pp. 412-415.

Buddha, Pascal and the Gospels. (He felt that anybody would profit from following this cycle as well.)[3]

From his very first contact with the thought of Lao Tzu, Tolstoy seemed to sense something true in it. In what seems to have been his first written remark about Lao Tzu (in a letter dated 3 January 1878), Tolstoy asked N.N. Strakhov "Where did you take Lao-Tzu's words [in an earlier letter] from?"[4]

By 1884, Tolstoy had begun translating the *Tao-Te Ching* (from the French translation by Stanislas Julian).[5] This was five years after his turning away from Orthodoxy (as mentioned above). It seems clear, therefore, that he had already embarked along the path of religious searching before he encountered Lao Tzu and his concept of the Taoist sage. Although he definitely derived some benefit from reading the *Tao-Te Ching*, however, it would seem to have been one more influence among the many.

Tolstoy read the work from a theistic standpoint, in that he equated the Tao with Heaven and God. Thus, his interpretation was weighted by his unusual form of Christian belief.[6] Whenever a concept found in the *Tao-Te Ching* disagreed with his own ideology, Tolstoy usually resolved the conflict by ignoring the particular tenet of Taoism.[7] (This is how he was able to use the teachings of so many different, often conflicting thinkers.) So, it would seem, Tolstoy studied the world's philosophies and religious searching for coreligionists as much as for guidance. His method was simply to find in each system of thought those precepts which he felt to be correct. He sought the "universal affirmations" of religious beliefs "which are the same for all religions."[8] It was the enunciation of things which all men knew in their hearts to

---

3. *Tolstoy's Diaries:* Volume I (1847-1894), edited and translated by R.F. Christian (Charles Scribner's Sons: New York, 1985), p. 204.
4. *Tolstoy's Letters: Volume I (1828-1879)*, selected, edited and translated by R. F. Christian (Charles Scribner's Sons: New York, 1978), pp. 309-310.
5. Derk Bodde, *Tolstoy and China* (Princeton University Press; Princeton, 1950), p. 13.
6. Bodde, p. 72.
7. Bodde, p. 68.
8. Bodde, p. 74.

be true that made a philosopher great.

To pose the question of Taoistic influence on (as opposed to agreement with) Tolstoy would be apt to lead to an academic steeplechase. It is difficult, if not impossible, to determine what in Tolstoy's life and thought was a manifestation of Lao Tzu's teachings, and what was derived from some other source, or even came from his own thoughts. This problem is pointed out by the article "Taoistic Patterns in *War and Peace.*" As its title suggests, the article points out that despite being written 20 years before his exposure to Lao Tzu, *War and Peace* did exhibit Taoistic themes in several places.[9] Thus, a more useful question to consider might be how Tolstoy's life and thought (particularly after his acquaintance with Lao Tzu and the *Tao-Te Ching*) correspond to Taoist teachings. Particularly appropriate would be an examination of such correspondence to one of the most important concepts of Taoism, that of the sage.

The Taoist concept of the sage, as expressed in the *Tao-Te Ching*, is based upon five basic principles which recur throughout the work. Although they are never explicitly listed in the work, they are distinguishable after some examination and thought. Not widely separate in nature, they are closely linked to each other, complementing and overlapping each other as they form the whole image of the sage. Often, one aspect is discussed in the same chapter of the *Tao-Te Ching* as one or more of the others. There are many instances in which a particular passage can be held equally applicable to two (or even more, sometimes) of the principles.

The first of the five principle characteristics of the sage is one of simplicity. To be a sage, one must manifest plainness and embrace simplicity;[10] discard the extremes, the extravagant and the excessive;[11]

---

9. Vytas Dukas and Glenn A. Sandstrom, "Taoistic Patterns in *War and Peace*," *The Slavic and East European Journal*, Vol. XIV, No. 2 (1970), p. 182.

10. *Tao-te ching*, Chapter 19. All citations form the *Tao-te ching* and its commentary come from *The Way of Lao Tzu (Tao-te ching)*, translated and with introductory essays, comments and notes by Wing-tsit Chan (The Bobbs-Merrill Company: Indianapolis, 1963).

11. *Tao-te ching*, Chapter 29.

be concerned with the fundamental ("the belly"), rather than the external and superficial ("the eyes");[12] and reject learning and extensive knowledge.[13] As the simplest element of society, therefore, the peasantry is held up as a source of wisdom and an example to follow – not despite their lack of sophistication and learning, but because of it. "The sage has no fixed (personal) ideas. He regards the people's ideas as his own...His mind forms a harmonious whole with that of his people."[14] As for too much knowledge being bad, it is written "Abandon learning and there will be no sorrow."[15]

Tolstoy's delight in the simple naive piety of the peasantry was well known. In the springtime, many pilgrims passed down on the highway near his estate at Yasnaya Polyana on their way to Kiev. Often, dressed in peasant clothes, Tolstoy went out to watch them pass. Occasionally, he would stop one to ask questions about his journey and religious faith.[16]

Tolstoy's faith in the ordinary muzhik, or peasant (as opposed to the "exceptional being") as the repository of religious insight and understanding was probably strengthened by his pilgrimage to the Optina-Pustyn monastery to see a famous *starets* (holy man). The monastery was well known for its devout monks, and its leader was almost considered a living saint. Tolstoy emerged from his meeting with *Starets* Ambrose unimpressed, dissatisfied and disliking the man.[17]

The *Tao-Te Ching* elaborates on this principle of simplicity when it states that people's hearts should be kept "vacuous," and that the sage should encourage this.[18] The term "vacuous" is not meant literally here, according to the commentary. Rather, it refers to a state of mind of "absolute peacefulness and purity of mind, freedom from worry and selfish desires, not to be disturbed by incoming impressions or to allow what is already in the mind to disturb what is coming into the mind."[19]

12. *Tao-te ching,* Chapter 12.
13. *Tao-te-ching,* Chapters 20 and 81.
14. *Tao-te ching,* Chapter 49.
15. *Tao-te Ching,* Chapter 20.
16. Troyat, pp. 398-399.
17. Troyat, pp. 399-400.
18. *Tao-te ching,* Chapter 3.
19. *Tao-te ching,* Commentary, p. 104.

It is probably this state of mind which attracted Tolstoy to the peasantry so much. As an illustration of this state in the peasantry, the impoverished peasants accepted their lot with resignation, without allowing their problems to ruin their lives. Also, their belief in God was like drinking vodka.[20] (When Russians drink vodka, they do it without flinching, without hesitating, letting it go straight into the core of their being. The ability to accept something as potent as faith in the Almighty without an emotional "shudder" or pause was something which he viewed as worthy of admiration.)

Excess in anything is also condemned when it states: "He who knows when to stop is free from danger. Therefore he can long endure."[21] Likewise, it says elsewhere that "It is by knowing when to stop that one can be free from danger."[22] Needless or gratuitous excitement and activity are also condemned when Lao Tzu states:

"The five colors cause one's eyes to be blind.

The five tones cause one's ears to be deaf.

The five flavors cause one's palate to be spoiled.

Racing and hunting cause one's mind to be mad."[23]

As for numbing the senses (and the mind as well) through needless sensual stimulation, one can look at the admonitions in the *Postface to the Kreutzer Sonata*, and later in *Christian Teaching*, to see his condemnation of sexual excess and call for living as chastely as possible (at the least.)[24] In the *Postface to the Kreutzer Sonata*, Tolstoy calls for sexual abstinence within and outside of marriage, and considers the birth and rearing of children "the *Raison d'être* of marital relations," and "an expiation of carnal love."[25]

Furthermore, Tolstoy completely abstained from tobacco and alco-

---

20. Troyat, p. 396.

21. *Tao-te ching*, Chapter 44.

22. *Tao-te ching*, Chapter 32.

23. *Tao-te ching*, Chapter 12.

24. Earnest J. Simmons, *Leo Tolstoy* (Little, Brown and Co.: Boston, 1946), p. 453.

25. Leo N. Tolstoy, *Postface to the Kreutzer Sonata*, in *The Kreutzer Sonata and Other Stories*, translated and with an introduction by David McDuff (Penguin Books: Harmondsworth, Middlesex, England, 1985), pp. 268-269.

hol. As he wrote in the essay *Why Do Men Stupefy Themselves?*, he felt tobacco and alcohol were means of escaping a guilty conscience, and that this refusal to face life honestly prevents men from living morally.[26] Lastly, Tolstoy gave up hunting as well, feeling embarrassed at the thought of trying to kill a rabbit or other animal for pleasure.[27]

The second aspect of the way of the sage is that the sage must reject selfishness and have few desires,[28] and be frugal (which will lead to generosity).[29] The reverse, having and showing off great wealth, is condemned when it is written: "Do not value rare treasures, so that the people shall not steal. Do not display objects of desire, so that the people's hearts shall not be disturbed."[30]

In a similar vein, it is also said: "To have little is to possess. To have plenty is to be perplexed,"[31] and "To be proud with honor and wealth is to cause one's own downfall."[32] Elsewhere, Lao Tzu writes:

"There is no calamity greater than lavish desires.

There is no greater guilt than discontentment.

And there is no greater disaster than greed.

He who is contented with contentment is always contented."[33]

Although he lived on his lands (and in his Moscow home) until his death, Tolstoy nevertheless did try to obey this precept as best he could. Despite the appearance of hypocrisy of the surface of the situation, Tolstoy followed what seemed to him to be the path of the lesser evil. While he was tormented by the thought of possessing enormous wealth while masses of the people suffered in poverty, he was forced to the conclusion that giving all his worldly goods to the poor was not the solution. While possessing so much wealth might be evil, he would fail in his duty to his family if he gave away all to the poor, reducing them to poverty themselves (and only benefiting the poor in the very

26. Morris Philipson, *The Count Who Wished He Were A Peasant: A Life of Leo Tolstoy* (Patheon Books: Harmondsworth, Middlesex, England, 1985), pp. 268-269.

27. Simmons, p. 385.

28. *Tao-te ching*, Chapter 19.

29. *Tao-te ching*, Chapter 67.

30. *Tao-te ching*, Chapter 3.

31. *Tao-te ching*, Chapter 22.

32. *Tao-te ching*, Chapter 9.

33. *Tao-te ching*, Chapter 46.

short term).[34] They were entitled to live in their accustomed manner, without being forced to change their way of life. Tolstoy resolved to attempt their conversion by setting a proper example for them to follow. Thus, he forsook the service of servants, performed manual labor, began to make his own shoes, etc.[35] This life of manual labor, which Tolstoy followed to his death, seems adequate proof that he was serious in his condemnation of wealth, despite his family's continued possession of it.

Additionally, the division of all his property, his money, and the royalty rights to his pre-1881 works (all those published after that year were to be in the public domain) amongst his wife and children in 1892 further illustrates his desire to deny himself wealth without penalizing his family for their lack of belief. (Even this measure was a compromise, as he earlier had considered giving all his land to the peasants!)[36]

Not only is possessing great wealth condemned, but the sin is compounded if the common people are poor while the nobles live in luxurious excess:

"The courts are exceedingly splendid,
While the fields are exceedingly weedy,
And the granaries are exceedingly empty.
Elegant clothes are worn,
Sharp weapons are carried,
Foods and drinks are enjoyed beyond limit,
And wealth and treasures are accumulated in excess.
This is robbery and extravagance."[37]

"Therefore the sage desires to have no desire, He does not value rare treasures."[38] "The sage does not accumulate for himself. The more he uses for others, the more he has himself. The more he gives to others, the more he possesses of his own."[39]

---

34. Philipson, pp. 100-101.
35. Simmons, pp. 379-380.
36. Troyat, pp. 511-512, 515.
37. *Tao-te ching,* Chapter 53.
38. *Tao-te ching,* Chapter 64.
39. *Tao-te ching,* Chapter 81.

Tolstoy showed his commitment to this additional doctrine of generosity during the famine of 1891. Despite his dislike for charity by the rich (he felt that their wealth had come at the expense of the poor to begin with), he saw no alternative in this instance. The government did nothing to help, and even pretended that the problem did not even exist. Thus, Tolstoy helped coordinate the efforts to provide aid to the starving millions. He spent "the better part of two years" in helping with famine relief. His efforts probably helped save thousands of human lives. However, he did not feel that helping the poor was something to be done only in time of famine, but rather at all times. The events of this period in all likelihood helped spark his decision (discussed above) to renounce all his property rights.[40]

The third commandment for the person who would be a sage is to have "deep love" for all men.[41] Tolstoy practiced this virtue as much as possible. The work with and for the poor during the famine of 1891 was just one example. This work went beyond that single great tragedy. For example, at the village at Yasnaya Polyana, Tolstoy received poor people needing help every day. He also cared for the widows and orphans of the village.[42]

This principle of brotherly love seems to be contradicted elsewhere in the *Tao-Te Ching* by the statement that "The sage is not humane. He regards all people as straw dogs." The same is said to be true of Heaven and Earth.[43] ("Straw dogs" refers to the ancient religious practice of sacrificing dogs made of straw, which were thrown away after use, and to which there were no sentimental attachments.) According to the commentary, however, "humane" is almost universally understood here to mean having favorites, showing partiality, and being humane "in a deliberate or artificial way."[44] "The Way of Heaven has no favorites. It is always with the good man."[45]

---

40. Philipson, pp. 117-118.
41. *Tao-te ching*, Chapter 67, and accompanying commentary on p. 220.
42. Martine de Courcel, *Tolstoy: The Ultimate Reconciliation* (Charles Scribner's Sons: New York, 1980), p. 182.
43. *Tao-te ching*, Chapter 5.
44. *Tao-te ching*, Commentary, pp. 107-108.
45. *Tao-te ching*, Chapter 79.

Tolstoy's dislike for such artificial, plastic humanity and caring can be illustrated simply by his revulsion for "normal" charity in cases (most of them) in which it would do no real good. While in his own village, giving to the poor could be effective. But in a larger place with larger problems, such as Moscow, such giving was embarrassing for the giver and the receiver both. There could be no long-term benefit for the recipients, and it was a waste of the giver's money.[46] The only good it did was to ease the conscience of the giver, helping him to ignore the evil of his position of wealth. Tolstoy was more interested in curing the cause of the situation – a lack of love – not its symptoms.[47]

As a part of this principle of deep love for mankind, violence is condemned. (It is probably spoken against also because of the fifth and final principle discussed, that of managing affairs without action. Violence is, after all, a rather dramatic sort of action.) "'Violent and fierce people do not die a natural death.' I shall make this the father of my teaching."[48]

Tolstoy's opposition to violence found a rather eloquent – if inelegant – expression in his reply to the question of whether "killing by a revolutionary was not superior to killing by a policeman." He responded by comparing the two to "'cat-shit and dog-shit,' both of which have unpleasant odors."[49] In a more scholarly vein, he wrote in a letter to Gandhi in 1910 that

"every reasonable person is bound to know that the use of violence is incompatible with love as the basic law of life, that once violence is tolerated in any cases whatsoever, the inadequacy of the law of love is recognized and therefore the law itself repudiated."[50]

The *Tao-Te Ching* deplores unnecessary wars, and attempts to "dominate the world with force" are condemned. If one does engage in war, it should only be "as an unavoidable step." The general who follows the Tao "achieves his purpose but does not aim to dominate."[51]

---

46. Henry Gifford, *Tolstoy* (Oxford University Press: Oxford, 1982), pp. 53-54.
47. de Courcel, p. 229.
48. *Tao-te ching*, Chapter 42.
49. William W. Rowe, *Leo Tolstoy* (Twayne Publishers: Boston, 1986), p. 15.
50. *Tolstoy's Letters: Volume II (1880-1910)*, selected, edited and translated by R.F. Christian (Charles Scribner's Sons: New York, 1978), pp. 706-707.
51. *Tao-te ching*, Chapter 30.

The wise ruler resorts to force of arms only when unavoidable, and then "he regards calm restraint as the best principle....Even when he is victorious, he does not regard it as praiseworthy."[52] Tolstoy himself condemned all war. In fact, he even renounced "the deliberate killing of living creatures,"[53] and felt that war was bred on "'cultural' barbarity."[54] He felt that although one side might behave worse than the other in a war, they were both to blame for its outbreak.[55] He felt that was a monstrous relationship between people, engaged in because people have lived so long under it that they feel it is normal.[56]

In a similar vein, violence and the threat of violence by the state against its people is deplored. "Fish should not be taken away from water. And sharp weapons of the state should not be displayed to the people."[57]

Tolstoy made his complete opposition to capital punishment – something almost certainly beyond the intent of Lao Tzu – known quite clearly and forcefully. Two examples should suffice. The first was his letter to Alexander III urging the emperor to spare the lives of his father's assassins. "Return good for evil, resist not evil, forgive everyone" was the request he made. Tolstoy argued that the only righteous course would be to spare them.[58] (The appeal was, of course, unsuccessful.)

A second example was Tolstoy's *I Cannot Be Silent*. Written in the aftermath of the execution in 1908 of 12 peasants (initial reports said 20, however) for an armed uprising, the article condemned the idea "that an evil deed committed for the benefit of many, ceases to be immoral."[59] He further deplored the state of things in which people talked and wrote "of executions, hangings, murders and bombs, as they used to talk and write about the weather."[60]

52. *Tao-te ching*, Chapter 31.
53. *Tolstoy's Letters: Volume II*, p. 692.
54. *Tolstoy's Letters: Volume II*, pp. 644-645.
55. *Tolstoy's Letters: Volume II*, pp. 584.
56. *Tolstoy's Letters: Volume II*, pp. 406-407.
57. *Tao-te ching*, Chapter 36.
58. *Tolstoy's Letters: Volume II*, pp. 342-343.
59. Simmons, pp. 692-692.
60. Troyat, P. 641.

The fourth aspect of sageliness is humility and refusal to exalt one-self. The sage is commanded not to be ahead of the world (and thus he shall become his leader)[61], nor to compete. "It is because he does not compete that he is without reproach,"[62] and "that the world cannot compete with him."[63] It is further commanded: "Do not exalt the wor-thy, so that the people shall not compete."[64] "The way of Heaven does not compete, and yet it skillfully achieves victory."[65] (Although the term "compete" is consistently used in this translation, it would seem reasonable to assume that this does not just mean competing, but at-tempts to set oneself ahead of others. Thus, it is more than just not trying to keep up with the rest of the world, but is more of a condemna-tion of attempts at self-aggrandizement.)

Lao Tzu continues, saying "The sage places himself in the back-ground, but finds himself in the foreground,"[66] and "Therefore humble station is the basis of honor. The low is the foundation of the high."[67] The sage is further described as being like water: "It is good; it ben-efits all things and does not compete with them. It dwells in (lowly) places that all disdain. That is why it is so near to Tao."[68] On the other hand, self-exaltation is condemned when it is written: "He who stands on tiptoe is not steady...He who shows himself is not luminous."[69] "He who boasts of himself is not given credit. He who brags does not en-dure for long."[70]

Tolstoy's humility was an incredible thing. After 1884, he preferred to be called simply Leo Nikolayevich by all, including servants, and quit using his title (Count Tolstoy).[71] But this was only the beginning. In a letter written some time in October of 1887, he expressed the

---

61. *Tao-te ching*, Chapter 67.
62. *Tao-te ching*, Chapter 8.
63. *Tao-te ching*, Chapter 66.
64. *Tao-te ching*, Chapter 3.
65. *Tao-te ching*, Chapter 73.
66. *Tao-te ching*, Chapter 7.
67. *Tao-te ching*, Chapter 39.
68. *Tao-te ching*, Chapter 8.
69. *Tao-te ching*, Chapter 24.
70. *Tao-te ching*, Chapter 24.
71. Simmons, p. 370.

conviction that he should do nothing bad, nor useless, but good for others. He believed that "The simplest and shortest moral formula is to be served by others as little as possible, and to serve others as much as possible. to take from others the least possible and to give them the most possible."[72] (translation mine)

He even took this principle of self-subordination so far as to empty his own chamber pot, and began to perform manual labor, whether for his estate or for a local widow. While he enjoyed doing this labor for the exercise, though, this was not the reason for taking up the new pursuits of plowing, timber-hauling, hut building and shoemaking. He felt that men have a moral need for physical labor.[73] He stated in the same letter of October 1887 that if a man frees himself from his mortality obligatory labor and lives a parasitical life (depending upon the work of others) for the sake of science or the arts, he will produce nothing but false science or art.[74]

Another example of Tolstoy's unwillingness to receive personal glory was his refusal to allow giant celebrations of his eightieth birthday. He referred to the planned jubilee as a burden[75], "stupid and disagreeable flattery," and said it was "offensive" to him.[76] As he requested, the jubilee was canceled.

The final principle which the sage must follow, and possibly the most difficult for Western minds to understand, is that he must manage affairs without action.[77] "He acts but does not rely on his own ability" is used to describe the sage in three different places.[78] Twice this is described as "profound and secret virtue."[79] (It is also the way of the Tao itself: "It acts, but does not rely on its own ability.")[80] The sage instead relies upon the natural order to assert itself, as a bowstring eventually returns to its neutral position if left alone.[81] "By acting with-

72. *Tolstoy's Letters: Volume II*, p. 422.
73. Simmons, p. 381.
74. *Tolstoy's Letters: Volume II*, p. 423.
75. *Tolstoy's Letters: Volume II*, p. 676.
76. Simmons, p. 695.
77. *Tao-te ching*, Chapter 2.
78. *Tao-te ching*, Chapters 2, 10 and 77.
79. *Tao-te ching*, Chapters 10 and 51.
80. *Tao-te ching*, Chapter 51.
81. *Tao-te ching*, Chapter 77.

out action, all things will be in order."[82] "Therefore (the sage) never strives himself for the great, and thereby the great is achieved."[83] "Tao invariably takes no action, and yet there is nothing left undone."[84] "Heaven's net is indeed vast. Though its meshes are wide, it misses nothing."[85] (This is not meant to be a total indictment of all action – just of unnecessary action. A useful analogy might be one of steering a boat by using the rudder, not by rowing harder on one side.)

Tolstoy echoed Lao Tzu's warning against such unnecessary activity (as opposed to performing necessary activities, which he viewed as a human need), saying "....external, feverish activity is not only not necessary, but is actually harmful....Work, *le travail*, is the only idol of people wishing to free themselves from the demands of Christianity..."[86] He also wrote that sin came from doing what we should not do, whereas the will of God is only performed by men when they do that which they cannot avoid. It is the turmoil arising from unnecessary actions which blinds us to the will of God, and only by refraining from such actions can we be opened to His will.[87]

Lao Tzu took this principle farther, proscribing active resistance to strength. (The analogy of the boat becomes relevant here as well. Rowing against the current will eventually lead to nothing but exhaustion, as eventually one will return downstream. "Going ashore" is out of the question, as one cannot leave the Way of the universe, the Tao.) "When man is born, he is tender and weak. At death, he is stiff and hard...The strong and the great are inferior, while the tender and the weak are superior."[88] "All the world knows that the weak overcomes the strong and the soft overcomes the hard."[89]

Along these lines is Tolstoy's doctrine of nonresistance to evil. Although it is closely related to the concept of deep love and nonviolence, it is even more applicable to this position of Lao Tzu's teach-

---

82. *Tao-te ching*, Chapter 3.
83. *Tao-te ching*, Chapter 34.
84. *Tao-te ching*, Chapter 37.
85. *Tao-te ching*, Chapter 73.
86. *Tolstoy's Letters: Volume II*, p. 494.
87. Bodde, pp. 82-83.
88. *Tolstoy's Letters: Volume II*, p. 494.
89. *Tao-te ching*, Chapter 78.

ings. His version of nonresistance was that the use of physical force of any sort in order to force a man to do or not do something against his will was wrong. He even extended this view – in theory, at least, although he held that in practice it would not be strictly adhered to – to say that it was wrong even to use force to prevent murder.[90]

On the other hand, there is a warning for not following the path of Tao: "Open the mouth. Meddle with affairs. And to the end of life there will be no salvation."[91]

Tolstoy affirms this by attributing all the evil in the world to acting when one should not. For example, he felt that worrying about freedom led to government and participation in it, which led to slavery. He added that one could not do good until one had ceased to do evil.[92]

Tolstoy looked at the *Tao-Te Ching* as a guide to everyday living, and was interested by its socio-ethical concepts, not by its theories on cosmology, knowledge, or elemental materialism.[93] It was in this way that its patterns were visible in his life. This is not to say that Tolstoy ignored the spiritual side of life, but rather that he was primarily interested by how a given teaching could be applied to daily life. Thus, he regarded the *Tao-Te Ching* as a moral-ethical guide to man's relationship to the world around him,[94] a guide which he followed in his daily life.

Whatever the source of inspiration for his actions, Tolstoy fit the criteria for being a Taoist sage. He embraced simplicity; rejected wealth; had deep love for humanity; demonstrated humility; and rejected unnecessary action. Despite disagreements with Lao Tzu on some occasional points (such as his total opposition to capital punishment), Leo Tolstoy clearly followed the commandments of the *Tao-te-Ching*. In his writings, his words and his deeds he truly showed himself to be a Taoist sage.

90. Simmons, pp. 436-437.
91. *Tao-te ching,* Chapter 52.
92. *Tolstoy's Letters: Volume II*, p. 494-495.
93. A. J. Shifman, *Lev Tolstoy i Vostok* (Moskva: Nauka, 1971), p. 43.
94. Shifman, p. 45.

BIBLIOGRAPHY

Bodde, Derk, *Tolstoy and China* (Princeton University
Press: Princeton, 1950).
de Courcel, Martine, *Tolstoy: The Ultimate Reconciliation*
(Charles Scribner's Sons: New York, 1980).
Dukas, Vytas and Sandstrom, Glenn A., "Taoistic Patterns
in *War and Peace*," *The Slavic and East European Journal*,
Vol. XIV, No. 2 (1970).
Gifford, Henry, *Tolstoy* (Oxford University Press: Oxford, 1982).
Lao Tzu, *Tao-Te Ching*, published as *The Way of Lao Tzu
(Tao-Te Ching)*, translated and with introductory essays, comments
and notes by Wing-tsit Chan (The Bobbs-Merrill Company:
Indianapolis, 1963).
Philipson, Morris, *The Count Who Wished He Were A Peasant:
A Life of Leo Tolstoy* (Pantheon Books: New York, 1967).
Rowe, William W., *Leo Tolstoy* (Twayne Publishers: Boston, 1986).
Shifman, A. L., *Lev Tolstoy i Vostok* (Moskva: 1971).
Simmons, Ernest J., *Leo Tolstoy* (Little, Brown and Co.:
Boston, 1946).
Tolstoy, Leo N., *Postface to the Kreutzer Sonata*,
in *The Kreutzer Sonata and Other Stories*, translated and
with an introduction by David McDuff
(Penguin Books: Harmondsworth, Middlesex, England, 1985).
Tolstoy, Leo N., *Tolstoy's Diaries: Volume I (1847-1894)*,
Christian, R.F., ed. and translator (Charles Scribner's Sons:
New York, 1985).

Tolstoy, Leo N., *Tolstoy's Letters: Volume I (1828-1879)*,
Christian, R.F., ed. and translator, (Charles Scribner's Sons:
New York, 1978).

Tolstoy, Leo N., *Tolstoy's Letters: Volume II (1880-1910)*,
Christian, R.F., ed. and translator (Charles Scribner's Sons:
New York, 1978).

Troyat, Henri, *Tolstoy*, translated by Nancy Amphoux
(Doubleday & Col, Inc.: Garden City, New York, 1967

CHAPTER SEVEN

SOME SIMILARITIES AND DIFFERENCES BETWEEN TOLSTOY'S CONCEPTS OF IDENTITY AND VOCATION AND THEIR PARALLELS IN HINDUISM

Dragan Milivojevic
University of Oklahoma

For Tolstoy, the study of major world religions was not a matter of the mind, a scientific and objective investigation of their principles and tenets, but a matter of the heart which should answer such vital questions for Tolstoy as Who am I? Where am I going? Tolstoy searched far and wide for an answer to these questions in his native Orthodox Christianity as well as in Oriental religions, including Hinduism.

An attempt is made here to compare Tolstoy's own answers to these fundamental questions with those provided by certain schools of Hinduism in view of presenting points of similarity and difference. Tolstoy's interest in Hinduism is selective, for him, Hinduism is an all-embracing concept, where differences among schools and movements are not clearly perceived and considered.

Identity in Tolstoy's Interpretation

Identity and vocation[1] are two coordinates of human life which indicate "consciousness of one's position in the universe (mir) and the actions that follow therefrom" (35, 170, 1902).[2] Human identity can

---

1. The terms "identity" and "vocation" are used by Richard F. Gustafson, *Leo Tolstoy: Resident and Stranger* (Princeton: Princeton University Press, 1986). English translations are taken from Gustafson.
2. Parenthetical references in arabic numerals refer to the Jubilee Edition, *Polnoe Sobranie Sochinenij* (Moscow, 1928-58). The first numeral refers to the volume, the second to the page, and the third to the year of composition or publication.

be located in one of the two conceptions of the self, the "animal self" and the "spiritual self." The former is framed by our body and lives through the body and its desires. The "animal self" consists in physical separation from our fellow human beings and spiritual separation from our divine source and it is perishable. The latter is the seat of our eternal soul; it is our divine self and the connection to our divine source. In general terms, Tolstoy's quest at human perfection is demonstrated in the transition from the "animal self" to the "spiritual self" representing a merger with the divine source. Tolstoy's fictional characters often in adverse circumstances of suffering, illness, and death find who they are where they are going. Pierre in *War and Peace* and Brekhunov in "Master and Man" are two examples. Human identity in Tolstoy's interpretation is a part of divine identity; it is related as a part is to the whole and this linkage is waiting to be discovered in each individual life. For Tolstoy, the concept of God is always known inwardly through the self's intuition of itself as a part of the whole. "I am a part. He is all. I cannot understand myself except as a part of Him" (52, 49; 1891).

This idea of the synechdochic relationship of the divine to the human is prevalent at different periods of Hinduism. Vivekananda, a neo-Hinduist and a contemporary of Tolstoy's, almost always uses the same words to express this idea, "God is one whole; we are the parts." Hinduism also posits a parallel to the Tolstoyan division between "the animal" and "the spiritual self." Nama-rupa (name and form) is a Hindu concept referring to the whole world as it presents itself to our senses. All schools and philosophies of Hinduism agree that this physical and sensual orientation will have to be transcended and the ultimate object of thought and the final good of knowledge lies beyond the range of names and forms. The relationship between the divine and the human is one of inclusiveness, "I am part; He is all," is also referred to by Hindu thinkers as a complementary relationship. Thus Namm'alvar speaks about "...the soul which the Lord has condescended to exhibit to me as a mode of himself, for I am related to him as the predicate to the subject, or attribute to substance."[3] Both Tolstoy and the Hinduist

---

3. R. C. Zaehne, *Hinduism* (Oxford: Oxford University Press, 1988), p. 128.

thinkers mentioned here, posit a duality between lower and higher states of consciousness and it is the higher state of consciousness which leads to the union with God. The fundamental question is how is this transformation of consciousness from the part to the whole realized, or to use the Tolstoyan dilemma of separation vs. belonging, when does the shift in consciousness from separation to belonging take place, and how is this process brought about? Does this insight and conviction of higher consciousness occur only when the human body is decayed and annihilated, as is the case with Ivan Il'ich or Brekhunov in "Master and Man," and is the physical and mental suffering which many of Tolstoy's fictional characters endure (see Nekhlyudov in *Resurrection*) a precondition for the attainment of a higher state of consciousness and eventually a merger with the divine source?

As is to be expected an identification with the lower consciousness, the five senses, would not lead to higher consciousness; such an identification will produce chaos, giving us various sensations. The way to reach higher consciousness consists, according to Tolstoy, in reaching outward, in transcending one's "animal self." "The other method is indicated in first having known yourself by loving yourself by thought into another person, animal, plant, even a stone... this method is what is called poetic talent, it is also love. It is the establishment of the unity among beings which has been as it were destroyed. "Go out of yourself and into another. You can go into everything. Everything merges with God, with the All" (52, 101; 1893). Olenin in the Cossacks after reaching the mountains of Caucausus, has this experience of self-transcendence, of a love for all God's world in which he feels himself not an isolated human being but a part of the whole. The opposition between a subject and an object is removed in this state of higher consciousness. Olenin's experience in this state of higher consciousness is ecstatic, devoid of physical and mental suffering, as was the case with Ivan Il'ich, Brekhunov and Nekhlyudov.

Hinduism through its long history has developed different spiritual techniques of reaching higher consciousness and some of them are directly opposed to Tolstoy's method of reaching outward in love. Some of the Yoga spiritual techniques lead to a state of pure isolation in which there is no sense of "I" or "mine," a consciousness of pure detachment both from the world and from other souls. This is a movement from the world in the quest for self-perfection. Tolstoy comments indirectly on the Yogic inward way of self-perfection. "Do not think that this [consciousness of God] destroys the energy of life, that it leads to an ascetic, mental-prayer and to staring at the end of your noses" (55, 49; 1904). This ascetic and self-centered ideal of sainthood in Hinduism was criticized by Neo-Hinduists and bhakti followers as not being conducive to charitable social action and a reaction took place in which the so-called bhakti cults became prominent. Bhakti, the religion of loving devotion, of reaching outward to merge with God and through other human beings, is similar to Tolstoy's notion of reaching out in love. In some of bhakti's believers, there is a theme of separation from God accompanied by guilt and belonging to God manifested by ecstasy. For Ramanuja, a bhakti philosopher, there are as many souls as there are bodies to house them, and souls, though like God and like each other are eternal, are distinct from each other and from God, who is their origin. Only on achieving moksha (higher consciousness) can souls enter into possession of their true, timeless nature by reaching God who is the supreme soul. For Ramanuja, God is benevolent and loving; He imprisons souls in matter, Tolstoy's "animal self," only to release them and unite them with Himself. The cause of the soul's imprisonment in matter is unbelief, or lack of faith. Ramanuja's beliefs are close to Christianity, as well as to Tolstoy's thinking.

Tolstoy favorite metaphors are pipes and conduits. Man is a "channel through which the immobile, non-material, non-temporal, non-spatial principle passes in this life" (57, 173; 1909). and "They speak of saving the soul. One can save only what can perish. The soul cannot perish because it alone exists. One need not save the soul but cleanse it of all that has darkened and defiled it, enlighten it so that God might more and more pass through it," (45, 42; 1910). This is what Gustafson calls salvation through deification, "...a total transfiguration of self, a turning away from all personal passion, desire, perception, and reasoning which returns you to your life in God."[4] In other words, it is a process of turning away from one's animal self and embracing one's

---

4. Gustafson, p. 104.

spiritual self. This process does not entail accumulation and acquisition; it is a negative, inward action of introspection and purification which brings it about.

The converse of this process of transformation, which results in unity with the divine source, is a state of separation from it, which is sin as Tolstoy understands, an act of separation from the God of Life and Love and a violation of the divine principle of love. Tolstoy calls this separation from God the "dissociation of people from God and each other" (63, 114; 1883) and his own personal crises bear testimony to the sense of acute isolation and guilt which such mental states produce. "All night and early morning I was visited of everything, of God, of the truth of my understanding of the meaning of life...it was all a punishment for unkind, unloving feelings which I allowed myself in the preceding days. And it serves me right" (57, 131; 1909).

Just as with Tolstoy, some of the Tamil Bhakti followers from South India show an intense sense of personal guilt in their separation from God; human beings, as they exist apart from God, are evil and corrupt, the slaves of their egoism.

Evil, all evil, my race, evil my qualities all,
Great am I only in sin, evil is even my good,
Evil my innermost self, foolish, avoiding the pure,
Beast am I not, yet the ways of the beast I never forsake.[5]

Vocation

Man's vocation in life is to do the will of God. Since man cannot grasp the will of God in its entirety one must look for some signs that God's will is being followed. Tolstoy mentions three such signs: (1) the absence of suffering, (2) the absence of hostility in oneself or toward oneself, (3) the sense of movement or growth.

One's vocation to do the will of God, the movement of growth, proceeds from one's positive identity with a higher state of consciousness which is an imperative for action. God wills and gives and man "collaborates." "Nothing spiritual is acquired spiritually, neither a religious sense, nor love, nor anything. The spiritual is created through

---

5. Quoted in Zaehner, p. 132, from the poet Apar in the collection *Devaram*.

material life, in space and time. The spiritual is created by doing" (54, 121; 1902). The mowing scene (iii, iv-v) in Anna Karenina is a concrete image of that spiritual endeavor. Levin begins his mowing in a self-conscious way as an effort and he ends it unconsciously in a state of self-forgetting. "You can forget yourself in plowing, mowing, or sewing. And in this way you must forget yourself and all of life, in the divine task. Don't ask yourself what will come of my labor, what will become of me after death, but give yourself to the task with the same – be it love or desire to do good – with which you plow or sew" (51, 76; 1890).

Selfless action, which Tolstoy advocates as man's vocation, resembles the Hinduist way of Karma-Yoga. In the Bhagavad-Gita three paths of the absolute are offered to the man who seeks liberation, the path of knowledge (jnana), the path of action (karma), and the path of bhakti (loving devotion). Karma Yoga requires that the individual continue carrying on with his usual duties and activities, but with a new attitude of detachment from their fruits, from the possible gains and losses that they will entail. The world is not abandoned, as it is in the different Hinduist ascetic practices, but the will of the individual is united in action with the universal ground, not with the vicissitudes of the suffering body. "Set thy heart upon thy work, but never on its reward. Work not for a reward; but never cease to do they work" and "Do thy work... free from selfish desires, be not moved in success or failure...."[6]

Tolstoy extends the path of bhakti not only to God as it is understood in Hinduism, but also to human beings, who participate in the divine creation. This is Tolstoy's path of love and compassion which is expressed in his fiction and writing. Tolstoy distinguishes between to kinds of love: love of and love for.[7] The former is personal and exclusive, centering on one person or object; the latter is universal and manifests itself as God's law, or compassion. Gerasim, the servant of Ivan Il'ich, sees in Ivan's predicament of illness and death a universal human fate, which deserves a universal feeling of compassion extended

6. *The Bhagavad Gita*, trans. by Juan Mascaro (London: Penguin Books, 1988), 2, 47 and 49 (p. 52).

7. These are Gustafson's terms in *Resident and Stranger*.

to all human beings who are or who will share Ivan's fate. Gustafson sees Tolstoy's "Master and Man" as "...an emblematic journey of discovery and a parable of the way to love."[8] Brekhunov is trying to save Nikita from freezing by lying on top of him. Now he knows that "he is Nikita and Nikita is him, that his life is not in himself but in Nikita, that if Nikita is alive, he is alive" (29, 44; 1895). This is a concrete image of the path of love in Tolstoy; humans are so close to each other that they live as one life.

The feeling of universal love which Tolstoy expresses is absent from early Hinduism but in later schools of Hinduism it found its representative in Vivekananda, who was a contemporary of Tolstoy. Vivekananda distinguishes, like Tolstoy, between two kinds of love. The love for our children and wives is for him a necessary animal love, corresponding to Tolstoy's "animal self." It is a selfish kind of love, "the love of" in Tolstoy's words. The love which is perfectly unselfish is God's love, "the love for" in Tolstoy's formulation. Men, if they love unselfishly, should imitate God's love in its impartiality. In Vivekanada's words, "a finite subject cannot love, nor a finite object be loved."[9]

Vivekananda also agrees with Tolstoy's statement that God's will is followed in a sense of movement and growth on the part of an individual who is immersed in the bhakti form of love for God and fellow human beings. Worship and ceremonies are something secondary. Vivekananda writes "Religion is not doctrines, nor dogmas, nor intellectual argumentation; it is being and becoming; it is realisation."[10]

Tolstoy's concept of love is rooted in this concept of being and becoming. It is realized on the part of particular being in the movement away from his self-centered ego toward God and human beings. The goal is to transfer oneself into "everything, to merge with God, with the All" (52, 101; 1893).

Tolstoy's religious and philosophical views have points of similarity and difference with those of Hinduism. The Hindu concept of karma-Yoga (Yoga of the action, the path of action) is echoed in Tolstoy's

---

8. *Resident and Stranger*, p. 197.

9. Swami Vivekananada, *Religion of Love*, (Ramakrishna Math: Calcutta, 1988) p. 20.

10. Ibid., p. 96.

views on selfish action. The path of bhakti (loving devotion) resembles Tolstoy's love of God and human beings. Tolstoy does not agree with the idealistic concept of classical Hinduism of the world being an illusion (Maya) and of the tendency on the part of some of the followers of this philosophy to withdraw from life and action into asceticism and isolation. It is with the followers of Neo-Hinduism, Vivekananda and his group, who preached bhakti, that Tolstoy found most in common. Tolstoy's assessment of Hinduism refers to Vivekananda's interpretation of Hinduism. "Last night I read books about Hindu faith. It was a superb book about the meaning of life.... Love not yourself but Atman, that is, an infinite spirit, and you will love everybody and you will live with the spirit, freely, and blissfully. How happy am I that I am beginning to understand, confirm and feel this not by reason but with the whole soul and most importantly through experience" (57, 166; 1909).

When Tolstoy started reading intensely on the subject of Oriental religions and Hinduism in the eighties, his views on "Who am I?" and "Where am I going?" were already formed. He found the confirmation of his views in some of the Hinduist religious writings. The similarity between Tolstoy's views on religion and those of Hinduism are not due to the influence of the latter on the former. The parallelism and the similarities are part of a universal religious and philosophical quest.

BIBLIOGRAPHY

The Bhagavad Gita. Translated by **Juan Mascaro**.
(London: Penguin Books, 1988.)
Gustafson, Richard F., Leo Tolstoy: *Resident and Stranger*.
(Princeton: Princeton University Press, 1986.)
Tolstoy, L.N. *Polnoe Sobranie Sochinenij*. Moscow: 1928-58.
Vivekananda, (Swami). *Religion of Love*.
(Calcutta: Ramakrishna Math, 1988.)
Zaehne, R.C. *Hinduism*. (Oxford: Oxford University Press, 1988.)

CHAPTER EIGHT

THE "INDIAN" IN TOLSTOY
(Part two)
A. Syrkin

Tolstoy's departure is manifoldly reflected in memoirs and research literature.[1] We shall not repeat here all the details of the respective evidence, which is well known, although from 1910 and up to now it has received different interpretations. Putting aside the most biased and one-sided opinions (as e.g. accusing V.G. Tchertkoff of the main responsibility for this departure[2]) and judging without prejudice, from the evidence of Tolstoy himself and those surrounding him, one can see that the desire to leave the family, to be able to follow his doctrine more closely had been characteristic of Tolstoy for a long time; this desire was permanently strengthened by the domestic situation but evidently could never have been fulfilled if this situation had not been extremely aggravated during 1910. Irrespective of giving preference to one or another factor (ideological or domestic), both of them appeared long before Tolstoy's departure, sometimes closely interwoven

---

1. See t. 58 (diaries and notebooks of 1910); *Dnevniki Sofi Andreevny Tolstoj*. 1910, Moskva, Sovetskij pisatel' 1936 (TD); S. Tolstoj, pp. 235-293; Suxotina-Tolstaja, pp. 369-426 (*O smerti...*); ST, pp. 186-244); I.L. Tolstoj. *Moi vospominanija*, Moskva, izd. Xud.lit-ra, 1969, pp. 254-266; Gol'denvejzer, II (1910); V.F. Bulgakov. *The last year of Leo Tolstoy*, London, 1971; V.F. Bulgakov. *Uxod i smert' Tolstogo* - in: *Lev Tolstoj, ego druz'ja i blizkie,* Tula, 1970, pp. 80-123; JZ, IV (July 1909 - November 1910); A.I. Ksjunin, *Uxod Tolstogo*, Spb, 1911; V.G. _ertkov. *Uxod Tolstogo*, Moskva, 1922; V. Xodasevi_. *Uxod Tolstogo - Izbrannaja proza*. N.Y. Russica publishers, 1982, pp. 109-122; *Smert' Tolstogo po novym materialam*, Moskva, 1929; B.M. Mejlax. *Uxod i smert' L'va Tolstogo*, Moskva, izd. Xud. lit-ra, Izd.2, 1979; Lanskoj, pp. 361-460.
2. By his son L.L. Tolstoy (cf. Mejlax, p. 59 sq.).

with each other (e.g. in his reaction to his wife's hostility to his spiritual quest).[3] We do not dwell on positive elements in Tolstoy's family life (which certainly existed) and in connection with the problem discussed, would note here that certain conflicts had begun in the first months and years of marriage. Respective feelings of S.A. Tolstaja and Tolstoy himself (who began at this time to think of leaving the house, under different pretexts), are often testified to in their diaries.[4] Tolstoy's spiritual interests turn him more and more to the idea of departure from the late eighteen seventies, when these interests come up against the lack of understanding and sometimes – the direct aggressiveness of his wife.[5] "He cried out aloud to-day that his most passion-

---

3. "All my works, which were none other than my life, interested and interest you so little" (see his letter to wife of 15-18 XII 1885 - t. 83, p. 546). In autumn of 1907 he says as if summing up: "I have been waiting for it for 45 years - that S.A. would listen to me - and I cannot achieve it" (Suxotin, p. 196).

4. Cf. already a record of 8 X 1862 in S. Tolstaja, I, p. 37. In autumn 1863 Tolstoy desires to go to war if it begins (ibid., pp. 61, 527; GT, 1855-1869, pp. 614 sq.). See also with respect to theses relations: Suxotina-Tolstaja, pp. 375 sq. (ST, pp. 190 sq.); A. Tolstaja, II, pp. 10, 136, 192 sq., 290; S. Tolstoj, pp. 240 sq.; D.P. Makovickij. *Uxod L'va Nikolaevi_a* - Gos. Literaturnyj Muzej. Letopisi, Kn. 2, Moskva, 1938, pp. 446 sq.; Mejlax, pp. 197 sq. etc.

5. "Alas! He is writing what you might call theses about religion ... My only hope is that he will get to the end of this work as quickly as possible and just get over it all like an illness" (in S.A. Tolstaja's letter of 7 XI 1879 to her sister - see: Suxotina-Tolstaja, p. 389; ST, p. 207). In *My Life (Moja _izn')* she remembered later how in 1880, when she was rewriting his religious works, "I was seized by mounting indignation. I snatched up all the pages, took them to Lev, and told him, that I would not be doing any more copying for him; I *cannot* - Suxotina-Tolstaja, p. 390 (ST, p. 207); cd. M.V. Muratov, *L.N. Tolstoj i V.G. _ertkov po ix perepiske*, Moskva 1934, p. 11. We do not dwell here on Tolstoy's relations with other members of the family, who did not play such an important role in his departure. However he suffered from misunderstanding not only on the part of his wife. In a letter to her of 15-18 XII 1885, cited above (see note 3) he goes on: "and as it to children, they do not care even to read" (i.e. his religious writings) t. 83, p. 546). His favourite son Vane_ka, in whom he placed his hopes as on his successor, died a child in 1895. Other sons were more or less alien to him (especially Leon, Andrew and Michael, who took their mother's side in the family conflict). The daughters stood much closer to him, especially Maria, who, however, left Jasnaja Poljana after her marriage in 1897 and died in 1905. The eldest daughter Tatiana married and left him in 1899. Of all the family only the youngest daughter Alexandra supported him actively in his last years. Cf. Suxotina-Tolstaja, pp. 297 sq (ST, pp. 215; 219 sq.; cf. ibid. 245 sq.); A. Tolstaja, II, pp. 82-82, 296; JZ, II, p. 312, A. _ifman. *Stranicy iz zhizni L'va Tolstogo*. Moskva, 1983, pp. 261 sq.; etc.

ate desire was to get away from the family" – runs her diary of 26 VIII 1882.[6] During the eighteen eighties Tolstoy already makes attempts to pass from words to deeds. On 17 VI 1884 he leaves the house but turns back half-way (S.A. Tolstaja was going to give birth to a child at this time). On 26 VII he records: "It is a pity that I did not leave. It seems that I shall not escape it" (t. 49, p. 113; cf. 104-105). The next crisis comes at the end of 1885 when Tolstoy writes her a letter cited above (cf. notes 3,5).[7] He makes another attempt to leave but again stays at home, trying to make his situation more bearable. In the end of 1890 his daughter Tatiana records: "He says that he sees only two ways to be quiet. First – to leave the house – he thought and thinks about it; and the second – to give all his landed estates to peasants and to make his works common property".[8] In April 1891 he divided all his estates between his wife and children – as if performing a traditional proce-dure of the householder (grhastha), prior to his going away to the for-est (cf. Br.had_ran.yaka upanis.ad, II, 4; IV, 5; cf. below). New com-plications arose in the eighteen ninetees when S.A. Tolstaja was enamoured of S.I. Taneeff. In May 1897 Tolstoy thinks of going abroad – alone or with her (t. 84, pp. 284 sq.). On 8 VII 1897 he writes her again – the main motivation here is the growing burden of discrepancy between his life and convictions. "The children have grown up and my influence in the house is no longer necessary" (TL, II, p. 561). These words seem to echo the important condition for leaving the house in Hinduist tradition (The "Laws of Manu", VI, 2; cf. above). And then justifying his intention, he resorts directly to an Indian model: "But the main thing is that just as the Hindus, when they are getting on for 60, retire to the forests, and every religious man wants to dedicate the last years of his life to God...so I, who am entering my 70th year, long with all my heart and soul for this tranquility and solitude, and if not

---

6. S. Tolstaja, I, p. 108 (cf. *The Diary of Tolstoy's wife*. 1860-1891, London 1928, p. 200). It was evidently still earlier that Tolstoy said to the tutor of his children, who lived with them: "I constantly think that I should renounce the life which I lead" (V.I. Alekseev, *Vospominanija*. – Gos. Literaturnyj Muzej. Letopisi, Kn. 12, L.N. Tolstoj, t. II, p. 263).
7. Cf. also P. Popov. Pis'mo Tolstogo k S.A. Tolstoj - LN, t. 37/38, L.N. Tolstoj, II, pp. 665 sq.; GT, 1881-1885, pp. 522 sq.
8. Suxotina-Tolstaja, p. 198.

full accord, then at least not blatant discord between my life and my beliefs and conscience" (t. 84, p. 288-289; TL, II, p. 561). As we see, the first motivation here is the need to coordinate life with moral convictions. This letter however was not given to S.A. Tolstaja. The next day a reconciliation followed, though Tolstoy did not abandon his plans – cf. his letters to A.R. Ernefelt in summer and winter of 1897 (t. 71, pp. 410, 517; in particular, about going to Finland). During the next years the domestic situation worsened and came to a head in 1910 (problem of Tolstoy's Testament; strained relations between S.A. Tolstaja and V.G. Tchertkoff; her obvious nervous disorder, etc.). On 14 VII 1910 Tolstoy writes her again that if she does not accept his conditions for a peaceful life, he will certainly go away "because it is impossible to go on living as we are doing now" (t. 84, p. 400; TL, II, p. 702). His argument here is not based on his ideas but on their domestic situation alone. Meanwhile this situation grew worse and on the night of 28 X hearing her burrowing in his papers, Tolstoy felt, as he wrote in his "Diary for myself only" ("Dnevnik dlja odnogo sebja" – t. 58, pp. 123-124) "the stimulus, that made me take a step which has been my cherished dream for thirty years". In a letter left to her on his night he refers first to his domestic position which "has become unbearable" and second – to his convictions: "Apart from everything else I cannot live any longer in these conditions of luxury, in which I have been living, and I am doing what old men of my age commonly do: leaving this worldly life in order to live the last days in peace and solitude" (TL, II, pp. 710-711). Here, Tolstoy does not mention explicitly the Indian tradition but the complete analogy with the respective passage from his letter of 8 VII 1897 seems to be obvious. At the same time in two variations of this letter he does not mention his domestic situation at all and begins directly with self-accusation about his sin – a life of a rich man among the poor, "of senseless luxury among common poverty". It is interesting that both variations contain similar additions to his words about departure where he stresses that his leaving is different from that of an orthodox Christian: "Most people go to monasteries, and I would also go to a monastery, if I only believed in the things in which the people in monasteries believe. But since I do not believe in such a manner, I go now simply to solitude" (t. 84, pp. 404-405).

Tolstoy dreamed of this departure for 30 years and being unable to perform it, he naturally tried to find some ethical justifications for his contradictory position. "Having once entered definite practical relations with people, one should not suddenly neglect these conditions for the sake of Christian renunciation of life... You should try to become higher not by denying your duties but by freeing yourself from them, that is: 1. carrying out those already undertaken (cf. below) and 2. not undertaking new ones" runs his record of 4 V 1895 (t. 53, p. 28-29).[9] However, his decision "to endure without changing the present state" proved to be impracticable. He was so obsessed by the desire to leave, that even on his deathbed in Astapovo he uttered repeatedly in delirium: "One must run away, run away".[10] "I confess to you that I am waiting only for any occasion to go away" – he said to his daughter several days before departure.[11] But in fact, he looked for such occasions still earlier and his reasons (besides ideological) were of every kind[12] – property relations, jealousy (of S.I. Taneeff in the late eighteen nineties), rivalry around him ("they tear me to pieces. Sometimes I think of leaving them all" – t. 58, p. 138), etc.

However, notwithstanding the substantial (sometimes – decisive) influence of the domestic situation (by no means connected with India) an obvious influence of a traditional Indian institution, which served

---

9. Cf. A. Tolstaja, II, p. 136; Mejlax, pp. 261 sq.; cf. t. 63, p. 198; t. 78, p. 114; Gusev, p. 107; etc.

10. S. Tolstoj, p. 280.

11. A. Tolstaja, II, p. 386. On the same day (25 X 1910) he wrote in his diary: "and on my side a sinful wish that she should give me occasion to go away" - t. 58, p. 143; cf. *Dnevniki Sofi Andreevny Tolstoj,* 1910, p. 242 (TD, p. 339); S.A. Tolstaja. *Pis'ma k L.N. Tolstomu.* 1862-1910, Moskva-Leningrad, Academia, 1936, p. 799. Cf. e.g. t. 58, p. 132; Gusev, pp. 147, 279, 286, etc.

12. Cf. above (note 4) about his desire to leave the house in case of war. Another ground for departure (though the whole family's transmigration was planned then) arose in autumn 1872, when after an accident with a shepherd, Tolstoy had to give a written undertaking not to leave the place, and indignant at the administrative tyranny wanted to leave for England (cf. his letters to A.A. Tolstaja – t. 61, pp. 314-319). D.P. Makovicky (JZ, IV, p. 26) suggests, that when planning to go to Stockholm in 1909, to attend the Peace Congress, Tolstoy intended to use this as a pretext to leave the house never to return, and that S.A. Tolstaja opposed this plan so violently, just because she suspected his hidden intention.

him as a model worthy of imitation and one of the basic arguments for his intention, can be traced in his departure. As we saw, his letter of 8 VII 1897 contains a direct reference to a Hindu custom of leaving the house, that is of passing from gr. hastha to vĀnaprastha (or saṃ nyĀsin) state. But apart from this letter, Tolstoy more than once referred to this custom in his later years. "He often spoke enviously of the way in which Hindu men, when they become old, withdraw from society and live in solitude" – recalls his daughter Tatiana.[13] Similar evidence is adduced by D.P. Makovickij as well – such is e.g. Tolstoy's narration in December 1906 about 60-year old Hindus who go to the forest and live on charity as recluses (JZ, II, p. 324; a description containing elements of the 3rd and the 4th Āśramas, while mentioning "the yellow robes" in this context is obviously called forth by Buddhist sources - cf. below). And though in his letter written on the night of departure he did not mention "Indians", the example as we have already said is the same. The words about life of "peace and solitude", of old men of his age, obviously correspond to the state of a forest recluse in India. It is noteworthy that departure such as in the Indian model was evidently so often in Tolstoy's thoughts and was so often and intensely lived through by him, that it became in his imagination quite a traditional act, even in his Russian surroundings. Hence a substitution of "Hindus, when they are getting on for 60" by "what old men...commonly do", made 13 years later (1897-1910). These variants obviously meant the same thing for him, though for an old Russian man such a change of state was not so "common". And the response of S.A. Tolstaja who wrote to her husband on 30 X 1910 is natural: "You say that old men go away from the world. But where have you witnessed it? The old peasant men live out their last days amid their families and their grandchildren, and it is the same among gentlefolk and all other classes of the community".[14]

The country where such a departure was common indeed – is India. Hindu sources (not only law books cited above) beginning in ancient times contain plenty such evidence. So we find a typical example

---

13. Suxotina-Tolstaja, p. 416 (TS, p. 234).
14. S.A. Tolstaja. *Pis'ma*, p. 800 (cf. TD, p. 396).

in Br.hadĀran.yaka up. (II, 4; IV, 5). A brĀhman.a YĀjñavalkya (one of the most authoritative Hindu sages) is about to leave the state of householder and to go into the forest. He had two wives: Maitreyī, who was "a discourser on Brahma = knowledge", that is living by spiritual interests, and KĀtyĀyanī who "possessed only such knowledge as women have". Before he leaves, YĀjñavalkya wants to divide his property between them. But Maitreyī rejects the wealth which cannot provide immortality and asks him to teach her the highest Truth. "You have been truly dear to me (even before), now you have increased your dearness", – answers YĀjñavalkya, and he teaches her the doctrine of Ultimate reality, the supreme Self, Ātman, for the sake of whom (but not for the sake of themselves) all is dear – the wife, the sons, wealth, the worlds, the gods and all that exists (one can find similar words in Tolstoy's record of 5 XI 1909).[15] And completing his precept YĀjñalkya leaves his house.[16]

However, the most famous case of departure in India, though performed in a mode substantially different from traditional prescriptions, was that of Buddha – a case well known by Tolstoy. Buddha had likewise abandoned himself to passions in his youth; then he felt the discrepancy between his luxury and human sufferings and still a young

---

15. It was called forth by reading the book of Swami Abhedananda; *Vedanta-Philosophie*. Leipzig u. Frankfurt a.M., which impressed him greatly: "You should love in you not *yourself*, but atman, that is infinite spirit". How happy I am that I begin to understand, to go through it, to feel it not by reasoning, but with all my heart and – first of all – from experience" (t. 57, pp. 166; cf. 383).

16. *The Principal Upanisads*, transl. by S. Radhakrishnan, London, 1953, pp. 195 sq.; 281 sq. S.A. Tolstaja (if we extend to her this analogy) was not devoid of religious interests, which sometimes even brought her closer to her husband's views. "What beautiful and simple truths are found in Buddhism" – she writes in her diary at the end of 1898, impressed by a book on Burmese Buddhism by Filding (*The Soul of a people* – cf. S. Tolstaja, I, p. 435; cf. similar impressions that Tolstoy also had – t. 71, p. 490; t. 84, pp. 335-336; t. 88, p. 141). In spring of 1902 reading the same book in Russian translation she adds quite in the spirit of Tolstoy: "How much better Buddhism is compared to our Orthodoxy" (S. Tolstaja, II, p. 67). Cf. ibid., p. 124; ST, p. 193 (about her efforts "to catch up to him spiritually" during the first years of their marriage); ST, p. 243 (about her spiritual evolution after Tolstoy's death), etc. At the same time there was enough of "such knowledge as women have" in her and she presented rather a combination of KĀtyĀyanī and a more orthodox-minded Maitreyī, though devoid of their submissiveness.

man left his house, became a recluse, grasped the Truth and preached it. Tolstoy doubtlessly was aware of certain of his own traits that paralleled Buddha's;[17] we have already mentioned his interest in this image, including its artistic aspect (cf. t. 30, pp. 109, 382, etc.). While mentioning Brahmanism in most cases impersonally, as certain texts, or trends, Tolstoy usually associates Buddhism with the name of Buddha, referred to by him (like that of Jesus Christ) perhaps more often than any other ancient teacher. In his last years Tolstoy was also inclined to connect the idea of departure especially with Buddhist tradition. "How good it is among Buddhists whose old men go into the forest" – he says in summer 1909, and several days later adds: "I want to go into seclusion, to retire from mundane vanity as old Buddhist men do" (JZ, IV, pp. 28, 35). Here leaving the Hindu Āśrama institution (absent in Buddhism), Tolstoy obviously approaches the usual (not only among old men) tradition of entering the Buddhist community (sangha) and becoming a monk; a tradition so often described in ancient Buddhist sources – cf. a typical description of a wandering monk (pAli: bhikkhu, pabbajĀ) who renounces his family and property, cuts off hair and beard, clothes himself in yellow robes and begins to wander in a homeless state (agĀrasmĀ anāgīriyam pabbajeyyan – cf. Dīgha nikĀya, II, 41; XII, 16 sq; XIV, 2, 8 sq; 15 sq, etc.).[18]

The plans for this departure and the beginning of its realization (which lasted but a few days) were naturally determined by Tolstoy's position and surroundings and they were far from the way of life led by traditional forest recluses or wandering mendicants. Nevertheless one can observe certain analogies with each of these states. On the one hand Tolstoy often spoke about the joys of a quiet solitary life[19] and expressed a desire to settle somewhere in this manner. The place had not been definitely decided upon by him – in this connection he spoke at various times about different places in Russia (Caucasus, Crimea,

---

17. Cf. in this connection, OT, 1886-1892, p. 79.

18. *The Dīgha NikĀya*, ed. by T.W. Rhys Davids and J.E. Carpenter, Vol. I; II, London, 1966; 1975. Cf. C.S. Upasak. *Dictionary of early Buddhist monastic terms*, Varanasi, 1975, s.v. pabbajĀ, pp. 137-138; S. Dutt. *Early Buddhist monasticism*, Bombay 1960; P. Olivelle. *The origin and the early development of Buddhist monachism*, Colombo, 1974, etc. (cf. analogous details in *Father Sergius* (TW, v. 16, p. 332).

19. Cf. e.g. his impressions of Crimea in 1885 (GT, 1881-1885, p. 396).

Odoev, a village Borovkovo in Tula province), or abroad (Finland, Bulgaria, Paris, America).[20] Sometimes his projects did not mention solitude but just a simple life of work.[21] Another substantial modification of departure for him was a life in a monastery, preferably small and secluded ("skit"). His visit to "Optina pustyn'" monastery on 28-29 X, his interest in the life of the elders ("starcy") there and the subsequent removal to Šamordino monastery on 29-30 X testify to Tolstoy's possible preference for such a life style. According to one evidence, during this last visit he said to his sister Maria (a nun in Šamordino): "Sister, I have just been in Optino. It is so nice there! How happy I would be to live there, performing most unskilled and difficult labour, with one condition only: not to be forced to go to church".[22] It is possible that such a solitary monastic life, even within the framework of old Orthodox tradition, could have pleased him, notwithstanding all his reservations (cf. above on his letter of 28 X 1910), if some mode of living in a monastery ("skit") could be found which would not contradict his convictions and would be acceptable to Church authorities. However, excommunication made this possibility too complicated,[23] while Tolstoy's fear that his wife might pursue him made him dart off and run further on the night of 31st October.

---

20. Cf. ibid., p. 524 (Paris or America); S. Tolstaja, II, p. 124 (Paris, Yalta, Odoev); JZ, IV, p. 287 (Caucasus, Crimea, etc.).
21. E.g.: "to renounce all the privileges...and to perform that ordinary work of peasants, that is almost of all people" (Alekseev, p. 263). Cf. also about his intention to live in a village, "in a peasant-house, among the working people, working together with them, as far as my strength and capacities permit" – t. 85, pp. 223-224 (cf. GT, 1881-1885, p. 414). Several days before his departure Tolstoy makes arrangements with M.P. Novikoff about renting a peasant-house in the village Borovkovo, and after his leaving, on 30 X, he tried to do the same in Shamordino (JZ, IV, pp. 390; 408; cf. S. Tolstoy, p. 269, etc.).
22. Cf. A. Ksjunin, *Poslednie dni Tolstogo v monastyre* – Novoe Vremja, 24 XI 1910; idem, *Uxod Tolstogo*, p. 81; Xodasevi_, pp. 116 sq.; 121; Bunin, pp. 19-22; Nabokov, p. 187. Cf. Mejlax, pp. 266 sq.; N.A. Pavlovi_. *Optina pustyn'. Po_emu tuda ezdili velikie?* – Prometej, 12, pp. 90-91.
23. Concerning the last attempts to reconcile Tolstoy with the Orthodox church there are noteworthy words spoken in those days by the bishop of Tomsk and the Altai Makarij: "One must know where he has gone to – to Orthodoxy or to Buddhism" – *Poslednie dni L'va Nikolaevi_a Tolstogo*, Spb, izd. Voskresenie, p. 30.

One may add that Tolstoy's apparent inclination and readiness to follow certain canons of monastic life in the forms that were most suited to Russian conditions, does not seem to be accidental. As we know, he was interested in "Optina pustyn'" even earlier and beginning in the eighteen seventies visited it at least six times. Other monasteries attracted his attention as well. For example, in summer 1905, talking about the Soloveckij monastery, Tolstoy praised its role in the education of the simple people and the local inhabitants' way of life, making a noteworthy confession: "I wanted all my life to go to the Soloveckij monastery, but did not succeed" (JZ, I, pp. 384-385; the Russian idiom: "želat [=xotet'] v monastyr'", used here, as a rule, suggests an unequivocal intention to take the monastic vows).[24]

Whatever these possible variants could be, there is no doubt that in some manner Tolstoy strove to be solitary, far from Jasnaja Poljana and among common people, and that he searched more and more for a quiet life during his last years. The words about seclusion and peace, about the necessity to be alone are also found in his departure letter, previously cited (t. 88, pp. 404-405). These words were perhaps not called forth only by his desire to prevent his wife from following him.[25] His physical and nervous state in those last days was such that the ideal of an active life "among people" could scarcely attract him more than the monastic peace and seclusion.

On the other hand renouncing family life was closely connected in his thoughts with the state of wandering (sam̩ nyĀsin). And though by the time of his departure from Jasnaja Poljana this state already could not be practically carried out by an 82-year old man, the ideal of wandering possessed him for many years. Already in the late eighteen seventies, admiring such traits of Jesus' image as his renouncing of family and lack of property, he speaks first of all about Jesus' wandering way of life.[26] This state seems to him the most important for a Christian and he often mentions it – not only with respect to Christian tradi-

---

24. Pavlovič, pp. 88 sq.; cf. *Memoirs of S.P. Arbuzov* (TV, I, pp. 293.); Gusev, p. 72.
25. Mejlax, p. 262.
26. GT, 1870-1884, p. 597 (in the exposition of the unpublished religious-philosophical work, written at the end of 1879 and not included in the "jubilee edition").

tion[27] but to Indian as well. "It is better to go around begging with a money-box as Buddhists do" he writes in a letter to N.N. Ge of 20 III 1890 (t. 65, p. 48). In February of 1910, answering B. Mandžos who urged him to give away his property, to leave the house and to move begging from place to place, Tolstoy wrote: "The thing, that you advise me to do is my cherished dream... There is no day when I do not think about carrying out your advice" (t. 81, pp. 104-105; it is interesting that, obviously in accordance with his plans, Tolstoy kept this answer a secret and asked his correspondent to act similarly). We shall see that the same ideal is more than once realized by his heroes.

The wandering ascetic-saṃnyĀsin overcomes not his worldly attachments only, but the traditional ritual as well and this reminds us of one more essential trait of Tolstoy's views, already noted above. Though this trait evidently does not go back to Hinduist of Buddhist influences, there are a number of significant parallels to these traditions. Tolstoy's continuous surmounting of ritualism, his evaluation of rites and of beliefs, connected with them, as useless and senseless can be (and already was) compared to a protestant reaction to Catholicism, or – in connection with the subject that interests us more – to a reaction to the traditional Vedic ritualism. The latter evidently began around the middle of the 1st millenium B.C. and became basic feature of some great religious trends in India – Buddhism and Jainism among them. Tolstoy's attitude to Orthodox Christianity is in some respects reminiscent of Buddha's (or partly the upanishadic teachers') approach to Vedic rites. We similarly find in these ancient trends a certain transformation of traditional dogmatics, a re-evaluation of ritual culminating in complete renunciation of it (as useless and not leading to liberation; cf. below), a recommendation of a definite "introvert ritual", i.e. a personal spiritual state[28]. Corresponding evidence of Tolstoy's views dates

---

27. Cf. V.V. Veresaev. *Xudožnik žizni (o L've Tolstom) – Polnoe sobranie sočnenij*, t. 8, Moskva, izd, Nedra, 1929, p. 149; S.N. Durylin, *U Tolstogo i o Tolstom* – Prometej, 12, pp. 225-226, etc.

28. Cf for example: H. Oldenberg, *Die Lehre der Upanishaden und die Anfänge des Buddhismus*. Göttingen, 1923, S. 31 sq.; 165 sq.; F. Edgerton. *The Upanishads: What do they seek and why?* – Journal of American Oriental Society, vol. 49, 1929, pp. 102 sq.; B. Mal. *The religion of Buddha and its relation to Upanishadic thought*, Hoshiapur, 1958; A. Ja. Syrkin, *Nekotorye problemy izučenija upanišad*. Moskva, Nauka, 1971, pp. 123 sq.; 148 sq.; etc.

from the eighteen fifties (cf. above, his letter to A.A. Tolstaja)[29]. Thus, substituting the "external" ritual for the "internal" one, he seemed to attempt long before his departure, to embody in his views and deeds some significant traits of saṃnyĀsin or a Buddhist monk.

One is reminded here of another characteristic type of behavior, pertaining to a person who renounces the world. It is connected first and foremost with the tradition of Oriental Christianity and at the same time it appears to be significant within the more general framework of the typology of religious behavior, and has, in particular, some parallels with Indian tradition as well. We mean here the state of "The fool for Christ's sake" ("jurodivyj"), which was realized most completely in Byzantine and Russian religious life[30]. Tolstoy more than once expressed his attitude to this state. "If I were alone I would be "jurodivyj" valuing nothing in the world"[31]. A 'specific jurodivyj's trait: to provoke consciously the abuse and condemnation of other people was

---

29. Cf. the evidence of his relation to the Orthodox ritualism in *Ispoved'* (t. 23, pp. 50 sq.), *Issledovanie dogmatičeskogo booslovija* (t. 23, pp. 248 sq.); in *Memoirs of S.A. Tolstaja* (about receiving the eucharist with wine – S. Tolstaja II, p. 14), of E.I. Sytina (concerning the chime – *Vospominanija E.I. Sytinoj;* LN, t. 37/38, II, pp. 410-411); of A.B. Goldenweiser (on a public prayer performed before the army – Gol'denvejzer, I, p. 156). One can add that the reaction against certain public conventions (with respect to etiquette, to clothes, etc.) was displayed by him already in his young years. Cf. GT 1828-1855, pp. 198-199; GT, 1855-1869, pp. 327-328; GT, 1870-1881, pp. 491-492. This attitude did not exclude of course the opposite feelings especially in the first half of his life – a young man's tribute to vogue, a temporary animation in 1876-1877 for the Church rituals, etc. (see below; cf. t. 23, pp. 49-50; S. Tolstaja I, p. 507; Suxotin, pp. 190-191, etc.).

30. Cf. I. Kovalevskij. *Jurodstvo o Xriste i Xrista radi jurodivye,* Moskva, 1900; Aleksij (Kuznecov), *Jurodstvo i stolpničestvo. Religiozno-psixologičeskoe issledovanie,* Spb. 1913; P. Hauptmann. *Die "Narren um Christi willen " in der Ostkirche* – Kirche im Osten, 2, 1959, S. 27-49; G.P. Fedotov. *Svjatye drevnej Rusi (X-XVII st.),* New York, 1960, pp. 191 sq.; A. Syrkin, *On the behavior of the "Fool for Christ's Sake"* – History of Religions, vol. 22, N. 2, 1982, pp. 151-171 (ibid., p. 160, n. 50 – a parallel with ancient Indian tradition of pĀśupata – cf. D. Ingalls. *Cynics and PĀśipatas: the seeking of dishonor* – Harvard Theological Review, v. 55, N. 3, 1962, pp. 281 sq.).

31. Bunin, p. 35; cf. Èixenbaum, *O proze,* pp. 53 sq.; Durylin, p. 225. Cf. ST, 225, Kuzminskaja, p. 197 (KT, 174: "Leo Nikolaevich honestly loved these "God's folk": the feebleminded, the half insane, the wanderers, religious pilgrims"). Cf. t. 41, p. 331, and another varient in: *Krug čtenija,* t. I, Posrednik, izd.3, Moskva, 1910, p. 338; Cf. Gusev, pp. 174, 207, etc.

also typical of him from his young years: "What I am...I am ugly, awkward, untidy...short tempered...I am almost a know-nothing...I am intemperate, irresolute, inconstant, foolish, vain...I am not brave, I am inaccurate, lazy..." runs his record of 1854 (t. 47, p. 8-9). This tendency is often displayed by him in the years following his spiritual turning-point. In a letter to N.N. Strakhoff of 1-2 XI 1890 he speaks of the necessity to describe himself in such a way as to "arouse aversion for his life in all his readers" (t. 62, p. 500). This purpose is reflected in his "Ispoved'"[32]. One is reminded here of similar motifs in "Father Sergius" ("Otec Sergij")[33].

In this connection we should like to touch upon the role of respective ideas, and first of all, the motif of departure, in writings of Tolstoy. A close tie between his "Dichtung" and "Wahrheit" goes back not only to the essentially autobiographical character of his main and best images, but – to no small degree – to his concept of the main purpose of the artistic work. All that he wrote – not only diaries, didactic treatises, letters, but his works of art as well – was never isolated from spiritual quest. This link can be traced back to his earliest writings (cf. his autobiographical trilogy) and he was aware of it himself[34]. The creative

---

32. GT, 1870-1881, p. 616; cf. A Tolstaja, II, p. 70 ("to always be ready to see my work abused and myself – put to shame"); Bunin, pp. 82, 163, etc. Cf similar behavior of a famous byzantine jurodivyj Symeon, of ancient cynics, and (though impelled by different purposes) of Indian pāśupata (Syrkin, *On the behavior,* pp. 156, 166 sq.).
33. "Only when he had perished irrevocably in the eyes of men, he learned what it means to rely upon God" (t. 52, p. 39; cf. t. 65, p. 268; t. 87, p. 71). It is characteristic of Tolstoy that he stresses the denouncing of mundane glory as the main purpose. Another note to *Otec Sergij,* also of 1891, runs: "He must fight the pride...and only after his fall and shame should he feel that he has escaped from this vicious circle and can be humble indeed" (t. 52, pp. 57-58). Cf. t. 41, p. 331; t. 52, p. 82. By the way, this last period of Father Sergij's life, which remind us of some "jurodivyj's" traits (see below), has been also interpreted in the sense of "un nihilismo buddista, una religione del Nirvana". Cf. R. Przybylski. *Un senzadio cercatore di Dio: Padre Sergij di L.N. Tolstoj* – Tolstoj oggi. Firenze. 1980., pp. 98 sq. (with reference to D. Mereśkovskij's essay on Tolstoy: D. Mereśkovskij. *Polnoe sobranie soćinenij.* t. 11, Moskva, 1914, pp. 91 sq. a.o.
34. So he advised his biographer P.I. Brukhoff to consider his artistic works biographical material (V. Šklovskij. *Lev Tolstoj,* Moskva, Molodaja Gvardija, 1963, p. 690). Cf. respective remarks of Anna Akhmatova in: I. Berlin. *Personal impressions,* London, Hogarth press, 1980, p. 196.

activity was conceived by him during his last decades as something
that can be justified only by spiritual, moral aims, as the expression
and transmission of corresponding values (cf. above on similar traits
of Indian didactic tradition, also used by Tolstoy)[35] . From this point of
view his writings irrespective of their artistic importance are
characterised by a high degree of pragmatism and it seems like a misunderstanding that he was able to censure later these very writings,
using the same pragmatic criterion.

For Tolstoy the idea of departure was a necessary step in the attainment of spiritual perfection in overcoming all mundane attachments,
and this act, which is so close to Indian religious tradition, is often
repeated by his heroes – though its reasons, forms and surroundings
may be quite different, according to real images and events that served
as prototypes for his heroes.

The combination of domestic and more speculative, ethical and
religious impulses for departure, that invariably marked the last decades of Tolstoy's life, is reflected symmetrically in the images created
by him. These images seem to supplement each other in their variety
and in the contradiction of grounds that influence them – emotional
and rational. It is typical however that with all this variety of motives
and characters, the ultimate result of departure is always the same – an
enlightenment which on the highest spiritual level justifies the act performed by the hero.

Let us begin with subjects where the departure is caused by a crisis
in family relations and a subsequent emotional explosion – the departure fated to become that of Tolstoy himself. One of the most characteristic works of this kind is "Father Sergius" ("Otec Sergij" – 1890-
1898, t. 31, pp. 5-46; cf. 203-210; 257-269)[36] . The hero, duke Kasatskij,

---

35. I.A. Bunin (pp. 33-34) speaks of the "obsession with monotony" in Tolstoy's
"late writings and records, which reminds one of the monotony typical of ancient
sacred books..." Cf. above on Tolstoy's great appreciation of Indian legends from the
artistic points of view (t. 30, pp. 109, 382 etc.).

36. We shall dwell only on separate details, that can be connected (though in most
cases – indirectly) with the analogy that interests us here. Cf. in this respect: Eixenbaum,
O proze. p. 59; Mejlax, pp. 254 sq.; K. Kedrov. *"Uxod" i "voskresenie" geroev Tolstogo*
– V mire Tolstogo. Sbornik statej. M. Sovetskij pisatel', 1978, str. 248-273; etc. The
subject of *Otec Sergij* is close to Tolstoy's unfinished sketch about the hieromonk

goes away twice. The first departure is caused by a discovery that
shatters his value system (his bride appears to have been a mistress of
the emperor Nicolas I, adored by him). He goes to the monastery "to
be above those who considered themselves his superiors", to "look
down on those he had formerly envied" (TW, v. 16, p. 307). The feeling of pride invariably takes hold of him in the monastery where he
lives 22 years in all (from the age of 34 to 43 and 43 to 56). Living in
solitude for the last thirteen years he is not satisfied with himself and
wants to leave again, to become a wanderer ("There was a time when
he decided to go away and hide... First he would go some three hundred versts by train, then he would leave the train and walk from village to village" (p. 332-333), as if renouncing the third Āśrama for the
sake of the fourth. However at the end of his monastic life a sudden
fall takes place – his adultery with an imbecile daughter of a merchant
who was brought to him by her father to be cured (Sergij had the
reputation of a healer by that time). This fall marks the second turning-
point in his life – he leaves again and becomes a wanderer imitating his
relative Pašen'ka – an insignificant, oppressed, wretched woman, but
full of kindness and resignation (another analogy with "jurodivyj"). Thus
he overcomes his pride entirely and in the end becomes a servant of a
rich Siberian peasant. Notwithstanding the role of carnal temptation,
the main purpose of his life is overcoming the pride, a struggle with
worldly fame (cf. note 33).

Another still more affected departure is presented in "Kornej
Vasil'ev" written in 1905 for "Krug čtenija" (t. 41, pp. 205-220; cf. t.
42, pp. 599-605). A rich 54-year old cattle-dealer, who has discovered
his young wife's infidelity, beats her brutally (mutilating the child as
well) and leaves the house. His departure however does not lead him to
perfection at once (here again Tolstoy stresses the arrogance of his
hero – cf. t. 41, pp. 213, 215; t. 42, p. 601). Kornej suffers setbacks in

("ieromonax") Iliodor – a duke Ivan Tverskoj, a retired colonel, who took monastic
vows but continued to torment himself with his doubts (t. 37, pp. 288-290; 379-380;
452-453), and to another sketch about father Aleksej (1909). Cf. V.S. Mi'in, *Na alo
nezaveršennogo rasskaza "Zapiski svjaščennika"*, LN, t. 69, kn. 1, pp. 443-444;
V.A. Ždanov, *Poslednie knigi L.N. Tolstogo. Zamyaly i sveršenija* – Moskva, izd.
Kniga, 1971, pp. 45-47. Cf. above, n. 98.

his enterprises, degenerates, takes to drinking and little by little becomes a wandering mendicant though deprived yet of samnyĀsin's
moral standards. An incitement to such perfection is his return to a
native village, already an old sick man, seventeen years after departure. He finds shelter in the house of a grown-up girl (the child whose
arm he has maimed). She does not acknowledge the old man, yet in a
touching way takes care of him. He dies in her house soon after –
reconciled and enlightened. Similar to "Otec Sergij" the pride is not
overcome here by departure; on the contrary, the latter is rather stimu-
lated by it. This departure brings new trials overcome by Kornej only
at the end of his life. At the same time death is preceded here by the
state of a wandering beggar.

In Tolstoy's life the emotional impulses for departure were combined with ideological ones – with his spiritual quest leading to more
and clearer understanding of the discrepancy between his life and ide-
als. This discrepancy, which tormented him for decades, plays a still
more prominent role in his heroes' departures than their domestic relations. This motif is displayed first of all in Buddha's image, which he
was interested in from the eighteen seventies, and which served him as
a personal example (cf. above part one, note 24). Though it is difficult
to separate Tolstoy's artistic work from his philosophical and religious
writings, there is no doubt as to the artistic value of this image in
Tolstoy's writings – cf. e.g. a short tale written, like "Kornej Vasil'ev"
for Krug čtenija" (t. 41, pp. 96-101; cf. t. 42, pp 592-593).

Another example is connected with Tolstoy's interest in the legend
about the elder Fedor Kuz'mič i.e. the Russian emperor Alexander I
who allegedly renounced the mundane life – "Posthumous notes of
the hermit Fedor Kuz'mič, who died in Siberia in a hut belonging to
Khromov, the merchant, near the town of Tomsk, on the 20th January,
1864" ("Posmertnye zapiski Starca Fedora Kuz'miča, umeršego 20
janvarja 1864 g. v Sibiri bliz Tomska, na zaimke kupca Xromova" – t.
36, pp. 59-74; 584-589)[37]. "Let it be historically proven that it is im-

37. Cf. Ždanov, pp. 26-30; see also A. Tolstaja, II, p. 285; *Tainstvennyj starec Feodor
Kuz'mič v Sibiri i imperator Aleksandr I.* Jordanville, N.Y., 1972; N. von Sementowski-
Kurilo. *Der Tote von Taganrog* – Damals, Hf. 10, Oct. 1976, S. 879-892; P.N.
Krupenskij. *Taina imperatora.* Orange, Conn., Antiquary, 1986, etc.

possible to combine the personalities of Alexander and Kuz'mič – the legend remains in all its beauty and truth", so he writes in his letter to the Grand Duke Nikolaj Mixajlovič of 2 IX 1907 (t. 77, p. 185). The scheme of "Zapiski" relates to 1900; Tolstoy worked on the novel in 1905, but did not finish it. It is a genre of fictional memoirs written allegedly by an old emperor who likewise strives for people's censure and blames himself: "I am the greatest of criminals, the murderer of my father, the murderer of hundreds of thousands of men in wars, I have occasioned, an abominable debauchee and a miscreant" (TW, v. 15, p. 387). In his 47th year he decides to leave and stages his death using the corpse of a soldier beaten to death, who resembled him. Alexander's departure opens a way to the attainment of perfection for him – the reader sees him as an old man of 72 who is joyfully waiting for death in his seclusion.

A sketch for a drama "Petr Xlebnik" (1884-1894, t. 29, pp. 281-291; 364-371; 433-434) deals with a legendary rich man who lived in Syria in the III century A.D. gave away all his property, overcoming his family's resistance, and sold himself as a slave (a motif of self-abasement) in order to distribute the gained money among beggars. In this sketch Tolstoy used the text of a "Word" ("Slovo") about Petr Mytar' from the Orthodox ecclesiastical "Monthly readings" ("čet'i minei").

One more variant of leaving the family apperas in his unfinished play "The light shines in darkness" (1896-1902, t. 31, pp. 113-183, 216-243, 291-306) – one of his most autobiographical artistic works which he called "his own" drama. The history of the couple Saryncev follows closely Tolstoy's own family conflict (cf. especially their dialogue from the IVth act – pp. 176-180). Saryncev suffers the discrepancy between his principles and his life and he is ready to leave the house and go to Caucasus, but in the end he is unable to abandon the family (the situation of Tolstoy himself in those years).

A motif of departure is found in some of Tolstoy's other works as well, though in somewhat different circumstances. First of all these variants are marked by an altruistic tendency of the hero, who tries in some manner to change his previous way of life, which has become more and more intolerable. Such is the play "The live corpse" ("Živoj

trup" – 1900, t. 34, pp. 5-99; 407-483; 553-545)[38]. Its hero first feigns
suicide, disappears and lives among the town tramps (one more variant of a wandering mendicant) and in the end commits real suicide. On
the one hand his motive is wholy altruistic – he looks for an escape
from a family conflict, trying to free ("to untie") his wife by disap-
pearing. On the other hand this deed brings him freedom as well –
"Forgive me that I could not...free you any other way... It is not for
you...it is best for me" (TW, v. 17, p. 290) – are his last words. Moreover this real suicide is motivated by his fear of becoming connected
with his wife again according to the court's judgment. We are again
reminded here of Tolstoy's own experience. One can suppose that this
situation (the case of the couple Gimer which served as material for
the play) seems to have given him a possibility – in a way typical of the
creative process – to live through his wish: a fantasy in which the
departure, so desired by him, should at the same time make his wife
happy (a situation, utterly impossible in reality).

Another variant is Nekhludov's departure in "Resurrection"
("Voskresen'e", 1889-1899, t. 32-33). A young single man renounces
his habitual well established life in order to follow the woman whom
he has ruined. This departure is also altruistic and at the same time
marks the hero's spiritual growth. One cannot speak here definitely of
any final stage (that of recluse or wanderer); the subsequent
householder's life is also possible (and in one of the novel's variants
Nekhludov marries here indeed). The author leaves his hero at the
moment when he discovers the Gospels anew.

As we see, Tolstoy's heroes reflect his own spiritual progress and
repeat, with necessary modifications, his states in different periods.
This refers to his earlier years as well, not yet marked by an idée fixe
of departure, though bearing already the germs of the future conflict.
This state (of the eighteen sixties-seventies) is reflected best in "Anna
Karenina" (1873-1877; t. 18-20)[39].

The spiritual quest of Levin (who before his marriage already thinks
of a new life among peasants – TW, v. 9, p. 314), reminds us of Tolstoy's

38. Ždanov, pp. 60-95.
39. Cf. S.L. Tolstoy. *Ob otraženii žizni v "Anne Kareninoj"* – LN, t. 37/38, L.N.
Tolstoj, II, pp. 566-590 (cf. KT, p. 239).

own experience during the first years of his family life. This quest results in Levin's enlightenment on hearing the peasant's words about a righteous old man Fokanych, who "lives for his soul and remembers God" (v. 10, p. 411). This turning-point described on the last pages of the novel (ibid, pp. 412-438) does not bring him yet to the idea of departure. Levin is still wholly absorbed by his family attachments, he is anxious about his wife and child, cares about people's opinions, gets inappropriately excited in discussions, sometimes he is rude to servants, etc., but henceforward according to his concluding words, "My whole life...every moment of it, is no longer meaningless, as it was before, but has an unquestionable meaning of goodness, with which I have the power to invest it" (v. 10, p. 438). At first he decides to share these new thoughts with his wife, but seeing her absorbed with household troubles, changes his mind ("No, I had better not tell her... It is a secret, necessary and important for me alone, and inexpressible in words...there will still be a wall between my soul's holy of holies and other people, even my wife..." – ibid, pp. 437-438). Thus the first happy years of married life are already marked by an an inner estrangement from his wife. One can observe, that from the very beginning it is justified in a certain sense by her attitude. While a bride reading his diaries, she pays no attention to his want of faith that tortured him so much (v. 9, p. 462). "She...smiled when she thought about his disbelief and called him funny. "Why has he been reading these philosophies for a whole year?" (v. 10, p. 400). And though such an approach was connected with her high opinion of her husband's moral qualities ("she was persuaded that he was Christian, like, and even better than, herself, and that all he said about it was one of his funny male whims" – v. 10, p. 71; cf. ibid., pp. 143,401), the very lack of attention to his spiritual quest, conceiving it as a whim, seems to be characteristic. We are reminded here of the respective lack of understanding on the part of S.A. Tolstaja and her dissatisfaction with her husband's interests even during the first years of marriage[40]. And though S.A. Tolstaja, to a

40. Ibid., pp. 571-572 ("One can find in Kity many traits that remind one of young Sofia Andreewna"). So already in November 1862 she records: "He disgusts me with his People. I feel, he ought to choose between me, i.e. the representative of the family and his beloved People" (S. Tolstaya I, p. 43; cf. *The Diary of Tolstoy's wife, 1860-1891,*

certain extent had similar interests (see note 16), this discord deepened
more and more[41] . In summer 1877 (the year when "Anna Karenina"
was finished), Tolstoy records in his diary: "Keep silence, silence and
silence" (t. 48, p. 185) sounding like a paraphrase of the novel's final
scene. The subsequent history of Tolstoy's family relations, as we know
it, goes beyond the frames of analogies to "Anna Karenia" – one can
only suppose, judging by later evidence, what the relations between
Levin and Kity could be like in a later embodiment by Tolstoy. The
novel however reflects only the first symptoms of estrangement, a
departure "into oneself" which became a link in the long process
crowned with a real and final departure.

We can conclude that the idea of departure in Tolstoy's artistic work
– irrespective of his heroes' personal experiences, and of immediate
reasons which served as a stimulus – is marked by certain traits typical
of the act of departure in Indian and some other monastic traditions.
We mean the connection of this act with the hero's search for moral
perfection, with his changing of his internal (resp. external, social)
state, and with his gradual attainment of highest bliss in this new state.

The above evidence shows the manifold reflections of Indian ethical and religious traditions on Tolstoy's life and creative work. These
reflections are called forth by his natural inclination to Indian spiritual
values, his acquaintance with respective sources and his putting these
sources into practice – in his artistic creations, letters, talks with friends,
personal reflections and plans and at last – in his deeds. A similar
inclination is testified to more than once with respect to different authors and thinkers of modern history who nevertheless yield to Tolstoy,
if we consider the intensity of this interest and the range of its influence. One should add that the "Indian" in Tolstoy is not limited by the
sphere of this direct influence. A number of traits defining him as a
writer and as a man suggest direct analogies with the world of Indian
values; analogies which are obviously free of any Indian influence and
which can be regarded as independent typological parallels. Within

---

p. 90). In the beginning of 1863 Tolstoy writes in his Diary: "I am afraid that she, being
young, does not understand and does not like many things in me" (t. 48, p. 51). Cf.
Suxotina-Tolstaja, pp. 375 sq. (ST, pp. 190 sq.); A. Tolstaja, I, pp. 252 sq.; GT, 1855-
1869, pp. 381 sq.; T. Polner, *Tolstoy and his wife*, London, 1946, pp. 62 sq.; 83 sq.
41. Cf. GT, 1870-1881, pp. 25 sq.; 505 sq.; Polner, pp. 105 sq.

the framework of all other evidence they do not seem to be accidental, and in a definite sense can be connected with this evidence by a kind of genetic link as well. Some of Tolstoy's character traits and some aspects of his mentality, which developed before his acquaintance with India and independently of it, could, to a certain degree, have motivated his later interests and aspirations which helped him to find the way to himself.[42] Among these traits, some of which are mentioned above, we should stress again his striving for perfection – in himself and others – his "Weltverbesserungswahn" ; his inclination to preaching displayed not only in everyday life but in his creative activity as well, whose moral aims were understood by him as close to those of traditional Hinduism. Hence the peculiar genres he chooses for his writings, and the principle of spiritual progress that plays so decisive a role in his heroes' images, and which is worked out so thoroughly in Indian religions. Among ideas and rules that inspired Tolstoy and were preached by him, we find again those consonant to Hinduism or Buddhism – such as e.g. non-resistence to evil expressed by him obviously independently of Indian ahim.sa and so ardently supported in India.[43] Another typical trait is his inclination to divide his life into periods, calling forth (beside direct allusions to Indian customs) a number of supplementary analogies with the institution of   ramas. At the same time, the character of aims formulated by him[44], the invariable prefer-

---

42. Cf. above, note 18. The idea of finding the highest spiritual values in one's own self was very dear to Tolstoy. Cf. the title of one of his most important religious works: *The Kingdom of God is within us (Carstvo bo   ie vnutri nas* – 1890-1893, t. 28); it is reflected in a number of thoughts (taken from different sources, or his own) which he inserted in his anthologies (cf. t. 43, p. 67; t. 44, p. 110, etc.).

43. See e.g. his correspondence with Gandhi (LN, t. 37/38, II, pp. 339 sq.; Markovich, pp. 25 sq.).

44. In this connection it is interesting to note his tendency to introduce classifications into respective rules, descriptions etc. (cf. e.g. the division of rules into the "positive and negative", "moral" and "practical" with subsequent division of each into the "constant" and the "accidental", etc. – cf. t. 46, pp. 264 sq.; 290, etc.). Cf. also the division of his own life into periods in *Vospominanija* (t. 34, p. 347; Bunin, p. 17 sq. – see above). Similar tendency is often displayed by him with respect to different objects and notions. Thus speaking about Jews he often divided them into different types (four types in JZ, I, p. 139; three – in JZ, II, p. 104; two – ibid., p. 317; a.o.); cf. also about the three kinds of vice (JZ, II, p. 593), etc. This trait is also characteristic of Indian culture with its classifying approach to different phenomena. Cf. B. Heimann, *Studien für Eigenart Indischen Denkens,* Tübingen, 1930, S. 185 sq.; A. Syrkin, *K sistematizacii,* pp. 146-164.

ence for the principle of moral duty, his family life, the full length of it, call forth an association with the traditional complex of dharma-artha-kama-moks.a. We should stress here that his example goes beyond the simple simultaneous pursuit of different spiritual and material purposes, which appears to be common enough. It is rather a combination of pragmatism with a logically consistent tendency to overcome and renounce material values in the pursuit of perfection. In this connection Tolstoy often expresses ideas close to the concept of moks.a: overcoming egoism, the difference between Self and not-Self (tat tvam asi), the fear of death (cf. his numerous records in diaries, images of Karataeff, Bolkonskij, etc.)[45]. Such overcoming appears in ancient Indian sources as a necessary condition for attaining the highest state – moks.a, nirvĀn.Ā[46]. At the same time, it defines to a great extent the mechanism of Tolstoy's appraisals, resp. his specific, sometimes paradoxical, relation to some phenomena of civilization: to scientific achievements, to separate genres of art, and personalities (Shakespeare, Beethoven, etc.). In the course of such an approach the notions, pertinent to respective systems of description or forms of expression, and accepted conventionally in different genres, seem to be neutralized and made senseless by him. Tolstoy's main argument for this "overcoming" was practical (in his eyes) uselessness, futility, and even harmfulness of respective institutions, branches of science, works, as against the values and purposes that were really important and necessary for him (spiritual unity of people, understanding the law of love etc. – cf. t. 30, pp. 66 sq; 109 sq; 185 sq, etc; see his words on G. Oldenberg's book part one, note 2). We find here one more noteworthy analogy – to the views and attitude of Buddha. As we know, negating Vedic rituals and traditional forms of seclusion, Buddha at the same time rejected dealing with a number of abstract problems and theories with which

45. Cf. about the attitude of his heroes to death: V.V. Veresaev, *Da zdravstvuet ves' mir! (O L've Tolstom) – Polnoe sobranie sočinenij*, t. VII, Moskva, izd, Nedra, 1929, pp. 145 sq. See respective pages of *War and Peace, The death of Ivan Ilyich, Hadji-Murad* (e.g. in the scene of his death: "all these images passed through his mind without evoking any feeling within him – neither pity nor anger nor any kind of desire: everything seemed so insignificant in comparison with what was beginning, or had already begun within him" – TW, vol. 15, p. 383).

46. See some examples of such overcoming: *Laws of Manu*, VI, 45; Br.hadĀran.yaka upanis.ad, III, 5.1; IV, 3.22; Kaus.itaki upanis.ad I, 4, etc. Cf. Syrkin, *K sistematizacii*, pp. 151 sq.

some of his contemporaries (and interlocutors) were pre-occupied – i.e. such questions as whether the world is finite or infinite, whether it is eternal or not eternal, whether the Self continues to exist without consciousness after death, etc. Buddha's argument is based on his assertion that a similar question, unlike the four noble Truths (ariya-sacca) about suffering and the Eightfold Path (at.t.hangikamagga) proclaimed by him, "is not calculated to profit (atta), it is not concerned with the Norm (the dhamma), it does not redound even to the elements of right conduct (brahmacariya), nor to detachment, nor to purification from lusts, nor to quietude, nor to tranquillisation of heart, nor to real knowledge (abhiññaya), nor to the insight (of the higher stages of the Path), nor to NirvĀnā (cf. Dïgha nikĀya – IX, 28; 33; cf. XXIX, 27 sq. a.o.)[46a]

On the other hand Tolstoy was aware of his personal duty, not on a higher spiritual level only, but in its social and pragmatic sense as well, i.e. as a definite set of obligations imposed by social and genetic ties. This reminds us of a Hindu concept of dharma as a definite principle of behavior prescribed to every separate estate and caste[47]. So in his last years, several decades after his spiritual turning-point, preaching non-violence, non-participation in military service, etc., Tolstoy displays quite unexpectedly a liking for some social institutions and prejudices. We can refer e.g. to his reaction to the Russian-Japanese War of 1904-1905. Taking to heart the defeats of the Russian army and surrender of Port Arthur he said in December 1904 that the fortress should have been blown up but not surrendered, and when his interlocutor raised an objection, referring to possible victims, he added: "What do you expect? If you are a soldier you've a job to do. And you do it properly."[48] On the same occasion he says in the beginning of 1905: "Not long ago dogs frightened away a hare; I wanted him to escape but

---

46a *Dialogues of the Buddha*, transl. from the PĀli by T.W. Rhys Davids, Oxford, pt. I, 1923, pp. 254-255.

47. Cf. e.g. the evidence of *Laws of Manu* on the dharma of different people with respect to their estate: II, 89; VIII, 41, 335; X; 77 sq.; etc. (especially: X.97 – "it is better to discharge one's own (appointed) duty incompletely, than to perform completely that of another" – cf. *The Laws*, p. 433 and note to X.97).

48. Suxotina-Tolstaja, p. 440 (TS, p. 164); P.I. Birjukov, *Biografija L'va Nikolaeviča Tolstogo*, t. 4, Moskva – Petrograd, 1923, p. 107. Cf. a record in JZ, I, p. 126.

if I were a hunter I should have hunted him... If you undertake to fight, you must sacrifice yourself for your cause. Such a thing could not happen in our time. Everyone should die but not surrender" (JZ, I, pp. 156; 163, etc.). Another noteworthy piece of evidence – Tolstoy's enthusiasm at the sight of the military bearing of two cadets he met in the street ("My God, what fine fellows!... What stature, freshness, strength!... Oh, how splendid, how charming!")[49]. Tolstoy proceeds thus from the concept of a soldier's duty. Though this duty binds him – a noble, a former officer, who has taken his oath – no more, it remains immovable in his ideas – in direct contradiction to his own teaching and to his numerous statements. Now and then he makes declarations of his patriotic feelings[50]. The same refers to some of his class preju-

49. Cf. L.A. Sulerzhicky (cf. Bunin, p. 71; TV t. II, p. 481). "Tolstoy liked the war not without reason, and he hardly restrained this passion on himself" (Eixenbaum, *O proze*, p. 85). Cf. Tolstoy's memoirs of military bearing in his Diary of 28 VI 1904 (t. 55, pp. 60; 649-470). See also S.S. Dorošenko. *Lev Tolstoj voin i patriot. Voennaja služba i voennaja dejatelmost'* – Moskva, Sovetskij pisatel', 1966, pp. 285 sq., in particular, about his enthusiasm on reading the description of the regiment review in the *Duel (Poedinok)* of A.I. Kuprin.

50. It was also connected, in particular, with the Russian-Japanese war. See t. 55, p. 111; JZ, I, pp. 156, 301, 378, 390-391; III, 138 ("L.N. wondered how Tatjana L'vovna remained indifferent to the defeat of the Russians in the Japanese war: "Is it possible, that you have no patriotic feeling?" Tatiana L'vovna answered that she was quite devoid of it. – "You have annihilated it in us, while it has been preserved in yourself"); IV, p. 192, etc. Cf. also Suxotin, p. 180 ("He says that the old patriotic manifestations of Tolstoy's (and, respectively, his negative approach to other peoples – cf. above, pt. 1, note 36). Such were e.g. his "slavjanofilic" and anti-Turkish feelings that little by little were taking hold of him during the Turkish-Bulgarian war of 1877. These feelings were rather far from his favourite hero's (Levin's) views (see the respective discussion in the end of *Anna Karenina)* and stood much closer to those of F.M. Dostoevskij (see his polemics with Levin – resp. Tolstoy – in *Dnevnik pisatelja*, 1877, July-August, ch. 3). Dostoevsky, however, could fully repeat following Tolstoy's words directed to his children's young tutor: "You have met on your way a lot of young men going...to defend their brothers, Balkan Slavs... If I had your aspirations...your young age, I would go without hesitation to defend my kinsfolk... What! Do you want muslims to reign over Christians... Do you want Turks to mock at Armenians and Slavs?" (Alekseev, p. 248; cf. GT, 1870-1881, pp. 443-434). Cf. more details in: Dorošenko. At the same time there was no lack of contrary (and mostly – public) statements. So in his article *Change your mind (Odumajtes'* – 1904) he writes: "the case of my life has nothing to do with recognizing Chinese, Japanese of Russian claims to Port-Arthur" (t. 36, pp. 129-130). Cf. also JZ, III, p. 350 (censuring N.V. Gogol for his Russian nationalism); Suxotin, p. 200 etc. In his *What my*

dices[51] , e.g. with respect to arranging his daughters' life, to different traditional occupations and the habits of his circle, etc.[52] .

It may be suggested that evidence of this kind can be (at least partially) explained by a pragmatic approach to everyday behavior, which made Tolstoy more than once recommend to his interlocutors and correspondents that they fulfill those obligations, which result from their present state and not change this state unless they have no choice. This approach could refer to military service as well[53] (hence the necessity to fulfill a soldier's duty), or to other cases or circumstances[54] . Thus

---

belief is (V čem moja vera – 1883) he says: "if I am able now in the moment of oblivion to help a Russian more than a stranger, to wish success to the Russian State or people, I am not able, however, in the moment of soberness to serve the temptation, that ruins me and other people" (t. 23, p. 461).

51. Cf. evidence of V.G. Bulgakoff, E.M. Lopatina, S. Samarina, about his interest in traditional estate and family ties, about his fear of mésalliance for his daughters, about the military service of his son Ilya, etc. (Bunin, pp. 82-86). Cf. T. 68, p. 230; a record of 31 XII 1904 about his personal, family and even aristocratic egoism (t. 55, p. 111); Suxotin, p. 200; KT, 207, etc. One can naturally draw similar examples from his earlier years. Cf. V.N. Nazar'jev's memoirs about Tolstoy's student years (TV I, pp. 22 sq.); t. 34, p. 399 (attitude to clothes in his youth; cf. KT, p. 416); t. 61, p. 315 (a letter to A.A. Tolstaja of 5 IX 1872 about the importance of the aristocratic circle for educating children); t. 62, p. 134 (to his brother-in-law A.A. Bers in the beginning of 1875 on the occasion of his marriage – about the importance of breeding).

52. E.g. to hunting, which had been his favourite amusement for a long time, remained so in the eighteen eighties (cf. t. 83, 394), and was naturally denounced by him in later years (cf. his foreword to V.G. Tchertkoff's article *A cruel amusement* – *Zlaja zabava*, t. 27, pp. 290, 554, 710-712). Cf. D.D. Obolenskij (in TV, I, pp. 194 sq.); A.L. Tolstoj. *O moem otce* – JS, 1965, p. 133; JZ, I, 165 (an example of hunting the hare, drawn above); 171 (another example – also on the occasion of the Russian-Japanese war: "hunting is stupid and evil, but if you go hunting you should not miss a fox").

53. Cf. also: X.N. Abrikosov, *Dvenadcat' let okolo Tolstogo* – Gos. Literaturnyj Muzej. Letopisi, kn. 12, L.N. Tolstoj, t. II, p. 379 (advice not to change the external conditions of one's life until these conditions become unbearable). Cf. on his conservatism: KT, pp. 235-236. See above, n. 9.

54. Cf. above, note 52 (about hunting). Another example – funny but characteristic – his relation to drinking bouts. I. Bunin recalls how on hearing his words about organizing the society against drinking, Tolstoy replied: "That is, when people gather in order not to drink vodka? Rubbish. To abstain from drinking, one need not gather. And if people gather, they should drink" (Bunin, p. 60). "The whole of Tolstoy is reflected here" notes his secretary about this story (V.F. Bulgakov. *Lev Tolstoj, ego druz'ja i blizkie*, Tula, 1970, p. 37). Cf. also about his love for drunk men – KT, p. 174; JZ, III, p. 57; IV, p. 384; Gusev, pp. 69, 142, 229.

he takes into consideration the real state of a man, in which the latter is naturally bound by certain traditions, obligations, duties (cf. above on Tolstoy's arguments against leaving the family).

In the broader context of Tolstoy's teaching, this attitude calls forth another, "double" analogy, which is still more interesting from the structural point of view: that with Kṛṣṇa's doctrine as taught to Arjuna in Bhagavadgītā (familiar to Tolstoy)[55]. It is noteworthy that the situation, in which Krsna expounds his teaching, is to a certain degree analogous to the conflict in Tolstoy's conscience, where traditional class and family obligations clashed with his moral principles. Finding himself between the armies, ready to fight, Arjuna is afraid of entering the battle and killing his relatives – even under the threat of death (I. 35 sq). Kṛṣṇa refutes him, producing beside more abstract proofs (impossibility to destroy our true essence by death – II, 17 sq), more concrete ones as well, based on the necessity to follow one's own duty (svadharma). Arjuna is kṣatriya (i.e. a member of the second warrior caste) and a "better thing than a fight required of duty exists not for a warrior" (II, 31)[56] – therefore he must throw away all his doubts and fight. As we see, in his later years, himself a teacher devoted to the ideal of mokṣa and preaching non-resistance to evil (cf. above on his reaction to violent exploits of the same Kṛṣṇa - t. 56, p. 340), Tolstoy, as if following Kṛṣṇa, more than once makes similar pragmatic state-

---

55. We have already said that Tolstoy was deeply interested in the image of Kṛṣṇa and in Bhagavadgītā. In the beginning of 1908 he writes to S.R. Chitale that he quite agrees "with the fundamental principle of the Bhagavad-Gita that man should direct all his spiritual force only to his duty" (t. 78, p. 32). Two months later he reads Bhagavadgītā, in particular, paying attention to its idea that "the work is not the most important thing; the work is good when you do not think about results" (JZ, III, p. 32; cf. IV, p. 102). In 1909 reading the Peterburg magazine *Vestnik Teosofii* he again pays attention to translation from Bhagavadgītā, published there (t. 57, p. 385; cf. JZ, IV, pp. 105, 446). Cf. Šifman, p. 135.

56. Cf. *The Bhagavad Gītā*. Translated and interpreted by F. Edgerton, Cambridge, Mass., 1972, p. 12. One can refer also to the image of another great teacher – the Buddha (ksatriya by birth!) who sometimes "faced the fact of fighting...however strange this may seem, by expressing a certain admiration for the soldier...there are several similes which are military in nature, their point usually being to encourage monks to be steadfast in endeavour as soldiers are steadfast in battle and to wage spiritual battles as they wage armed ones..." (I.B. Horner, *Early Buddhism and the taking of life*, Buddhist Publication Society, Kandy, 1967, pp. 16 sq.).

ments, urging Russian soldiers to fulfill their duty and to stand up to the enemy till the end. He appears here not only as teacher, but, notwithstanding his doctrine, as a former soldier, a nobleman who was fulfilling his duty in the past and recalls this duty again and again, depending on the circumstances.

It seems that until the end of his life Tolstoy did not cease to experience at heart this duality – of a wise teacher moving towards a final liberation, and of a soldier bound by his duty – that is the duality of Kṛṣṇa and Arjuna in BhagavadgītĀ, or of Kṛṣṇa himself, whose ambiguous image combined the traits of a warrior destroying his enemies (the demons, asuras) and of a wise preceptor[57]. Here, one should be reminded of some noteworthy evidence – an interesting dream[58] that greatly impressed Tolstoy: On 29 XI 1908 Tolstoy records the following in his diary: "I have dreamed by night that I partly write, compose, and partly experience the drama of Christ. I am Christ and I am a soldier at the same time. I remember myself putting on a sword. Very lively" (t. 56, p. 158). Some parallel, partly complementary, evidence is found in V.G. Tcherkhoff's record of 4 XII 1908: "Several days ago L.N. told me about his dream. I have seen a dream so lively – a drama about Christ, performed by characters: I imagined myself in the place of certain personages. I was now Christ, now a soldier, but more often – a soldier. I remember very distinctly how I put on a sword. But it made a powerful impression on me"[59]. The character of the experience lived through in this dream is scarcely accidental [60], and it

---

57. Cf. above on the noteworthy connection between Tolstoy's and Kṛṣṇa's images in the lost letter of S.R. Chitale ("He writes that Lev Nikolaevich is the incarnation of Kṛṣṇa" – t. 78, p. 33; see pt. 1, note 12).

58. One can observe in this connection, that dreams played a prominent role in Tolstoy's personal life and creative activity. His own dreams were more than once embodied in his works (cf. *Ispoved'*, XVI; *Tri dnja v derevne; čto ja videl vo sne; Son*, etc.), and were reflected in his artistic plans. A hero'd dream, having an important semantic function, is often introduced by him in the narration (as e.g. in *War and Peace, Otec Sergij*, etc.).

59. Cf. *Tolstoj o literature i iskusstve. Zapisi V.G. Čertkova i P.A. Sergeenko* – LN, t. 37/38, L.N. Tolstoj, II, p. 530. Cf. Gusev, p. 92.

60. One can suggest that this experience, motivated by a certain ambivalence of the Christ image, reflects in a peculiar manner the character of the Gospel's tradition. This ambivalence is displayed in the combination of Christ's attributes (cf., in particular,

presents a peculiar correspondence – at a subconscious level – to the duality mentioned above.

It goes without saying that there is much in Tolstoy's individuality and writings, that should be studied within the framework of other, not necessarily Indian traditions, as well. This refers, in particular, to the problem of departure, which cannot be understood completely outside traditional Christian institutions, and to the sources of Tolstoy's ethical and philosophical views, arrived at initially under the influence of European spiritual tradition, beginning with ancient stoics and also including modern Western thinkers. Nevertheless, when one considers that in comparison to antique, Christian or new European sources, the Indian spiritual values were much less accessible, more distant in the historical perspective and much more alien to the society in which Tolstoy grew up and lived all his life – the disproportionally great role of these values in his spiritual quest becomes obvious. In the course of time they occupied a more and more important place in his life among other oriental traditions, seeming to drive them back. Notwithstanding all the reservations that arise with respect to Tolstoy's handling of Indian sources (lack of professional and sometimes of general know ledge, contradictory judgements, mistakes) his experience in this domain seems to be unique. It is not an exaggeration to suggest that such an intensive Indian influence, touching upon creative activity, world-outlook and everyday behavior, cannot be found in any non-Indian author whose significance is equal to that of Tolstoy's.

However voluminous the literature about Tolstoy is, it seems to be impossible in essence to render an exhaustive interpretation of his personality and writings – one can speak only of separate descriptions, complementing each other and to a certain degree drawing us towards this ideal. In this advancement, in as much as we are capable of it, an investigator should not lose sight of the Indian heritage which Tolstoy for decades realized in himself on his way to "The Kingdom of God within us".

---

the motif of a sword, appearing in the dream, as well: "I have not come to bring peace, but a sword" – Matthew 10, 35) and in the attitudes of those surrounding Christ. Cf. C.G. Jung, *Answer to Job*, London, 1955, pp. 89 sq.; 127 (Christ is a "wrathful lamb"); A.Ja. Syrkin. *K xarakteristike induistskogo panteona* – Učenye Zapiski Tartuskogo Gos. Universiteta, Vyp. 309, Trudy po vostokovedeniju, II, 1, Tartu, 1973, pp. 165 sq.

Bibliography

References to volume and page without further designations indicate the "jubilee" edition of Tolstoy's complete works: L.N. Tolstoj. *Polnoe sobranie sočnenij.* (jubilejnoe izdanie), tt. 1-90, Moskva, Gos. Izd. xudožestvennoj literatury. 1928-1958. (Following abbreviations are used below:

Biblioteka – *Biblioteka L.N. Tolstogo v Jasnoj Poljane. Bibliografičeskoe opisanie. t. I. _. 1;* 2, t. II, Moskva, Kniga 1972-1978.

Bulgakov. *Knigi* – V.E. Bulgakov. *Knigi ob Indii v biblioteke L.N. Tolstogo* – "Kratkie soobščenija Instituta Vostokovedenija AN SSSR", XXX, Moskva, 1959, pp. 45-56.

Bunin – I.A. Bunin. *Osvoboždenie Tolstogo* – *Sobranie sočnenij,* t. 9, Moskva, Izd. Xudožestvennaja literatura, 1967, pp. 7-165.

Gol'denvejzer I; II – A.B. Gol'denvejzer. *Vblizi Tolstogo,* Moskva, Gos. Izd. Xudož. lit., 1959; *Vblizi Tolstogo,* tom II, Moskva – Petrograd, Kooperativnoe izdatel'stvo, 1923 (memoirs of A.B. Goldenweiser).

Gusev – N.N. Gusev. *Dva goda s Tolstym.* Moskva. Xudožestvennaja literatura, 1973.

GT 1828-1855; 1855-1869; 1870-1881; 1881-1885 – N.N. Gusev. *Lev Nikolaevič Tolstoj. Materialy k biografii s 1828 po 1855 god,* Moskva, Izd. AN SSSR, 1954; iden – *s 1855 po 1869 god,* 1957; idem – *s 1870 po 1881 god,* 1963, idem – *s 1881 po 1885 god,* izd. Nauka, 1970.

JS – Jasnopoljanskij sbornik, Tula.

JZ – *U Tolstogo. 1904-1910. "Jasnopoljanskie Zapiski" D.P.*

Makovickogo, kn. 1-4; Ukazateli – LN, t. 90, Moskva, Nauka, 1979-1981 (diaries of D.P. Makovicky).

Kuzminskaja – T.A. Kuzminskaja. *Moja žizn' doma i v Jasnoj Poljane. Vospominanija.* Tula, 1959 (memoirs of T.A. Kuzminskaya).

KT – Tatyana A. Kuzminskaya. *Tolstoy as I knew him. My life at home and at Yasnaya Polyana.* N.Y. The Macmillan company 1948.

LN – Literaturnoe Nasledstvo, Moskva, Izd. ANSSSR; Nauka.

Nabokov – V. Nabokov. *Leo Tolstoy* – in: *Lectures on Russian Literature.* London. Pan books Ltd., 1983, pp. 173-243.

OT 1886-1892 – L.D. Opul'skaja. *Lev Nikolaevič Tolstoj. Materialy k biografii s 1886 po 1892 god.* Moskva, Nauka, 1979.

Suxotin – M.S. Suxotin. *Tolstoj v poslednee desjatiletie svoej žizni* – LN, t. 69, kn. 2, 1961, p. 141-236 (memoirs of M.S. Sukhotin).

Suxotina-Tolstaja – T.L. Suxotina-Tolstaja. *Vospominanija.* Moskva, Xudožestvennaja literatura, 1976 (memoirs of T.L. Suxotina).

ST – Tatiana Tolstoy. *Tolstoy remembered,* tr. by D. Coltman, London, Michael Joseph, 1972.

Šifman – A.I. Šifman. *Lev Tolstoj i Vostok.* Moskva, Izd. Nauka, 2nd ed. 1971.

A. Tolstaja I; II – A.L. Tolstaja. *Otec,* t. I-II, New York, Izd. imeni Čexova, 1953 (memoirs of A.L. Tolstaja).

S. Tolstaja I; II – S.A. Tolstaja. Dnevniki, t. I-II, Moskva, Xudožestvennaja literatura, 1978. (diaries of S.A. Tolstaja).

S. Tolstoj – S.L. Tolstoj. *Očerki bylogo.* Tula, 1965. (memoirs of S.L. Tolstoy)

TD – *The final struggle, being countess Tolstoy's diary for 1910,* transl. with an introd. by A. Maude, London, G. Allen and Unwin, 1936.

TL, I; II – *Tolstoy's letters,* vol. I-II, selected, ed. and transl. by R.F. Christian, New York, Ch. Scribners' sons, 1978.

TV, I; II – *Tolstoj v vospominanijax sovremennikov,* tt, I-II, Moskva, Xudožestvennaja literatura, 1978.

TW – (The works of Leo Tolstoy) *Tolstoy* – *centenary edition,* vol. 1-21 Oxford, London, 1928-1937.

Zajdenšnur. Fol'klor – È.E. Zajdenšnur. *Fol'klor narodov Vostoka v tvorčestve L.N. Tolstogo* – JS, god, 1960-j, pp. 19-39.

CHAPTER NINE

LIFE AND TEACHING OF SIDDHARTHA GAUTAMA CALLED THE BUDDHA, THAT IS, THE MOST PERFECT ONE

In the second half of the sixth century B.C. in south Asia, in India, in the city of Kapilavastu, almost at the foothills of the highest mountains in the world, the Himalayas, in the family of the Indian Prince Suddhodana from the Shakia tribe, Siddhartha was born, who was given the name of his mother's relatives – Gautama.

Siddhartha, named later by his followers Buddha, that is, the most perfect one, was the founder of the most widespread religion in the world – Buddhism. This religion has up to 500 million followers [and there are 1250 million people on the earth.]

The princedom of Siddhartha's father was small, around 25 square versts.* The land there was very fertile. The climate was gentle; everything grew in abundance. The people were industrious [and that prince Suddhodana was considered to be rich]. He surrounded his son with all kinds of care; Suddhodana attempted to give him the best education available. The father dreamed of his son becoming a good warrior, a skillful shot and he dreamed that he would take care about expanding the power of his rule. This seemed to him very important because petty rulers fought each other and each one of them aimed at conquering others and forming a big state.

In Suddhodana's court there were different learned men, who tried to educate Siddhartha in the sciences. The most important science was considered to be knowledge of the correct way of living and of how to live a better and happier life. Literacy did not exist and learned men knew by heart the holy tradition preserved from deep antiquity. The

---

*Versta is equivalent to 3500 English feet.

most ancient tradition was considered to be the Vedas. In them, it was told which Gods exist, how the world was created, how a man should behave in order for him to be well not only in this world but after death as well.

In that country, traditions and the way of life based on them divided people sharply into masters and slaves, the nobility and the lower classes. There were four ranks of people: 1) warriors or noble men – they defended the country from enemies; 2) Brahmins or the learned men – they taught the people religion and sciences; 3) peasants and tradesmen; 4) slaves. People of one rank were not permitted to mix with people of other ranks. Not only could they not marry a woman from another rank but they could not even eat and drink from the same dishes.

People in India believed in this difference. So when princes of separate princedoms fought each other, the peasants did not take part in the war but continued their work on the land. Warriors considered it unworthy of themselves to even offend the lower class of people, the peasants, and to spoil their fields and gardens. Wars were then competitions of only noble people – the warriors.

Until he was sixteen Siddhartha was instructed in the military art and in different sciences. When he turned sixteen, he married Iazodhara, Kalris's daughter, who was a chief of a tribe. Soon, the couple had a son named Rahula, and they lived happily without cares.

Different philosophers often visited Siddhartha's father and the young Siddhartha often listened to their discussions and arguments about religion, the origin of the world, about good and evil and so on. Then and later the Indian people were very interested in religions questions. Governments were tolerant toward religion – everybody was allowed to believe and reason as he pleased. Because of this many religions and beliefs existed but everybody was tolerant toward each other and other religions. Other religions and beliefs were viewed with interest. The young Siddhartha listened to different arguments on religions and became increasingly interested in the most serious questions about life. The Brahmin or learned men around Siddhartha taught him to believe that life was wonderful – and the future life would be good for anyone who fulfilled the duties of that rank of people to whom he or she belonged. They thought that Siddhartha as the first ranking soldier must know how to fight and how to defeat enemies, how to defend the fatherland and eye all the goods, which others would readily provide. And, according to the Brahmin if they don't provide them willingly, then, they must be taken by force – there is nothing bad about it. They told Siddhartha that one should only offer sacrifices and often bloody sacrifices and the Gods would by force of habit bless anything that Siddhartha would do.

Siddhartha, in the beginning, like all others, believed in what he was told but later he started having doubts. Some said that cows should be sacrificed, while others said that cows feed us and that it is a sin to offer them as sacrifice. And as Siddhartha was compassionate by nature the thought of killing a cow, such a meek and useful creature, was repulsive to him. They discussed the necessity of war and Siddhartha thought, whether it was good of him to wage war with close relatives of his mother, his friends and the princes from surrounding regions. The Brahamins kept saying that there was no evil in it and that before God there were no relatives. Each person should fulfill his obligation. Siddhartha felt that this would be painful for him to do.

Such questions appeared to Siddhartha ever more often but mundane cares and his scattered way of life distracted him from a deeper and more serious resolution of his doubts. Moreover, his father, King Suddhodana, who was getting old, because of his son's pensiveness tried, in all possible ways, to have Siddhartha care more about government and military accomplishments and to be less pensive. According to King Suddhodana, warriors should not think about what is the best way of life. This is a Brahmin's work. A warrior should just believe in what the Brahmins teach. Suddhodhana tried to remove from his son's life everything unpleasant and difficult, and when Siddhartha became bored his father would set up a feast at which they would drink much and having drunk they would forget everything.

– 11 – 11 – 11 – 11 –

What about present happiness? After several decades you won't notice it and you will be in the same condition as an old man. Then there will be no happiness nor enjoyment and one will have to live in such a pitiful state.

And to Siddhartha it became ever more clear that the Brahmins were not right in saying that one has to be just a good soldier and fulfill one's obligation and one will benefit from all the good of life and one will always enjoy life. The young and healthy Siddhartha could not imagine what kind of happiness could be for him when he would become a decrepit old man. Thinking about his old age Siddhartha was overwhelmed by despair.

He started looking at his surroundings more closely and more attentively and he was more and more convinced that not everybody was happy. He became convinced that if some had happiness and joy, the majority had much more grief and suffering. Siddhartha, somehow, met an unfortunate man covered with sores and reluctantly imagined that he, too, could be sick and suffer. Sickness, suffering and the irrevocable old age are a part of life. Not everything is well ordered.

Heavy thoughts were more and more frequently on Siddhartha's mind and he fell into despair. Stale to him became all joys. He became evermore firmly convinced of the impermanence of happiness and ever deeper he sank into himself, trying to understand what life was about and to save himself from those horrors which frightened him now at every step.

Year after year went by in this way. Siddhartha continued living while he painfully tried to resolve what to him appeared intolerable. When he was twenty-nine years old he met a funeral procession. The inevitability of death presented itself to him with extraordinary clarity and this thought finally poisoned his life. "What are we all living for. What are our joys for, if death will finally come which is inevitably for everybody and anybody. Neither wise nor stupid, neither rich nor poor, neither high nor low – nobody will avoid death. But the most frightful thing is permanent suffering. Everything we hold dear in this life will fly away, death will destroy everything."

Siddhartha felt that he could not live any longer. To live longer meant to suffer unbearably with the thought that everything will end. It is better not to live.

Bordering on despair and ready to kill himself, Siddhartha met a tramp. The tramp's appearance astounded Siddhartha. In spite of his beggarly clothes and exhausted appearance the tramp's face was content and calm and shone with a tender, peaceful smile. Everything in this tramp revealed nobleness and contentment with life. This amazed Siddhartha. He spoke with the tramp and learned that this man had left his home, friends, cut off all attachment and had gone to the forest to live as a hermit. The tramp told Siddhartha that many hermits lived a life of poverty in the forest. These hermits realized the meaning of their life by having a clear mind and they learned how to deal with people who were dissatisfied with their life and who search for its meaning.

Siddhartha listened to the tramp intently. He thought about the tramp's life and realized that the tramp by giving up his home, relatives and friends, had now nothing to lose and regardless of what he had lost he was still content with life. "It is possible to struggle with suffering and death," decided Siddhartha, "but how?" If I don't know this and learned men and the Brahmins don't know it, then perhaps these beggar hermits who left everything and departed this world, know it."

And Siddhartha was encouraged. He felt that one can still live and search for the meaning of life but one had to learn a new science of the knowledge of life. Luxury, riches and power did not fascinate him anymore; it was even painful for him to think about all this. He knew that the more he held things precious, the stronger he got accustomed to them, the more painful it was to give up that to which he had become attached. One had to give up attachment in view of irrevocable sickness and death. One had to learn.

At that time in India people learned not in the way they do now in our country. Even now in India people who want to realize the meaning of life and learn about a virtuous man who realized it, act the same way as they did in old times. They leave their home and go to the virtuous man to be instructed. The instruction proceeds in the following way: These people settle near the virtuous man and live with him one, two, or three years. They live the same way as their teacher and they listen all the time to what he says, questioning him about what they don't understand and about the most important things. They live the way he teaches them.

Siddhartha decided to go and study with the hermits but he did not dare announce this to his father and wife for fear that their persuasion and tears might hinder the realization of his intention. Siddhartha revealed his intention only to his favorite and faithful servant Channa. At night when everybody was asleep, Siddhartha set on horseback with Channa to the border of his kingdom. There, Siddhartha took off his rich clothes, put on a simple garment, cut his hair, gave Channa his horse and clothes, parted with him and hid in the forest.

From that time on a new life began for Siddhartha – a life of learning. Siddhartha went to the Brahmin Kalama. This hermit was a follower of one of the most ancient wise man of India – Kapila.

The teaching of this wise man could be summed up as follows: The Soul exists in a universe where everything is matter in a constant state of flux. The seed is an example of matter. From it a tree grows, which, finally, dies, but this only seems so. The *true* substance of the tree does not perish but turns to the earth and the earth's juices again enter into a new tree and so on, endlessly. The matter which permeates the universe does not perish; it just changes constantly.

In the beginning, this matter from which the universe consisted did not change as it was in an undeveloped state of balance. As soon as this balance was upset, the undeveloped and unchanging matter of the universe began to change and receive different forms. Separateness of the matter appeared that way and somehow a separate life of every form started: of human beings, beasts, trees, stars and of everything animate and inanimate in the universe. Often the matter became diversified and personal, five fine essences with the corresponding five gross essences appeared in it. These five essences are: 1) sound (fine) and ether (gross), 2) touch and air, 3) color and fire, 4) taste and water, 5) smell and earth. It only appears to a human being that he is what he is. As a matter of fact he is a part of nature, of that universal material, which is constantly changing, in a human being as well as in everything in the universe. Fine essences are called 'manas' and the corresponding gross ones – feelings (hearing, touch, sight, taste, smell). When a human being, for example, sees a red flower, that does not mean that the red flower actually exists. In fact, there are no differences in nature, as there is only an unchanging material from which nature consists. It only appears to a human being that he or she sees a red flower because of the fine human essence – man receives an impression from the gross essence – the feeling of sight and the fine essence made this division of the universal matter. If the fine essence or manas is concealed by the gross one or feeling of sight, a human being would not receive the red flower as a red flower.

As a part of the whole matter of the universe a human being changes. At one time he could be a human being, at another an animal, a plant, a stone and so on. The meaning of human life consists in stopping these external changes. This can only be achieved when he learns the cause of the changes, that is when he learns to strive for the original state of matter -balance and nonexistence. This can be done when consciousness and the separateness of a human being from the rest of matter is destroyed, that is when the consciousness of his separateness as an individual is destroyed. This can happen when his fine essences or manas cease creating his isolation from the rest of nature. Then the insensitive gross essences will become feelings. A human being will stop feeling and stop being conscious of his separateness from nature and thereby he will put a stop to the changes of matter which constitute the eternal transformation from one being into another. Then, the balance of all the matter in the universe will be again re-established.

In order to reach this higher state long study, introspection and thought is necessary. By way of the most profound introspection and rejection of everything that provides food for feelings, a human being will finally reach the highest state – Buddha. After reaching that state, a human being disposes of supernatural powers while he accomplishes what to others appears miraculous.

Siddhartha lived for a long time near Kalama learning from his wisdom. He lived the way Kalama taught in deep meditation and introspection but at last he realized that Kalama's teaching did not explain to him life as it is. Moreover, Siddhartha's common sense could not accept on faith that which his reason did not verify. Siddhartha did not find in this teaching a solution to the questions tormenting him about suffering, sickness and death. Not seeing in Kalama's teaching a solution to these questions, Siddhartha went to another wise man named Udraka Ramaputra.

Udraka Ramaputra followed Patanjali's teaching. It was completely different from the teaching which Kalama followed. Udraka believed that there was a supreme beginning, Brahma, which created everything in this world and established the order which exists in it. A part of the Supreme Being or Brahma exists in every human being and the meaning of human life consists in the union with Brahma, to merge with this Supreme Beginning in one whole. This is realized through gradual human reincarnations into new existences. The being, enclosed in a human being, gradually passes from one form of life to another. That which a human being has done is never extinguished but influences his life in a new existence. So, if for example, a human being has sinned, then he would pass into a lower form of existence – a beast, a plant, a stone and so on, or having been in a lower form and having committed in it good deeds he would pass into a higher form of life – into a human form. This is a law, to which everything is subject, existing in this world and this law is called Karma.

Brahma created everything in this world in a certain sequence and everybody should fulfill his obligations in order to ease and raise his karma. Brahma created four groups of people: noblemen – warriors, learned men – brahmins, tillers of soil and slaves. Only when everybody fulfills his assigned activity will a real order be established in the world and only then can everybody speed up his union with Brahma and thereby decrease his further reincarnations into other existences. This means that a warrior should destroy enemies, brahmins – teach people Brahma's will, tillers – create food and slaves serve everybody.

Siddhartha lived near Udraka, learned his teaching and absorbed the meaning of holy, ancient traditions but his spirit was not calm and he was not content. There was no solution in this teaching to the questions which had been tormenting him. He saw that in this teaching all human beings were different and that God assigned to some an easier fate than to others. Siddhartha understood that as a result of the difference in status of human beings, suffering in the world was only increased and instead of allowing salvation from the unavoidable evil of death warriors were assigned to kill others. Siddhartha realized that under this teaching instead of justice, injustice was increased in the world. But more than anything else Siddhartha could not reconcile himself with a teaching which affirmed the existence of a God who created evil and injustice on earth.

And Siddhartha, having lived a long time near Udraka Ramaputra, left him. Siddhartha heard at that time that five hermits were saving themselves in the Uruvili forest. One of these hermits was called Kaundaynoya. The hermits used to be Undraka Ramaputra's disciples but left him because they found a more correct way of life and salvation from the evils of the world. Siddhartha went to them.

From these hermits Siddhartha learned that all suffering, all evil in the world is caused by the existence of the body. The body possesses feelings, feelings call forth desires and when desires are born in us, which cannot be satisfied, then suffering proceeds from them. Therefore, in order that there will be no suffering and evil in this world, one has to be liberated from the source of evil or from the body. One should exhaust it and bring it to nothingness. Only then can a human being experience bliss and reach holiness.

For the first time Siddhartha found an understandable explanation of suffering and the means of liberation from it. He joined these five hermits gladly and started to wear out his body. Six years passed, while he lived in this forest in deep meditation exhausting his body. His strength was decreasing and he often fell unconscious from weakness. But the meaning of life had not been revealed to him completely. Along with horrible weakness he felt that his mind was weakening and he was aware he was going towards the unavoidable death, to that death whose meaning he was not able to divine.

Once Siddhartha bathed in a river and from weakness he felt faint. Siddhartha managed to grab a tree branch and he did not sink. With the greatest difficulty, he crawled on the shore but he felt faint again and for several hours he lay motionless dying from exhaustion. Sadzata, a shepherd's daughter, was passing by then and she took pity on Siddhartha, revived him and fed him with rice milk. Coming to his senses and after being strengthened by food, Siddhartha suddenly realized that by emaciating his body, he was consciously extinguishing in himself that only light which illuminated everything for him in the world – his reason. Siddhartha understood that while he was alive he should not reject his reason, that it is the only thing that he can trust and that only reason can show him the way. For this reason one should reject deliberate exhausting of the body.

Siddhartha started eating better and wondering. He was reassured and happy that he changed his mind in time, believing that reason would put him on the right path. As soon as Siddhartha changed his life, his hermit friends, who had treated him with the greatest respect, seeing now, that he had changed his life and stopped exhausting his body, treated him now with contempt and indignation and they left him.

Siddhartha remained alone, but now he was not despairing. Reason told him that the way of salvation from suffering and death was near. Siddhartha spent day after day in deep meditation under an enormous fig tree and only seldom went to the nearest village for food.

Sitting once at night under the fig tree, Siddhartha finally understood the meaning of life and solved the questions which had been tormenting him. He also saw clearly the errors of the teachings which he had studied before. They allowed that which reason could not verify and understand, and having allowed that they came to the wrong conclusions. He understood more clearly where the source of all suffering came and he understood the way of liberation from suffering. The cause of suffering as Siddhartha saw it now was rooted in the selfish attachment to life. Liberation from suffering consisted in living the true life.

Suffering comes from ignorance of the true life. This ignorance is total blindness and the one who uproots in himself this ignorance will realize knowledge and he will not enter the impermanent life. As the people don't know the true life, they, in their blindness, attach themselves to all the temporary things which cannot belong to them and which are constantly changing and being destroyed. Human beings give themselves to passions, wishes and strivings; they are eager to possess things, they are excited, happy and embittered, not realizing that the cause of happiness and suffering resides in the corporal, perishable and transitory, which is not a part of the true rational life. A human being as a rational creature can only be satisfied by the rational way of life. If human beings find the source and the meaning of life in the perishable or corporal then they must unfailingly suffer and die. Human beings are searching for enjoyment, but from enjoyment originates sorrow and the fear of losing the object of enjoyment; he who is free from joy is also free from suffering. People, who think that they own horses, fields, cattle, riches, that they own sons, daughters, wives – such people are irrevocably destined to suffer. All this is temporary and subject to destruction and therefore one should not attach one's thoughts to all this and should not strive for possessions. The only object of possession for human beings should be the wisdom of knowledge and that is the only thing that should be coveted. A person who strives for the possession of something other than wisdom, who indulges in enjoyment, who feeds only his lust, that person forges for himself ever more lasting chains tying him to the life of suffering.

Siddhartha realized that what he understood earlier by life was not the true life. That what human beings understand their life to be is a soap bubble. Such a life is transitory.

Life is that which proceeds from our thoughts and that which is born in our heart. Human beings create for themselves a false life which death destroys but it is possible to create a life over which death has no power – a true life. The only way to eternal life is knowledge of the true life.

And when to Siddhartha the reasons of his former agitation, suffering and fears became clear, so did the further way in life.

Having explained to himself the cause of suffering, Siddhartha found what brings about the birth of passions and desires and how by avoiding them a human being can reach full freedom and perfection. But how can one reach this freedom and how can one liberate himself from suffering?

If a person becomes loving, good-natured and helpful to others, he will thereby assist others in discontinuing to be a source of anxiety for him. As everybody else is striving for happiness, so every person should try to save others from suffering and sorrow. Another human being is not something separate from oneself. Another human being is another I. Consequently if I want to liberate myself from difficult circumstances I should assist others to liberate themselves from difficult circumstances and in no way cause them suffering. Although a body consists of different members, only one member can be hurt for the whole body and all other members to suffer. In the same way, the world consists of many creatures and the suffering of one is reflected in another. If a person wants to save himself from suffering, he should subject himself to the law of goodness.

For Siddhartha the way to the true life free from suffering and death was clear. He arrived at five commandments which when followed can bring human beings to perfection and eternal life.

Here are these commandments.

Commandment 1. Do not kill. Kill neither human beings nor all living creatures. "Everything that is alive trembles before torture, everything that is alive is afraid of death; recognize yourself in each living creature, don't kill and do not cause death."

But Siddhartha understood that reaching such a state in which a human being is adverse to murder and causing harm is only possible when a human being learns to love all other human beings and everything alive. One has, however, to love with true love. This love is called "Maitri" in a Hindi dialect. This love should not be confused with the love a lover bestows on his beloved (in Hindu "Kama") or with the love parents bestow on their children, or the love brothers bestow on their sisters, or the love friends bestow on their friends (in Hindi "Prema"). These last two kinds of love are not true love but only an obstacle against it. Human beings should love and be loved with a love free of egoism and the desire for reciprocity. "And the way a mother loves her child and is ready to sacrifice her own life for it, let everybody love everybody else, ready to give up life for others. Let every human being grow in himself the feeling of love for the whole world, let him not allow differences between people. Let a human being be always awake in that state of loving, whether it be walking, sitting, standing or lying. This state is the highest state accessible to a human being."

In such a state of loving there cannot be differences between people, there cannot be higher and lower, masters and slaves, rulers and subjects. "Not by birth but through life one becomes noble or ignoble. A person who is free of sin is noble. A noble person is the one who fully depends on himself." In such a state of love, relations between people are understandable. "Conquer anger by love, overcome evil by goodness." To a person, who because of stupidity or on account of ignorance treats me badly, I should respond with true love and good will.

And the more evil that emerges from such a person, the more goodness and love should emerge from me toward him. "It is good to pay
with goodness for goodness, but to pay with goodness for evil, this is
the true, higher life, this is the noble path. Your enemy, if you learn to
love him, is the person who can help you reach perfection."

One should relate to people with love even in one's thoughts. "Fill
the world with friendship, let all creatures – weak and strong – see in
you nothing that can cause them harm and they will find out a way to
peace."

Commandment 2. Do not steal. One should neither steal nor rob
others. But one should with all one's forces assist everybody to use
fully the fruits of one's labor.

"A person, who has known the true path, would abstain from stealing anywhere and anything and he would not agree to help those who
are engaged in any kind of theft or robbery."

"The one who receives the greatest advantage is the one who gives
to others and the one who looses more than anything else is the one
who takes from others without giving anything in return."

The main goal of abstinence from stealing and robbery in all their
aspects should be a contempt for riches and a conviction that the acquisition of property appears to be only an obstacle for living the true
life. "Passion for the acquisition of property and riches, this is what
enslaves a human being," spoke Siddhartha. "If you receive something,
keep it in your heart, so that this is not only yours but everybody else's."

Therefore those who follow the path of the true life cannot be rich
as the gathering of riches in some hands means unavoidably that something was taken now or earlier from somebody else and that somebody
else was deprived the fruits of his labor.

People often understand that they should abstain from the accumulation of riches exclusively for themselves and they are toiling not for
themselves only, but for the benefit of their family. This is, however,
only the step on the way to a true life. A human being should see
himself not only in the people close to him or his family, but in all
people. One should abstain from the fruits of one's labor not only for
one's family but for all people. Only then will a person enter the true
path of life.

If a person realizes success in his business ventures, if he manages to amass much money, land and cattle, – let him think about how he achieved that, and after thinking he will see that he acquired what he owned by underhanded means, by taking or stealing from others. That what has been taken from others cannot be beneficial.

"Do not envy the good fortune of others, rejoice in it. Generosity, love and good will for everybody-this is for a human being, what a linch pin is for an axis."

"Only he can be truly respected by people, who is loving, generous and ready to share with everybody."

Commandment 3. Do not commit adultery. The sexual life is not good as it serves as a source of strong attachments and is, therefore, for us, a source of suffering and disturbance of the true life. Although the goal of marriage appears to be only preservation and continuation of the family, people, in fact, derive from it enjoyment and thereby destroy their true life.

A wise man should avoid sexual uncleanliness, as a man avoids lying down on a bed of red-hot coals. If a man cannot preserve full virginity, then let him be content with his wife only and let him not commit adultery.

Beware of looking at women. If you see a woman then look at her as if you don't see in her a woman. If you talk to a woman, then talk to her with a pure heart and pure intentions. If a woman is old, look at her as if she were your mother. If she is young as if she were your sister and if she is very young as if she were your daughter."

Commandment 4. Don't lie. Speak the truth only with full sincerity not with the aim of hurting or insulting somebody but wisely and lovingly.

Love for other human beings should unavoidably bring us to the attitude that we should not only not lie, but that we should not communicate bad information about other people. One should look for the best in other people and this will help us to devote ourselves to sincere love for them. "One should see in oneself evil and in others good, one should not notice in others evil and imitate only what is good in them."

"If you go to a meeting, don't utter any lies to anybody. Don't act in any manner that which would allow them to speak lies because of you, don't agree with a lie, avoid all kinds of injustice. Avoid taking part in gossip, during empty conversations try speaking with dignity or remain silent."

There is no such crime, in which lies would not enter in as a main component "A lie is a desire to gain some advantage or cause insult or injury, which we don't dare do openly or it is a desire to avoid a deserved punishment or a loss." Envy, flattery, intrigue, all these are different forms of lying.

Commandment 5. Do not drink intoxicating beverages. The most precious quality in a person is his reason. It should be guarded in every way possible and preserved pure. All intoxicating beverages obscure reason and they make a rational human being irrational. When reason is obscured a person is deprived of the ability to distinguish what is true from what is false; he becomes side-tracked from the true path and is ready to commit any mistake and any crime.

Siddhartha after much thinking and after experiencing much suffering and despair finally achieved complete peace. He was steeped in the living of love – maitri – without which, he knew now, there was no life in this world. This love and the feeling of love and compassion issuing from it for everything that is alive in the world made him leave the hermit way of life which he had led until then. It was now necessary to go to people and tell them about that joy which is accessible to everybody. Humanity should be helped to wake up from a long sleep, be liberated from blindness and get to know the true life.

All of Siddhartha's later life was spent in wandering from one place to another explaining to people the true life. Siddhartha's first followers were those five hermits with whom he lived for a long time trying to emaciate his body. They had turned him down with contempt when he refused to follow this practice. Siddhartha found them in the forest and they, after seeing him, decided initially not to greet and associate with him. That did not trouble Siddhartha at all, approaching them, he started to talk to them about the mistake of pursuing self-torment. By killing our body, he told them, we deprive the possibility for reason, our sole light in this life, to illuminate our path. We should be concerned about our body and not kill it so that the life of understanding will burn brighter and that the concern about our body will interfere with the rational life.

Siddhartha told his former friends everything that he realized with gentleness and that permeating light, which after spiritual liberation, illuminated all his words and acts. He told them how happy and understandable his life became after that. His former friends understood him completely and agreed with him. With them, Siddhartha now went to the people.

Siddhartha's gentleness, love, compassion and reason began to attract people to him. Everybody started wondering at his wisdom; from all sides people gathered to him to study, as to a wise and just person. Siddhartha never got tired and he did not decline to answer questions addressed to him.

Siddhartha never judged the teaching of other wise men and the teaching of other religions at the time, although he did not agree with them. When they asked his opinion about religions and teachings in which they believed, he always tried to find in them the most essential feature and have people take notice of it.

When Siddhartha was asked questions about the definition of God, the soul and so on he was always silent and then when his closest followers and friends asked him why he didn't answer these questions he said: "We can discuss only that which can be conceived by our reason, only through reason can we get to know our life. Reason cannot entertain these questions and therefore one should be silent about them." And he told them a story in connection with it. "A physician was summoned to a man wounded by a poisoned arrow. The wounded man, before he allowed treatment, asked to what caste the physician belonged, who he was, and so on. (The physician, on the other hand, asked before the treatment started who was the person who wounded him, what kind of weapon was used, how tight was the bow, etc.,) Therefore let that which our reason has not revealed remain concealed and let that which is accessible to our reason remain open. It is necessary to live and do the work of life."

Although in India at that time everybody was allowed to believe as one wanted and Siddhartha was not persecuted, his teaching caused indignation. Siddhartha did not see differences between people and he treated everybody equally kindly. In India, at that time, as has been mentioned previously, people were divided into four castes. Before

Siddhartha custom and religion strictly forbade people from one caste to be friendly with people from another caste.

Siddhartha did not admit this. He associated equally with everybody and he taught his followers the same. That was difficult to accomplish. Even people from the lower classes with whom one was not supposed to associate were dismayed to see how Siddhartha and his disciples spoke, drank and ate together. The lower classes were not accustomed to being treated equally.

This feature of Siddhartha's teaching was not pleasing to Brahmins, especially to those in power. Siddhartha experienced much unpleasantness because of this. He often had to repeat and demonstrate that a human being does not become noble or ignoble by birth but by the life he leads.

Many, especially Brahmins, treated Siddhartha with contempt and ridicule. Once Siddhartha walked through a field where Brahmin Kazibharadvagi worked. That Brahmin, seeing a tramp, recognized in him Siddhartha, addressed him and said "Here you are loafing without work, it would have been better instead of wagging your tongue, to take up some work, to plough and sow and then to feed yourself from the labor of your hands."

Siddhartha had a ready answer. He told his disciples, which work is the most important in life. The most important work should not be to produce something, to gather and accumulate. The most important work is to work on yourself; to strengthen reason in oneself, to enlighten it, to extinguish passions. In that consists true goodness, the bread of life.

Siddhartha's teaching was very much to people's liking. Brahmins in whom the people believed in matters of truth before Siddhartha, were dissatisfied with the new teaching which they considered to be seducing people. They often came to Siddhartha with their disciples in order to argue with Siddhartha and prove to him the incorrectness of his teaching. Siddhartha in his discussions with Brahmins would usually find some higher truth in the teaching they professed and he would say that everybody should bow down, respect and follow it in life. Along with this Siddhartha would remember the life of some righteous Brahmins, who gave up property, different wishes and passions, and spend their entire life in love for other people. Siddhartha, having explained that, would say that in essence, he was trying to follow what the wise, righteous Brahmins followed and his advice was the same as theirs.

Usually, proud and self-confident Brahmins left Siddhartha and were ashamed. Often, they agreed with his assertions, became his disciples and changed their lives.

Many rich people, seeing how Siddhartha lived in a forest, one after the other offered Siddhartha their gardens so that he would live in them with his disciples. Siddhartha would live for some time in the garden given and then move on. These constant wanderings strengthened his body. He became inured to all kinds of weather and hardships and died in a forest when he was eighty years old in the arms of his disciples. While dying he said to his disciple Ananda "perhaps, you will think the teaching has lost its teacher, that we don't have a teacher anymore. You should not think so. The truth, about which I told you and your reason – there are your teachers when I leave." Regardless of how simple his teaching and understanding of life was, his close disciples often did not understand their teacher. Many of his disciples thought that Siddhartha was special and not like everybody else, a holy man and they ascribed to his reasoning a super-natural quality. According to them, this reasoning was inspired by his direct communication with God. His disciples thought that their teacher could perform any miracle. Siddhartha heard and knew all this and was very saddened by such a lack of understanding of his reason and his teaching by his disciples. He used to tell his disciples "that one, who looks at me as some special being, as a holy person, who values me because of my corporal cover, steps on the wrong path and will not reach the true life." And wishing to affirm even more that he could not save a person and direct him on the true path and that each human being carries in himself a higher source of the true life, he would tell his disciples "Be Ananda, a light to yourselves. Be a refuge to yourselves. Don't seek refuge in anyone, but in yourselves". It was obvious, however, that his disciples still continued to think that Siddhartha was a supernatural being although Siddhartha repeated again that there was nothing supernatural about him. He said "All those who, either now, or after my death, will be lights to themselves and will find refuge, only in themselves, only those will be able to reach the highest state of perfection."

Many times Siddhartha stopped his disciples from their enthusiasm for the supernatural. The disciples asked Siddhartha to perform a miracle thinking that their teacher could do anything. Siddhartha was amazed at such ignorance of his disciples and he would tell them with sadness that miracles can never convince a human being who has a powerful weapon for the knowledge of life – reason.

So, even during Siddhartha's life not all of his disciples understood his teaching the way, Siddhartha, himself, taught it. Soon after Siddhartha's death, his disciples and followers differed in the interpretation of his teaching. Much was attributed to Siddhartha which he did not say and which he could not say according to the basic meaning of his understanding of life. That upset the people who understood Siddhartha's teaching correctly and they started petitioning a convocation for a council of righteous people who remembered the pure teaching of Siddhartha. They thought that if a council of such people agreed on single philosophy, then the teaching would not be perverted any more. At this council the main basis of the teaching was established and later people dedicated to the teaching started writing down the decision of the council and everything else that was preserved in the stories of others about Siddhartha's life and teaching.

Other people, who understood Siddhartha's teaching in their own way, did not agree with the decision of the council and they propagated the teaching the way they understood it. They tried to prove their piety by founding communities of monks and nuns, by writing statutes for monasteries saying that this was established by Siddhartha. They convinced lay people to give up land, homes and gardens to monasteries, violating Siddhartha's teaching that one should not have property. They said that even meat could be eaten and that animals could be killed. They established complicated rites and furthermore worship of Siddhartha as a deity.

This is how the schism took place. Some followers of Siddhartha's teaching propagated this teaching primarily in Northern India, others did so in the South. Although in the beginning the two branches who understood his teaching differently and argued a lot, they never resorted to force and persecution.

After more than two hundred years after Siddhartha's death the powerful emperor Asoka took power. He lived 250 years before Christ. Asoka's empire included many small regions and princedoms into which India was divided. Asoka learned about Siddhartha's teaching, liked it very much and proclaimed himself its follower. He refused to kill animals and eat meat and announced it with a special proclamation to his subjects. In addition, the Emperor Asoka issued many imperial edicts about this teaching and inscribed them on stone columns. In these edicts and inscriptions, the Emperor praised Siddhartha's teaching and advised people to follow it. At the Emperor's court many preachers were gathered, who were then sent out to Asoka's state as well as to foreign countries to preach Siddhartha's teaching.

It seemed that this devout Emperor helped Siddhartha's teaching but it turned out otherwise. It is true that Siddhartha's teaching and his name were spread but on the other hand his teaching was even more perverted than before. Many followers of this teaching appeared but the teaching itself suffered significantly from it. Asoka, himself, remained an emperor, thinking that while remaining an emperor he could still follow Siddhartha's teaching. Asoka forgot that Siddhartha himself was a prince's son and refused to be a ruler of his estate, because that would contradict the realization of that true life which he sought. The Emperor Asoka accepted much that he liked in Siddhartha's teaching and that which he did not like he interpreted in his own way. The Emperor fought wars defending his people, judged and punished criminals, gathered riches at the same time as building everywhere in his Empire not only hospitals for the sick but also for animals.

The preachers whom the Emperor sent to spread the teaching understood it differently. To please the Emperor they tried to have the people believe in this teaching as much as possible and therefore tried to win them over in all possible ways. There, where the people were especially ignorant, missionaries talked about Siddhartha as a deity, about miracles which he performed during his life, about the bliss which awaits believers after death.

Soon everyone in Asoka's enormous empire began to practice the new teaching but this teaching was strongly distorted. Rich monasteries appeared in which monks lived. They went around collecting alms for the sake of appearances but in fact not living the life of poverty which Siddhartha led. They built rich temples and in these temples and monasteries they placed images and statues of Siddhartha, which they worshipped. They established a multitude of rites and they began to celebrate Siddhartha as the most perfect, holiest and divine.

Brahmins significantly contributed to the darkening and distortion of the meaning of Siddhartha's teaching. Before Siddhartha people respected and followed Brahmins in everything but the more Siddhartha's teaching spread, the clearer people realized the deception of Brahmins who advocated the inequality of human beings. People stopped respecting and following Brahmins. Siddhartha's teaching was more understandable and closer.

Then Brahmins started telling people that Siddhartha did not reject their teaching and as a support they cited Siddhartha's words. Siddhartha, in fact, said that he respected the righteous wise men who Brahmins honored and he advised that the righteous life of these wise men be followed. He never said, however, that everything Brahmins taught was correct. Afterwards Brahmins also began teaching that Siddhartha was a reincarnation of God Brahma and that they honored him as a deity. In this way they retained many of their followers who were inclined to accept Siddhartha's teaching.

People gradually became accustomed to Siddhartha's distorted teaching. Regardless of how distorted it was, its essence still remained clear and people under the influence of this teaching gradually changed for the better, becoming more loving, gentle and compassionate to their neighbors and to everything alive on earth. This teaching of gentleness and love soon spread throughout India and in the second century after Christ came to China and soon became there one of the most widespread religions. Several hundred years after its growth in China it spread to Tibet and then went further to Siberia and to the Volga steppes of Russia.

After the fifth century after Christ, new conquerors, Arabs, surged to India, believing fervently in the teaching of their prophet Mohammed. Arabs tried to convert everybody to their faith and they used fire and the sword to accomplish this. Gentle Buddhists submitted to the new rule, their temples were destroyed but their faith could not be exterminated even by Mohammadans, in spite of all their force. The population of India gently endured the rule of these conquerors through many centuries. Although they brought to the population much misery and grief, they did not exhaust the country with enormous taxes. Afterwards religious persecution quieted down and India began to live peacefully again.

About one hundred fifty years ago new conquerors entered India. In the beginning they were merchants – the English and the Dutch. These merchants tried to win the confidence of the people and having entered at the outset into commercial relations, started selling them their goods or in exchange for their goods they took what the Indians produced: precious stones, rice, coffee, silk, etc. Seeing the gentleness and good disposition of the population, the merchants lost all scruples and began cheating. They took by force the riches which the people did not want to give up. They began finally to grab rich land and even whole districts. Then they brought the army and guns to defend the expropriated estates, which they already considered to be their property. People even then did not resist. Then, the English merchants sold their estates to the English government, which was not content with what the merchants took, but soon declared the whole land of India to be their colony and assigned there governors to rule with the army and guns.

The gentle people for the most part endured silently the new rule. If somewhere mutinies and riots flared up, people considered the rioters and rebels brigands, who deviated from the teaching of love.

The new conquerors or English burdened the people with enormous taxes and by way of these taxes they seized all of their fruits of labor. The inhabitants of India became poor. Almost every year in this rich, fertile land hunger reigned. Almost every year hundreds of thousands of people died there of hunger.

The English used to send to India for the most part rude and cruel officials, who, after leaving their country tried to become rich as soon as possible and for this reason did not have any reservations about insulting the gentle people. They were not interested in the life and the religion of the people among whom they lived. They considered them pagans, turned them to slavery and robbed them brutally. Some good people however, were among the Englishmen who came to India. They looked closely at the life of the people, studied their religion and became familiar with their holy books. In the past fifty years the best

English, French and German scholars translated the majority of the holy books of the Indian people into their own language. Europeans began to admire the noble teaching which was set forth in these books. Many were found among Englishmen, who were ashamed of their government for its merciless treatment of this gentle, intelligent people who lived a good life. An Englishman, by the name of Fielding, wrote a wonderful book (*A Soul of a People*) about the life of the Indian people who professing Buddhism or Siddhartha's teaching lived in the enormous area of India-Burma. This book and many others caused great compassion for the exploited people and the English government is now beginning to take measures to ameliorate the oppression from which the gentle people of India, who follow for the most part Siddhartha's teaching, suffer.

P. Bulanzhe
Translated by **Dragan Milivojevic** from
Zhizn'Dl'a Vsekh, Nr. 3, March 1910, pp.110-127

To the Editor of the Journal
Zhizn'Dl'a Vsekh
V. D. Posse
February 24, 1910
Yasnaya Poalyana
Vladimir Aleksandrovich:
I have conceived for a long time an exposition of the world's major religions which is short and accessible to the majority of readers. I have done something in this direction. Lately my friends and I have intended to tackle this in a more thorough way. Articles about the world's major religions in the form of separate booklets have been published and others are prepared for publication. There are several of them, namely, "Confucianism," "The Sayings of Mohammed," and "Krishna" (according to the old Indian religion). And now an article about Buddhism which I am sending to you with a suggestion to publish it in your journal before it appears as a separate booklet.

This article is different from other learned descriptions of Buddhism which I know. In the majority of such works, the main interest is in scientific and historical facts about the appearance and spread of Buddhism, while the religious-moral teaching is treated mostly only as historical material. Here, on the contrary, the very essence of the religious-moral teaching of Buddhism is set forth in the full breadth of its meaning in a manner understandable and accessible to even the most unprepared reader.

Now a few words about the significance which I ascribe to the exposition, one accessible to the majority of readers, which will present the essence of all the great world religions including the most widespread one – Buddhism. I am attaching special significance to such kinds of expositions because I think that the knowledge of the foundations of these great world religions, with which all humanity lived and lives, is one of the most important and necessary forms of knowledge every person should have. Ignorance in this regard is one of the main reasons for the weakening of religious consciousness nowadays among the so-called simple people as well as the so-called intelligentsia. This weakening among the working class originates, in my opinion, primarily because the common fall to an education which exists in full ignorance of other peoples' religions and they persist in the conviction of the exclusive truthfulness of their own religion. The educated people and the working class people in their present mental development encounter in what is taught to them as doubtless true religious instruction in which they can no longer believe. The tenets of the faith taught them are inseparably connected with the recognition of God-inspired writings and the infallibility of the church. As they are not capable of separating the more essential truths from the lesser ones, they stop believing in the entire teaching of the church. There are ever more such people among the working class. Some of them hide their disbelief with outward appearances partly because of fear, partly because of inertia or propriety; others openly confess their full disbelief in the church teaching. The working class, in my opinion, can successfully counter this dangerous situation of our times by acquiring a knowledge of all major world religious teachings. I think that such a knowledge will show those who doubt that the religious tenets which cause them to doubt do not comprise the main essence of religions. By knowing other religions such people would learn that in all great religions, as well as the ones they profess, there are two kinds of religious tenets;

some which are infinitely different and varied depending on the time, the place and the character of the people in which they appeared and others which remain the same in all religions. These tenets, common to all religions, not only should be believed but they must be believed because they are the same in all world religions. In addition, they are inscribed on the heart of each human being as certain and happy truths.

And for this reason I think that especially in our time communication of the basic foundations of all world religions to our people is a work of utmost importance.

Now, about the consequences of such ignorance for the second group of people – the so-called intelligentsia. The ignorance among this class of people is staggering. No matter how strange it is to say, but not only young people, but old, respectable people, who are considered to be fully educated, professors and scientists, have for the most part about this very important subject on the essence of the religious teaching of other peoples, either a very vague, or more often, the falsest idea. These people, even if they know from history that Zoroastr existed, that there are Vedas, that there was Buddha and Confucius, don't have, for the most part, the vaguest idea about the essence of all these religious teachings. Not having any idea about the essence of the great, ancient religious teachings, the so-called educated people, like the common people, do not separate basic truths from distortions and additions which characteristically accompany the spread of religious teachings. They do one of two things: Either for the sake of propriety, vanity and mercenary goals they pretend that they believe in everything that the established church teaches. However, it is impossible for them to fully pretend because they believe that religion, on the whole, is a psychic condition which humanity has outlived and that science will answer questions more exactly and clearly than in their opinion were answered so frivolously by religion. These people, most of them publishers, men of letters and teachers of every kind and in general people who consider themselves educated, think that religion is completely useless. They think that the fundamental questions of life are quite satisfactorily answered by science, by their so beloved teaching of evolution, according to which a human being appearing in infinite space and time with all his spiritual qualities is only a consequence of the motion of infinitely small particles of matter as a continuation of infinite time in infinite space. Moreover, as it could not be any other way, in place of Buddha, Confucius, Christ, Augustine, Pascal, Rousseau, Kant and Emerson are Darwin, Hegel, Marx and others. In place of the moral teaching of love and self-renunciation is the teaching of conflict and violence.

Yes, regardless of how pitiful the situation of the working class, who are deprived of the benefit of religious leadership as a consequence of their inability, even of their impossibility, to separate the most essential from the inessential in the religious teaching taught to them, the so-called educated people are still in much worse a position. The common folk *cannot* separate in religion the essential from the inessential because they don't have enough knowledge for that. But the people who consider themselves educated, *not that they cannot* but they don't want to separate from the inessential the essential or they pretend to believe in that which one should not believe, or, not being able to understand higher human spiritual activity deny it with the unshakable conviction of ignorance.

And I think, therefore, that for this group of people, it would not be useless to become acquainted with the basic foundations of the world's religious teachings. After knowing them they would realize that coarse mistake which they make in their thinking when they accept the greatest manifestations of human reason as superstitions and when they accept for true knowledge these contradictory and often ridiculous scientific superstitions, which to them appear quite clear because of their thoughtlessness.

Forgive me for being so talkative about a subject which is only indirectly related to my article but which is very close to my heart.

It is understandable that both the previous articles about ancient religions as well as this one, which I will succeed in writing or at least in editing, are far from being perfect. I can only say this, that recognizing the enormous importance of this work, I tried to do what I could. I hope that others will do better.

Translated by **Dragan Milivojevic**
Leo Tolstoy 24 February 1910
Yasnaya Polyana

CHAPTER TEN

SIDDHARTHA, CALLED THE BUDDHA, THAT IS THE HOLY ONE... HIS LIFE AND HIS TEACHING
Part I

If one goes from the middle of Russia towards East straight, then one thousand and ten versts[1] from us[2] through Saratov, Uralsk, the Kirgizian steppe, Tashkent and Bukhara, one will arrive at high, snowy mountains. These mountains are the highest in the world. Pass over these mountains and you will enter the land of India.

The land of India is smaller than Russia by half, but their land is fertile and warm – there is no winter there; therefore, there are many more people there than in Russia. The population is considered to be up to 240 million. Englishmen have ruled Indian now for 150 years. Before the English conquered India the Indians lived freely and were governed by their own Tzars.

In this country and among these people was born approximately 2500 years ago, 600 years before Christ's birth, the holy Siddhartha Buddha and he was the founder of the great Buddhist religion, the one now in which one-third of the people on earth, more than 400 million people, believe.

At the time Buddha was born, the millions believed in their own ancient religion. The teaching of that religion was written down by them in books more than 3000 years ago and it began as soon as the Indians began to remember their history. The Brahmans' books are called the Vedas in their Sanskrit language and they are considered to

1. 1 verstan = 3500 English feet
2. Moscow

be revelation from above. The Indians say that the Vedas were not written by people, but that they were always in the mind of the deity. The Indian faith was the same faith written in the hearts of all people and without which there would be no people on earth. The Indian faith was the same as the faith of other peoples – the Persians, the Chinese, the Egyptians, the Greeks and all other people who live in the world – the faith that human beings live and die by God's will and that he who fulfills God's will be rewarded and he who does not fulfill it will be punished. All human faiths have always had that in common. They all agree that we don't exist by ourselves but through God's will and that God is merciful and in order to fulfill God's will, one should not do evil but one should do good. Such was also the Indian faith.

They called God by different names: Agni, Varuna, Indra, Brahman but they knew that there was one God. They understood the will of the one God in the same way as it is understood by all people, the way it is written in human hearts. They knew that God's will is to do good and to do evil means to contradict God's will. They knew what is good and what is evil as all people do. In accordance with this, in one of the ancient books it was written that people should restrain themselves from killing not only human beings but from killing everything animate. They should also restrain themselves from anger, adultery, drunkenness, gluttony, laziness, from judging others and they should be meek, abstemious, honest, just, pure and they should return good deeds for evil ones. The Indians knew all this and they based God's will on these precepts.

There is much that is high and noble in the Vedas but in time much superfluous and empty material was added to these books. It happened that lying and greedy people became established among the teachers of God's will. These people began teaching Indians that God's will consists not only in abstinence from willfulness and in the fulfillment of good but in many other things presumably necessary for God. Their agents, Brahman-priests, began introducing in their teaching of God's will much that was superfluous, unnecessary and harmful to people, but useful to themselves. They introduced sacrifices, sequences of prayers, ablutions, cleansings, they introduced the division of all people into different castes, having convinced the people, that all this was done by God's will; they obscured all that was true, with their own deception. The Brahman-priests taught that sacrifices protect people from all evil and sin. They taught that in order to save oneself from sin one should go to the forest and then torment one's flesh through fasting and all kinds of suffering. And so it happened that worldly people lived like beasts, expiating their sins through sacrifices, while monks left the world and in the wilderness tormented their flesh and lived without any use for mankind. The faith in the truth that was their in holy books had become gradually weaker by the time the holy Siddhartha Buddha was born, grew up and began propagating his teaching.

When Siddhartha Buddha was born, India was divided into many small kingdoms. They were sometimes friendly, at other times warlike to each other. In the south, from the Himalayan mountains the small river Raesti and another small river Roshni flow. Between these two small rivers, at the foothills of the Himalayan mountains, 2500 years ago, there was the small but rich Kingdom of Shakyas. They ruled one area of thirty-thousand acres of fertile, dark earth. The rule in their kingdom came to them from grandfathers and fathers and it went well. People sowed rice on irrigated lands, traded and paid a rich tribute to the kings. The kings were rich and they led a life of luxury. From this descent of kings was King Sudhodhana, the father of Siddhartha Buddha.

King Sudhodhana ruled 600 years before Christ was born. He married when he was young to a beauty, a daughter of a king whose name was Maya. The king did not have any children. In the eleventh year of their marriage queen Maya had a dream. She dreamt that she was lying on her bed next to the king, her husband, and suddenly the roof and the ceiling blew open and above her were starry skies. She looked into the skies and she saw into their very depth, behind all other stars, one star emerge larger and larger. The queen, then, saw six bright rays radiating from the star. The star became even brighter and lower and Maya saw in the middle of the star a seal – a white elephant with six tusks and each tusk shot a ray. Maya just saw that, then the star flew even faster, blinded her and burned her and like an arrow pierced her in her left side under the heart. Maya became frightened, woke up and told her husband about the dream.

The King called on his dream interpreters and asked them about the message of her dream. The dream interpreters said: "The dream is a very fortunate one, the dream means that the queen will bear a son and that son will be holy and wise and a boon to humanity. He will liberate the world from illusion and he will reign over the people."

And it happened – Maya conceived on that day and when the time came she bore a son of unusual beauty.

II

The king was happy the prophecy of his soothsayers was realized and he waited for the prediction that his son would reign over the people to come true. The king understood that his son would be a great warrior and that he would conquer other kings and be emperor of the whole world. The king rejoiced and ordered that the birth of his son be celebrated across his whole kingdom.

The people came from all over his kingdom to pay homage to the baby. Among them came a wise old man who had lived in the wilderness for 50 years, without ever leaving it. The old man approached the king; everybody knew who he was and they made way for him. When the old wise man approached the cradle, the king said to the women: "Place the infant Siddhartha at the feet of the old man!" The old man looked at the infant and said: "Don't touch the baby: He should not be lying at my feet, but I should be lying at his," and he prostrated himself on the ground before the baby and having gotten up he said:

"On the tree of humanity only once in a thousand years blooms a flower, such a blooming flower fills the world with a sweet smell of wisdom and love. On your branch, oh, queen this little flower blossomed. You did your part and you will die in seven days."

The old man left, and it came to be that the queen died quietly, assigning her servant Magapra as a wet nurse.

The King Suddhodhana was embittered by his wife's death, but was consoled by his son and by that which was foretold.

The son grew in body and spirit and it was time for him to be taught. The king invited the most learned man in his kingdom, Visvamitr, to educate him and Visvamitr moved to the king's palace and began to educate young Siddhartha.

SIDDHARTHA, CALLED THE BUDDHA, THAT IS THE HOLY ONE HIS LIFE AND TEACHING
Part II

The Wise man Visvamitr began teaching the young Siddhartha and was amazed at the understanding of his pupil. Whatever Visvamitr would say, Siddhartha would understand and remember immediately. He would often continue and complete by himself what Visvamitr had not yet explained. When Visvamitr taught his pupil for the first time how to count to one-hundred, the boy understood immediately, and he counted till one-hundred and then right away counted to one-thousand, ten-thousand, a hundred-thousand, one-million, and many millions. Regardless of what science his teacher explained Siddhartha knew it better than the teacher himself.

And when they covered everything in science then the old man stood up from his place and prostrated himself in front of his wonderful student and said:

"It is not for me to teach you, bright young man, but it behooves you to teach your teachers. It is for this that you started studying with me, so that you could show me how you mastered all the sciences without books. You also showed that your knowledge did not turn your head and it did not prevent you from being humble in your soul before the older persons." Siddhartha had a quiet and modest disposition. With his words he was careful and wise. He had a tender, sorrowful but fearless heart.

None of the young men of his age were equal to him in the art of riding. Nobody else managed a chariot better while hunting; he was always in the forefront pursuing a wild beast regardless of obstacles and dangers.

But having pinned down a deer he often preferred to let him go unharmed and during races, having overtaken his friends, he often held his horse back on purpose to let them go ahead because he did want to make them feel embittered. At the very height of their happy amusements, Siddhartha often hid from the eyes of his friends and in solitude he gave himself to his thoughts.

Every year Siddhartha became more compassionate to the living beings surrounding him – to human beings and animals. Yet he did not know anything about sorrow, suffering and tears. He knew by hearsay only that these strange words were avoided in conversations with kings.

Once, Siddhartha, the boy, walked in his palace garden and he heard above his head a frequent, even rustle. He looked up and saw a flock of swans above him flying in the direction of the North. In front of them flew as a leader the biggest one and behind him stretched the others. Siddhartha stared at the swans and he saw the one in front suddenly start waving his wings faster, become unsteady and fell (head over heels) faster and faster. It hit the prince's hand with its chest and landed right at the feet of the prince. The swan's wing was pierced by an arrow and scarlet blood smeared its snow white feathers.

Siddhartha sat on the earth and carefully raised the wounded swan to his knees and with a steady hand removed from the wing the arrow. Then with the swan in his hands he picked up some healing herb growing there, went to a stream, washed the swan's wound and put on it leaves from the healing herb. The swan became more alive bit by bit and trustingly snuggled up to his savior's chest. His cousin Devadata breathlessly ran up to the Prince then and shouted: "It was I who shot him. I killed that swan. He is not yours, he is mine. Give him to me!"

"No, brother," answered Siddhartha, "If the swan were dead I would have given him to you but he is alive and suffering and I cannot give him up because I have to serve him."

"Whether this wild bird is dead or alive, it belongs to the one who shot her. Give me my bird."

Siddhartha just tenderly pressed the leaves of the healing herb to the swan's wing and said: "No, dear brother! I cannot give you the swan – it is mine because I pity him and love him." And Siddhartha further added:

"Yes, I see how necessary it is to introduce to the world compassion for all living creatures and to hold down the flow of earthly sorrow! But if you insist that the swan is yours, let us rather go to the oldest and the wisest – let them judge between us and we will submit to their decision."

And so the brothers did. King Suddhodhana summoned a council of the wisest of his subjects, and they started to discuss the matter. Some said one thing, others said something else and they could not come to any decision. Then an old unknown man stood up and said:

"Life does not belong to the one who destroys it but to the one who saves it. Give the swan to the one who restored its life!"

So said the old man and all present admitted in their soul the wisdom of this judgment. When the king wanted to give praise to the just wise man, he was nowhere to be found. He left as suddenly as he had appeared. In such a way the Prince Siddhartha laid the beginning of his works of love and compassion.

Siddhartha grew in body and spirit. He carefully sized up everything and he asked the meaning of what he saw. He still did not know anything about human unhappiness, need and sorrow. The swan's blood for the first time showed Siddhartha that there was suffering in the world and he began suspecting that not everything was always good and happy on earth.

King Suddhodhana noticed that the Prince became steeped in dark thoughts more and more often and he wanted to amuse his son.

The King summoned Siddhartha once and said:

"What is the matter with you?, my dear son. It looks as if you have become depressed and sad. It is spring now; one should be happy and enjoy it. Who should feel himself fortunate if not the King's son? I want to ride with you today through our kingdom. Let us love and enjoy our kingdom. Let us love and enjoy our fertile land in its spring glory, let us look at our people as their joyous work fills our royal treasury. The time will come and my bonfire will burn* and you will have to rule the country and dispose of the fate of our people. It is time

---

* Referring to the burning of the body after death according to the Hindu's religious custom.

that you got to know the kingdom. And the king ordered a chariot to be ready. He went with the prince to look round the country. It was the happiest season, streams flowed everywhere, the grass was turning green, the flowers were blooming and the trees had leaves. Birds sang in the forests, small insects swarmed in the grass and motley-colored lizards lolled in the sun. Fish played in ponds and streams. Tillers following ploughs could be seen in the fields; children-drivers, waving their whips, were conducting oxen. Sowers stepped from one foot to the other in a measured way scattering their seed.

Everybody rejoiced that spring was here. Looking at his son, King Suddhodhana rejoiced, too. After this outing he ordered the Prince to be driven around neighboring fields and villages more often.

But the Prince's happiness did not last long. Little by little he started examining closer what his eyes saw and he noticed that the tillers breathed heavily and they barely managed their heavy labor and that sweat flowed from them in streams. He saw that the oxen became exhausted under their heavy yoke, driven by their merciless drivers. Siddhartha also noticed that the lizards ate ants, that the snakes ate the lizards and that the kites ate both of them. A fisherman deprived an otter of its booty, a shrike hunted a nightingale and a nightingale caught motley-colored butterflies.

No matter where the Prince looked – everywhere he saw one and the same thing: creatures devoured each other, they lay and waited enticing and deceiving their prey. Everywhere the strong destroyed the weak. Everywhere were robbery and murder, everywhere life was nourished by death. And Siddhartha understood that human beings like animals live at the expense of their kin, oppressing in a beastly way, robbing and killing each other. And Siddhartha's soul was full of sadness and compassion.

"Is this the unhappy, evil life that we so praised," he thought. "Is it possible to find in it peace and happiness?"

And the Prince sat, bending his head, in the shadow of a tall tree and became steeped in thoughts about how much suffering, sorrow and evil there was in the world. And he thought, trying to find the reason for all this unhappiness and a way to liberate the world from it. And often long after sunset he sat motionless in the same place having forgotten about himself, absorbed in thoughts of the struggle with evil and the victory over suffering and sorrow. Among the people a legend was preserved that holy, invisible spirits floated under the clouds as Siddhartha thought. When they gathered around the tree where Siddhartha sat, their wings swayed and an unknown force pressed them down to Siddhartha's feet. And they saw the wonderful youth, steeped in thoughts with scarlet light surrounding his head. And a voice from the heavens was heard. Here is the redeemer of the world. Bow before him! And the spirits sang praise to Siddhartha Buddha and the clouds rose again and flew further, in a hurry to speed the happy news about the redeemer of the world.

After that day Siddhartha began to avoid people more and more and to spend time in seclusion and deep contemplation. The luxurious palace life lost for him all its charm and the courtiers tried in vain to amuse him, thinking up for him new games and pastimes.

King Suddhodhana was upset and called to a council all his grandees and officials and told them:

"My faithful servants: Remember the prediction of the dream-interpreters and the mysterious old man that my son Siddhartha will become a great man and that he will rule over the people. These words must be fulfilled. I hoped that my son would become a King of Kings and that he would trample his enemies under his feet, conquering the whole world. But, alas, we all see in him other inclinations; it seems that he is attracted by the hermits' way of life, the way of renunciation and the taming of the flesh. Let those who are deprived of real, earthly treasures look for illusory, spiritual treasures. It is not becoming for my son to pursue a pitiful hermit life. He was born for great honors and I want to awaken in him love for all the joys of life. Let him wish for power and glory burn in him, let him step on the valiant path of a courageous warrior and the urge to rise higher and higher above all human beings will appear in him. Then the prediction of wise men will be finally fulfilled. You are the wisest of my subjects, give me advice on how to realize this."

And the oldest advisor stood up and said: "Great King! The Prince's ailment is easy to cure and the love for women will cure it. The youth's heart has not yet known tender passion, it is not familiar with the charms of female beauty. What iron chains cannot hold, feminine caresses will strongly bind. It is necessary to find a woman for the Prince."

They all agreed, but the king said, "If we choose a wife for him it is doubtful that he would like her, but if we suggest to him to choose one himself, then we will smile because he cannot even imagine the delights of married life."

Then the older royal advisor said, "Summon to the palace for celebration all the noble girls in your kingdom. Let them compete in beauty and charm and instruct the Prince to be a judge and to distribute presents to those whom he finds worthier. From all these girls one will appear to his liking more than the others. We will be watching carefully from the sides and we will notice which one. And then let that girl become his wife."

The King approved of this advice and he sent out messengers across the whole kingdom to summon to the palace all the noble young girls for the beauty competition. He promised presents to all and the greatest present for the most beautiful of them all.

At the appointed day from all sides girls conveyed, one more beautiful than the other. They were dressed up in multi-colored silk fabrics, made up and perfumed. And the grandees placed the prince on an elevated throne and the presents were laid out around him.

And the girls came up to him one day after the other. They approached him timidly with lowered eyes, not daring to look him straight in the face as he looked at them without passion, calmly and majestically. Each one of them received a gift from the Prince's hand but none shook his serenity.

Finally, after all of them approached, young Iazodhara came forward and having seen the Prince trembled. Without bending her head, the girl stood and looked at him calmly with her dark eyes. She smiled and asked softly, "Is there a gift for me too?"

"All gifts have been given," answered the Prince, "But instead of a gift, dear sister, receive this. Your beauty is beyond all comparison!"

And the Prince took from his neck an emerald necklace. He bent down and began placing it around Iazodhara's neck. While placing it, he raised his head and looked at the girl's dark eyes; the eyes of the girl and the boy met and from this glance love was born between them.

The grandees noticed that the Prince liked Iazodhara and they hurried to let the King know. King Suddhodhana was happy and without delay he asked from Iazodhara's father his daughter's hand for the Prince.

"Tell the king," answered Iazodhara's father to the messengers, "that I am proud of his proposal and that I will agree wholeheartedly to this marriage. Being myself of royal blood I keep to ancient traditions religiously. By the ancient custom in our family I can only give my daughter to that bridegroom who is victorious among all the men of his age in war games. If the Prince wants to be the husband of my daughter let him be the winner of such a competition."

Having heard these words King Suddhodhana became sad, "How is my son going to be equal with other young men in physical competition? During all these last years all he had done is sit in seclusion, steeped in his own thoughts."

Siddhartha, however, found out the cause of his fathers grief and told him, "Let the competition take place, I studied that, too!"

At the appointed day a multitude of viewers gathered at the majestic competition for the beautiful hand of Iazodhara. To the great amazement of all the viewers Prince Siddhartha remained the winner in all the competitions, in shooting with a bow and arrow, in the sword competition and in the horse riding.

Then Iazodhara stood up from her seat taking a flower wreath, approached the Prince and hung the wreath around his neck. Blushing, with lowered eyes, she said quietly.

"Take me – I am now yours!"

And the people rejoiced looking at the bridegroom and the bride and they shouted: "Long live the glorious Prince, our Siddhartha, and his bride Iazodhara."

The wedding was performed according to an old ritual. Then they bound together the clothes of the newlyweds and placed on their heads wreaths as they sang wedding songs.

But King Suddhodhana's heart was not calmed down by the wedding. He did not place hope in the lore of female beauty and he kept thinking about what would be a better way to protect Siddhartha from sorrow and heavy thoughts, fearing that the Prince would leave to become a hermit and renounce his glorious royal fate.

And the King devised for Siddhartha a safe jail from where he could not and would not leave. And the king ordered for Siddhartha a palace to be built as the world had never seen it. The whole palace was of white and rosy marble, with golden pillars, high attics and towers, and with decorated and gold-plated chambers.

This palace was built on a beautiful place above a small river. Around the palace, on both sides of the river Rogina, shady and fertile trees and flower gardens were planted so that the noise and torment of the village life would not reach the Prince's ears. Only the singing of birds was heard filling the gardens among the fountains and ponds. Silver and golden fish swam and played in the ponds. Under the roofs of the palace, swallows made their nests while white turtle doves cooed in the gardens. Tamed chamois nibbled flowers while peacocks strutted, wiping with their slimy tails the stairs of the marble staircases. There were no beasts or birds of prey. Everybody lived peacefully and happily. Male and female slaves, all young and beautiful, lived in the magnificent mansion. Among them were signers, dancers, musicians and story-tellers. Tasty food was available on golden dishes day and night, as well as different sweets, rare fruit and cool drinks from precious glasses. Day and night intoxicating scents floated from high incense-burners as the bright fountains murmured. At the heat of noon, it was comfortable and cool, while at night fragrant lamps were lit and under their light the prince could listen to music or stories, or look at the dancing of the beauties if he did not feel like sleeping.

When the palace was completed and everything was established in it, King Suddhodhana looked it over, was happy with it and settled Siddhartha there with Iazodhara. And in order to accustom the Prince even more to the joyous life, the king selected for him two more beauties, Gotami and Mimodara, and gave them to him as wives.

In addition, the King ordered all his servants to never mention in the presence of the Prince human sorrow, need, suffering or death. The Prince should never see human tears, nor sickness nor gray hair, nor old age or even exhaustion. If it happened that a dancer would be out of breath or that her leg would slip or that somebody would be hurt, then these people would be hidden from the Prince so that he would never see the suffering and he would not know that there was suffering in the world. A sick bird, a dead insect, a faded leaf and a withered flower – anything which would induce Siddhartha to thoughts of suffering and death and awaken in him the sorrow which he felt before – was quickly removed from his eyes by the royal overseers attached to him. Even that seemed to King Suddhodhana was not enough. He was still in the fear that his son might become sad again and leave. He then ordered the whole estate to be encircled by cast-iron bars with brass gates and strong locks. Behind that gate he put a second one which was higher and behind the second one a third one. At each gate he placed a hundred men of his faithful guard and he ordered them on the threat of capital punishment not to let in or out anyone without his royal knowledge, even if this were the Prince himself.

And Siddhartha moved into his new place and began living in it. In the beginning, it appeared to the royal overseers that Siddhartha had calmed down and that he lived carefreely and happily in his new palace. Time passed in unceasing enjoyment. Day after day passed in merriment and nothing ever reminded the Prince of human suffering, old age or death. He completely forgot the horrible meaning of these words, he forgot about everything he had sensed in his youth, what his soul had been sad about, and what he had wanted to help. The memory of the suffering world flew away from him as if it were a bad dream he had once.

But Siddhartha's soul could not be put to sleep for long by the wonderful songs and fanciful stories of the beauties or the slaving love of the mistresses, or the sly deceits of the royal overseers. Not even beloved Iazodhara, herself, with her tender caresses could contain the Prince's restless thoughts. Suddenly, everybody realized that he had become sad again. Often, for days on end, Siddhartha sat silent and thoughtful. Among the loud merriment of his courtiers he was pale and trembling as if he had remembered something frightful. At night he restlessly tossed on a soft, silken bed, breaking loose from Iazodhara's hot embrace, screaming, "I remember!" Human beings – brothers, suffering brothers, I remember you, I know everything, I know everything, I am coming!" In these moments his pale face shone wonderfully and his meek eyes were bright with compassion and love.

Then, Iazodhara, frightened, would wake up and would ask him timidly "What is the matter with you, master, where do you want to go?" And she would snuggle up to him covered with tears.

But Siddhartha became steeped again in his sad thoughts. He was tormented by the same obsessive memories and the same unanswerable questions. While the merry sound of music and song was heard, he thought:

"My life passes away like an eternal feast. It is complete with luxury, comfort and merriment but it does not have any meaning or goal. What kind of life is that? What will be the end of this empty and stupid amusement? Is my life given to me for my fun only? And if this were so, why did I find myself neither peace nor happiness among all this luxury, merriment and voluptuousness? Why are my thoughts carried far away from here to that other, hardly seen or known suffering where injustice and evil rule? Why in my dreams does the suffering of my distant brothers appear all the time? Why is my soul straining for this unknown world where unhappy people, overtaxed by excessive work, sink in a boundless sea of blood and tears? Whose mighty voice is calling me and saying, `Stand up, Siddhartha, Maya's son! You are not here for sweet and senseless comfort, nor for delights and indolence. The world needs a savior. Wake up! Unknown, helpless brothers are waiting for you. Help them, love them and you will find the true purpose of your life. Go and save!'"

The merrier the female slaves danced, the louder they sang, the clearer Siddhartha heard that mysterious, inviting voice and the more insistently rose before him that other life of the far away, perishing world. Iazodhara again noticed a change in the Prince's face but she could not understand why he was sad.

Once, in the evening, Siddhartha sat surrounded by his merry court, while the skillful storyteller Chitra told him ancient tales of famous heroes and princes, of gold maned horse and of wondrous distant lands.

Siddhartha heard the tales and smilingly said, "A wonderful tale! Iazodhara, give Chitra your emerald necklace! And what do you think, dear wife, is there really such a wide, big world, such lands overseas? Are there, there such living souls, like yours and mine – such loving hearts? Yes, dear, there are, I know! There are many souls there, dear, and perhaps, they suffer and they are unhappy. They should be loved and helped. Shouldn't they, Iazodhara. You and I don't see them and don't know them. We live in this palace as in a jail; we are feathered by comfort and luxury as by heavy chains and we cannot help our fellow human beings, our brothers. If I had a winged horse as in your tale, Chitra! If I had wide, eagle wings... I would fly above our mountains, I would see everything, whatever is there, behind our high, golden bars, I would see how my brothers live there."

And the courtiers told him, "There, there is the capital of the King, your father, master. There are temples and palaces and royal chambers and your happy and loyal people live there."

And the Prince jumped form his divan and his face lit up.

"Give an order to Channa, my driver, for the chariot to be ready tomorrow at noon! I will drive to the capital to visit it and look at our happy people!"

The King was informed immediately that Siddhartha was about to drive to the city and he said: "Well, fine, let him go! It is time for him to get to know our people."

And the king himself sent messengers and town-criers to all the streets of the city to announce to the people the following order:

"The great King commands all his faithful subjects to clean, tidy up and adorn the whole capital during the night in a holiday spirit. There will be no working or trading tomorrow; there must be neither dirt, nor dust, nor blood, nor smelly hides, nor beggars, nor sick people, nor the blind, nor cripples on the streets. Corpses should not be carried around the town and bonfires should not be prepared. All citizens, young and healthy men, women and children should run up to meet the Prince at noon. They should wear their festive clothes and present gifts to him and greet him. He who does not carry out this royal order will be punished by death.

And the town criers announced the King's order with a loud voice in all streets of the town, from one end to the other, with drums thumping. And the obedient people prepared to realize the order to the fullest.

As soon as the Prince's adorned chariot had appeared from the main gate, hitched by snow white oxen under a brilliant yoke, everyone, as one person, happily ran up to meet him. Men, women and children covered the path of the chariot with sweet-smelling flowers, expensive fabrics, bringing gifts and shouting, "Long live Prince

Siddhartha!"

The Prince was happy, having seen, how his people loved him and said, "Our kingdom is good! Everyone is happy! How easy it is to make everyone happy! I just had to ride out and how happy they are! Even small children know and love me. Drive on, Channa! Go to all the streets. I will enjoy our capital and our amusing gardens!"

And Channa drove him, while a happy crowd surrounded the chariot and ran after it, accompanying it with loud cries, "Long live our gracious prince Siddhartha!"

Translated by **Dragan Milivojevic** from
Yedinenie, No. 2, 1916, pp. 15-35.

CHAPTER ELEVEN

SUNDAY READING
THE BUDDHA

Two-thousand-four-hundred years ago, King Suddhodhana lived in India. He had two wives, two sisters, but he had no children from either. The King was very embittered by it and suddenly when he lost hope, his older wife, Maya, bore a son.

The King could not be happy enough with his son and he did not spare anything to make the boy merry and happy and to teach him all the sciences. Siddhartha—that was his son's name-was a smart, beautiful and good boy. When Siddhartha turned nineteen, his father had him marry his cousin and he settled the young couple in a majestic palace, among beautiful gardens and groves. In the palace and in the gardens, there was everything a human being could desire.

Wishing to see his favorite son always happy and merry, King Suddhodhana gave strict orders to Siddhartha's retinue and servants not to embitter him in any way and to hide him from anything that might make the young heir to the throne sad or bring him melancholy thoughts.

Siddhartha did not leave his estate and he did not see anything spoiled, unclean, or growing old therein. The servants tried to remove or clean everything that might be unpleasant. They not only removed anything unclean, but they also plucked and threw away from the trees and bushes all the faded leaves. Young Siddhartha saw around him everything young, healthy, beautiful and happy.

So lived Siddhartha for more than a year after the wedding. Once, wandering in his gardens, Siddhartha desired to leave his estate, so that he could see how other people lived. Siddhartha ordered his driver Channa to drive him to the city. Everything that he saw, the streets, the houses, the men and women in different clothes, the shops, the wares, all this was new to Siddhartha and it was a pleasant pastime which entertained him.

But, suddenly in one of the streets he saw such a strange man, as he had never seen in his life. The strange man sat contorted by the house wall and groaned loudly and pitifully. The face of the man was pale and wrinkled and he shivered.

"What is the matter with this man?", asked Siddhartha, as he sat in Channa's chariot.

"He must be sick", said Channa,

"What does it mean to be sick?"

"It means that his body became upset."

"And is it hurting him?"

"It must be hurting him."

"Why did it happen to him?"

"Sickness attacked him."

"Can sickness attack anybody?"

"Yes, anybody."

Siddhartha did not ask any more questions.

A little further on an old beggar came to Siddhartha's chariot. Decrepit, with a bent back, with watery red eyes, the old man with difficulty moved his withered, shaking legs and mumbling with his toothless mouth he asked for alms.

"Is he sick, too?", asked Siddhartha.

"No, this is an old man,"said Channa.

"What does an old man mean?"

"It means he became old."

"Why did that happen?"

"He lived for a long time."

"Do all people become old? Does it happen to all who live long?" "To all."

"Will it happen to me, if I live long?"

"It will happen to you and everybody else,"answered Channa.

"Take me home,"said Siddhartha.

Channa drove the horses but at the exit the city they were blocked by people carrying on a stretcher something resembling a human being.

"What is this?" asked Siddhartha.

"It is a corpse,"answered Channa.

"What does a corpse mean? asked Siddhartha.

"A corpse means that life has ended."

Siddhartha stepped down from the chariot and approached the people carrying a corpse. The dead man, with open, fixed, glassy eyes, with bared teeth and ossified limbs lied motionless as only dead people do.

"What happened to him?" asked Siddhartha.

"Death has arrived. Everybody dies."

"Everybody dies," repeated Siddhartha and having returned to the chariot, not raising his head, he reached his home.

Siddhartha sat through the whole day alone in a tucked-away corner in the garden, thinking unceasingly about what he saw.

"All human beings get sick, all human beings die. How can human beings live, knowing that they may become sick at any time, that with every hour they are becoming older, and more disfigured, that they are loosing their powers and moreover they are aware that they may die at any moment and that surely they will die sooner or later. How can you rejoice at anything or do anything, how can you live, knowing certainly that you will die? This should not be so—Siddhartha said to himself. One should find a refuge from this and I will find it and when I find it I will give it to human beings. But, in order to find it, I should leave this palace, where everything diverts my thoughts, I should leave my wife, father and mother and go to hermits and wise men and ask them the meaning of all this."

And having decided on this course of action, Siddhartha called his driver Channa the following night, ordered a horse to be saddled and the gate to be opened. Before leaving the house he went to his wife. She slept. He did not awaken her but he parted with her in his thoughts and stepping lightly, trying not to awaken the sleeping male and female slaves, he left his palace forever and he rode out along on horseback from his father's house.

Having gone as far as his horse could carry him he got off and let her go while he exchanged clothes with a wondering monk. After cutting his hair, he went to Brahman hermits and wise men and asked them to explain what he could not understand: why is sickness, old age and death present and how do we get rid of them? A Brahman accepted him, and explained to him the Brahmanic teaching. This teaching was as follows: the human soul moves from one creature to another, every human being was in his previous life an animal and after death, depending on his life, will migrate into a higher or lower creature. Siddhartha understood this teaching but did not accept it. He lived with Brahmans for half a year and went away to the virgin forests, where there live famous teachers or hermits and he lived with them for six years in fasting and labor. He labored and fasted so much that his fame spread among the people and disciples gathered around him and people began to praise him. But in the teaching of these hermits he did not find what he had been searching for. Temptation came upon him; he began to regret that which he had left and he wanted to return to his father and his wife. But he did not go home. He left his admirers and disciples and went to a place where nobody knew him and he kept thinking about the same thing, how to save oneself from sickness, old age and death.

He was tormented for a long time, even injured once. While he sat under a tree suddenly what he had searched for revealed itself. The way of salvation from suffering, old age and death was open. The way of salvation appeared to him in four truths.

The first truth was that all human beings are subject to suffering. The second truth was that the cause of suffering was passion. The third truth was that in order to escape suffering it is necessary to destroy passion in oneself. The fourth truth was that in order to destroy passion four works are necessary.

In the first place, the heart should be awakened; in the second place, thoughts should be purified; in the third place, one should liberate oneself from malevolence and irritability. In the fourth place, one should awaken in oneself love not only for human beings but for everything alive.

To mortify one's flesh is superfluous, cleansing of the soul from evil thoughts is more necessary than anything else. The true liberation is brought about through love only. Only a human being who has replaced his lustful wishes by love, breaks the chains of ignorance and passion and is saved from suffering and death.

When this teaching was revealed to him, Siddhartha left the wilderness, stopped fasting and mortifying his body and went to the people to preach the truth that he had discovered.

In the beginning, the disciples abandoned him but later, having understood his teaching, they joined him. And in spite of the Brahman's persecution of Siddhartha-Buddha, his teaching spread ever more.

Siddhartha preached his teaching to the people in ten commandments:

The first commandment: Do not kill, save the life of everything alive.

The second commandment: Do not steal, do not rob, do not take away from people the fruits of their labor.

The third commandment: Be chaste in your thoughts and in your life.

The fourth commandment: Do not lie, speak the truth, if necessary fearlessly but lovingly.

The fifth commandment: Do not speak bad about people and do not repeat bad things that are spoken about people.

The sixth commandment: Do not swear.

The seventh commandment: Do not waste time on empty talk, speak your business or be silent.

The eighth commandment: Do not profiteer and do not envy but be happy about your neighbor's happiness.

The ninth commandment: Cleanse your heart from malice, do not hate one but love everyone.

The tenth commandment: Try understanding the truth.

Buddha, moving from place to place, preached his teaching for sixty years.

In his last years, Buddha was weak but he still kept on preaching. On one of his outings he felt death rearing and he stopped and said, "I am parched." His disciples gave him water, he drank some, sat for awhile and went further. Near the river Kharaneavata he stopped again and having sat under a tree he told his disciples, "My death has arrived. Remember, without me, all I have told you." His favorite disciple Ananda, listening to him, could not restrain himself and going aside, he started crying. Siddhartha sent for him right away, saying "Enough, Ananda! Don't cry, don't be upset. Sooner or later we have to part with everything that is dear to us here. Is there anything in this world eternal? My friends, he added, addressing his other disciples, live the way I taught you. Liberate yourself from the web of passion which entangles human beings. Follow that way which I showed you. Remember always that everything corporal breaks down, it is only the truth that is indestructible and eternal. Look for salvation in it." These were his last words.

Set forth by **L. N. Tolstoy**
Tolstoy's Collective Works, Vol. 41, pp. 96-101.
Translated by **Dragan Milivojevic**

CHAPTER TWELVE

KUNALA'S EYES

The King Asoka had a son whose name was Kunala. This name was given to him because he had wonderfully beautiful eyes, as beautiful as the eyes of the Kunala bird. He lived far from the palace steeped in the contemplation of God and eternity. One of the queens fell in love with him but he rejected her love. The queen felt insulted and decided to take revenge on him. When he was sent to a faraway district, she with the help of some girls, enticed from the King his ivory seal and composed an order that the prince's eyes should be gouged. She sealed it with the king's masthead and sent it to the head of the district.

The head, having received the order, did not dare carry it out but the prince, himself, insisted on it. A man was found who agreed to gouge the prince's eyes. When he, with the sound of the crying and the screaming of the crowd, took out one of Kunala's eyes, the prince took the eye in his hands and said: "Why don't you see anymore those shapes, a while ago you saw that coarse flesh fall. How deceived and lost is that one, to whom you are precious and who says: this is I."

When they gouged him in the other eye, he said: "The fleshy eye, the envious treasure, it was gouged from me but I obtained a perfect, unblemished eye of truth. The King does not allow me to be his son any longer but I have become a Son of the Supreme King. In truth, I lost the kingdom with all its connected griefs and sorrows, but I obtained the kingdom of truth which destroys griefs and sorrows."

When he was told that his eyes were gouged at the highest point of their green color, he said, "Let her who sent the order enjoy happiness and life. Thanks to it I received great treasure."

Having lost his sight, he traveled together with his wife through cities and villages, singing songs and playing the flute. When he arrived at his father's city and began to sing under the windows of his palace, the king recognized his voice and ordered that he be invited inside. Having found out that he was deprived of his eyes by an order from that queen, the King ordered her execution. But Kunala told him: "King, if she acted unnobly, you act nobly. The greatest virtue is compassion. I don't feel any anger. I wish only good to the mother or father that had my eyes gouged. If I speak the truth, let my eyes become the same as they were before."

And his eyes shone again with that beautiful and wonderful brightness.

A Buddhist Legend
Translated by **Dragan Milivojevic**
from the Reading Circle: Krug Chtenia
No. 6. Biblioteka L.N. Tolstoi, Moskva, 1912, pp. 125-127

CHAPTER THIRTEEN

IT IS YOU

A tyrant invited a wise man to ask him what was the best way to take revenge on an enemy.

*Tyrant:*Name the fiercest and the slowest torment by which I could torment a criminal to his death.

A Wise Man: Make him recognize his sin and lead him to his conscience.

Tyrant: It seems, in your opinion, there is such a thing as conscience. Listen, my relative insulted me gravely and I cannot be happy and calm until I revenge myself on him. I have thought of the fiercest torments and have not found one equal to my anger.

Wise man: You will not find one because there are no torments with which you can destroy the criminal act itself or the person who committed it. Therefore, the only reasonable thing to do is to forgive.

Tyrant: I know that I cannot undo the things which have been done but why are you saying that I cannot destroy the criminal.

Wise man: Nobody can do that.

Tyrant: What nonsense you are saying. I can destroy him right away in the same way I destroy this lamp here so it will never shine again.

Wise man: You destroyed the lamp but not the light because light is everywhere when it burns. This light exists by itself in everything. You cannot kill a criminal, because you are the one whom you wanted to kill.

Tyrant: You are either crazy or a joker.

Wise man: I am speaking the truth. You are the criminal.

Tyrant: It seems I insulted myself and I will have to destroy myself to atone for the insult?

Wise man: Not at all, no evil can be atoned for by shedding blood;

in order to atone for your insult, you will have to destroy the whole of humanity because it bears the guilt. But even in that case something would remain because as you yourself, aptly said, one cannot undo things which have been done.

Tyrant: No matter how strange your words are, there is a grain of truth in them. Make it clearer.

Wise man: Look around at everything that lives and say to yourself: All this is one. All human beings are brothers, all human beings are in their essence one and the same human being. Before a higher justice there is no evil which can be punished. When you raise your own against your enemy then you are striking yourself because the offender and the offended are in their essence one and the same being.

Tyrant: I don't understand you. I rejoice at the suffering which I cause my enemy. If I were to have been one with him, could that have happened?

Wise man: You rejoice at the suffering you cause your enemy and you don't feel his pain because you are entangled in the illusion of your revengeful, imaginary, personal 'I'. Wake up to the consciousness of your true 'I' and you will feel all his suffering.

Tyrant: This resembles nonsense. Make it so that I would feel one with the criminal.

Wise man: It is hard to do that which you don't want but I will try. I will bring you to such a state where you will share unity with all human beings.

And the wise man, having had this ability brought about in the tyrant's soul the same impressions and feelings which were the consequence of his enemy's offense. In this state the tyrant saw himself as the person that he hated. The motivations of his enemy were clear to him. From this point of view, he could not find any reason for hating him, because he understood that personality is not the true human essence, the knowledge of unity with the whole of mankind. This is the basis for all personalities which appear at different levels.

When the tyrant returned to his previous state he posed to the wise man the following question:

Wise man: Go ahead.

Tyrant: I saw the truth as if through a shroud and found out that behind this shroud the whole of humanity exists as one essence, my friends and enemies are its members, as you and I are. The person who offends his neighbor offends us, as well as the whole of humanity.

Wise man: This is the truth, which I wanted to suggest to you and which is expressed in your words.

Tyrant: How does one live after that in the world.

Wise man: A farm laborer works, a merchant trades, a soldier defends a state, a prince rules. Everybody has his own sphere of activity. An enlightened person does not have such a sphere of activity. What for others in their circle consists of high virtue, for the enlightened person is crime and insanity. Now when you became enlightened you saw a ray of light from the other world, which shines for everybody but is perceived only by a few. Now you cannot return any longer into darkness.

Tyrant: Help me find pure light. I don't want to be an 'I', I don't want anything impermanent, I want to be eternal and impersonal, as you are.

The tyrant after this reconciled with his enemy, realized the purpose and the goal of life and went on the path leading to eternal peace.

Tolstoy's Collective Works, Vol. 34, pp. 138-140.
Translated by **Dragan Milivojevic**

CHAPTER FOURTEEN

MI-TI...
A CHINESE PHILOSOPHER...
THE TEACHING OF ALL-EMBRACING LOVE

Composed by P.A. Bulanzhe
Under the editorship of L.N. Tolstoy
Publishing House "Posrednik" No. 773
*Translated by **Dragan Milivojevic***

Two thousand five hundred years ago, about 500 years before Christ's birth, Confucius' teaching appeared in China.

People in China believed that their dead ancestors should be honored and for this purpose many ceremonies were invented. They believed also that the only good thing in life consisted in honoring one's parents, older people and rulers. If the possibility of taking up an official duty presented itself, it was considered by people to be the highest honor and they all aspired to it. The higher ups treated the lower ones condescendingly and the rich people considered it incompatible with their dignity to accept in their homes a poor person.

In such an official and well-off family Confucius grew up. His father was an official and preparing his son for the same profession, he gave him a good education, as good as it was possible to receive at that time. While reading ancient chronicles and stories of sages, Confucius soon understood that the faith which the people around him professed was not right. Confucius, pondering on the meaning and the purpose of human life, came to the conclusion that each human being has in him a divine origin and that human beings should understand the demands of the divine origin and serve it rather than the deceased ancestors in whose honor different, complex ceremonies were performed.

Having strengthened his understanding of life, Confucius started preaching his teaching that all human beings were brothers and that realizing in themselves the same divine origin, human beings should relate to each other in a friendly way. In such a relationship of human beings to each other there would be neither outstanding persons, nor beggars or the sick or poor. He taught that in order to realize the law of life a person who wants to serve his country in the best way should try in the first place to correct in himself all that is bad and to live virtuously.

Having clarified to himself the true meaning of life, Confucius gave up the office he occupied and started wandering from one region to another explaining to people the importance for them of the new meaning of life.

Rulers of the regions often called on Confucius but after learning from him that they had to change, that they had to forget about themselves and their interests and serve the people and consider only what was good for the people, drove him away, finding his teaching harmful. They drove away also those people who followed Confucius.

The learned sages who lived at the court of the rulers and who were their advisers and who enjoyed their charity behaved towards Confucius in the same way as the rulers of the regions. These sages praised the rulers of the regions and kept explaining to the people the importance of respecting the past, the ceremonies and illustrious persons. Confucius' new teaching appeared to them dangerous and they considered it necessary to fight it in all kinds of ways.

Confucius, nevertheless, inspired by the persecution of the people attracted more and more followers. He, himself, did not write any works, in defense of this teaching although he was an educated man. He did not leave behind him any writings of his teaching. Only his followers wrote down his teaching and wrote works in his defense.

With the death of Confucius in 478 BC, many disciples appeared, and his teaching spread among the people even more. Many writers emerged who occupied themselves with the study of how one should live and what is the meaning of human life, etc. Among them was the philosopher Mi-Ti. This philosopher preached that people should not draw differences among each other, they should not insult each other or cause injury to each other but in all their relationships they should be guided only by love. Mi-Ti believed that if rulers themselves were to be guided in life by love and if they encouraged in people love for each other, then the heavenly (god's) kingdom would appear on earth.

Mi-Ti had many followers and his teaching, as well as that of Confucius, his predecessor, quickly spread in China. But about 150 years after Confucius the philosopher Mencius, who was born in 371 BC and died in 288 BC, appeared as an opponent of Mi-Ti's teaching. Mencius was educated, rich and a clever debater. He proclaimed himself to be Confucius' follower and many consider him to be so even today, but in fact he held to views which were quite different and incompatible with Confucius'.

Mencius, in the first place, thought that sages like himself should be respected by everybody and that they should be honored at the ruler's court. He, himself, during his life, was at the court of two rulers and received for this much money. Mencius held strictly to the former faith of respect for parents and elders. He did not admit that all human beings were equal and that everybody should be treated equally, respecting in everybody the divine origin, as Confucius spoke about it. Mencius considered especially necessary the beneficial position of individuals who were rulers of regions and their assistants, and he heatedly disputed the teaching of philosophers who recognized the equal right of all people to the goods of life.

When Mencius lived at the court of the ruler Tang, the philosopher Hin-Hing came there with his disciples. Hin-Hing arrived with a plough on his shoulders, poorly and coarsely dressed. Hin-Hing taught that everybody should work on the land, earning his bread and that rulers, their officials and sages should also be equally involved. Hin-Hing demonstrated this with his own life. During his wanderings he and his followers made mats and sandals from grass and thereby earned their living. Mencius did not agree with Hin-Hing and argued with him that the division of labor was necessary and that educated people should be at the head of the government. He said that educated people are useful to the country, and that they teach and warn people how to avoid evil and that for this alone, they should be rewarded with supplies and money by uneducated, working people. Tang, the ruler at whose court Mencius lived, liked Hin-Hing's teaching and Mencius, insulted, left this region for good.

Mencius also disagreed with Mi-Ti's teaching. When Mencius saw how Mi-Ti's teaching was spreading he started preaching against it, demonstrating to people that the teaching of all-embracing love was harmful and dangerous. Mencius considered it harmful and dangerous because Mi-Ti preached that no differences should be made among people and that they should be all loved equally. From Mencius' viewpoint rulers and ruled, rich and poor, educated and uneducated were not equal. Mencius also considered this teaching harmful and dangerous because it undermined the power of parents and the respect for them. A human being, in Mencius' opinion, should love and respect his parents and elders above all. According to Mi-Ti's teaching (in Mencius' interpretation) with an equal love for everybody, the love for elders might weaken and as a consequence anarchy might rule in the country,

Mencius' teaching triumphed over the teachings of all other philosophers. There was a time when all of Confucius' followers were executed and exiled and in 213 B.C. by decree of the Chinese emperor Tsing-chi-hoang-ti all the writings of Confucius and his followers were burnt with the exception of Mencius' writings.

Hundreds of years have passed and sages have added so much to Confucius' teaching which he did not preach. It was distorted in such a way that it was completely replaced by Mencius' teaching. And the Chinese began honoring Mencius as one of the closest followers of Confucius. Fortunately, however, Mi-Ti's teaching of the all-embracing love was preserved. A translation of his teaching about the all-embracing love is cited further.

On the All-Embracing Love
Part 1

The task of wise men is to teach people to live in such a way that everybody in the country will live well. And therefore wise men should know why dissatisfaction, squabbling and injustice happen. If they do not know this, sages cannot teach people how to live well. A sage can be compared to a physician, who is called to see a patient. A physician must first determine the course of the illness, only then can he successfully treat the patient. Without a determination of the cause of the illness, all treatment will be useless. Wise men should act in the same way. They should know why squabbling and injustice arise and only after that will they be able to remove them.

The task of wise men is to make life good for all the people in the world. And for this reason they should investigate why squabbles and injustice take place and why the majority of people are dissatisfied. When they find out this, they will realize, that this occurs because of a lack of mutual. When a ruler does not love his sovereign and a son does not like his father, then squabbles and injustice come about. If a son loves only himself and does not like his father, he will act in such a way to make his father's life bad and his own good. A younger brother loves himself and does not love his older brother, therefore he acts in such a way to make his older brother's life bad and his own good. A ruler loves himself and does not like his sovereign, therefore he will act so that his sovereign's life will be bad and his own good. And only because of this squabbles come about. And the same squabbles and injustice would occur if the reverse were true: if a father does not like a son, an older brother does not like a younger one and the people do not like their ruler. If there are squabbles in life, they happen only because of the absence or a lack of mutual love.

Why do stealing and robbery happen? Because a thief loves only himself or his own family and he does not love the family of his neighbor and therefore he steals from his neighbor; he steals in order that he and his family will live better. A robber loves only himself and he does not love his neighbor and therefore, in order to improve his life, he robs and violates his neighbor. Why does all this happen? Only because of a lack of mutual love.

Imagine what would happen if people would love others in the same way they love themselves ... Where would squabbling and injustice come from? If people were concerned about their sons, younger brothers and their ruler as much as they were concerned about themselves how would squabbling and injustice occur? Would it be possible for thieves and robbers to be among people? If everybody would treat other people's property as if it were their own and would respect it as if it were their own—who would rob then? If everybody respected and honored others with the same feeling with which they respected and honored themselves who would steal and kill? There would be no thieves and robbers. Heads of families would not destroy each other, princes would not attack other states. There would be nothing of that.

Only then would order take place in the country, only then would good government be established. And therefore wise men whose task is to participate in removing squabbles and injustice cannot do anything else except profess love and show the destructiveness of hatred.

Therefore it follows it should be preached everywhere that if people start believing in mutual all-embracing love, then, there will be order in a country. If they believe and guide themselves in life by hatred, then there will be squabbles and all kinds of injustice. Therefore, if there is anything which one could advise people it is to love each other.

Part 2

"Yes, learned men and rulers say," it is true. If all-embracing, mutual love were to become supreme, it would be really good. But, the trouble is, it is very difficult to realize this."

Learned men and rulers say this because they do not understand the enormous benefit which would occur if all-embracing love were to be become supreme—that is why they reason like this. But let them remember what happens when they conduct war or seize some city. When men do this they sacrifice their lives for glory and the sacrifice of life is always considered the most difficult matter. Subordinates and common people are ready to do what a ruler commands. Love does not demand such sacrifice, because if a human being loves others, then others respond in the same way, they love him or her; when a human being does good turns for others, they respond in the same way. Only when a human being insults others do they respond to him in the same way and insult him or her. When a human being hates others, then they hate him or her also. Why is it difficult for everybody to live guided by feelings of mutual love? If there is difficulty then it lies in the fact that rulers do not want to guide themselves by a feeling of mutual love and therefore officials and the common people are not guided by it as well.

A Prince named Van lived once. He liked his servants to dress poorly and all of them tried to please him by dressing poorly to the point of indecency. Dressed like this they appeared at the prince's court, walked through the city and were not ashamed. Why? Only because the prince liked it. Another prince, Lin, liked thin officials and his officials tried to eat as little as possible; they were almost starving. They, finally, sunk to the point of having to lean against walls in order not to fall. A year passed and these officials looked as if they were going to die of hunger. Why did they act this way? Because their ruler liked it. Emperor Kou-tsen wanted his officials to be courageous and he taught them courage and bravery. When his officials gathered around him, he ordered a ship to be burnt and in order to test them, he said: "All my treasure is there," he began beating a drum and commanded them to save the treasure from the burning ship. As soon as the officials heard the drum beat, they threw themselves on the ship into the fire and died. And when more than a hundred men had died he called upon the other remaining men to save his treasure.

When people refuse food and wear rags, bringing shame upon themselves, when they sacrifice even their lives for glory, they must suffer through exceedingly difficult things but when a ruler wants this his subjects are ready to do all these things. People could bring enormous benefit to themselves and to others if they were guided in their lives by mutual love, by doing good to others; this is much less difficult than pleasing their rulers.

"Yes, rulers and officials would say, "all this would be good, if people were to show mutual love; but to realize this, is just as impossible as raising a mountain, and moving it to another place."

No, it is not true, this comparison is not appropriate. In order to raise a mountain and move it to another place a supernatural force is needed and this, as a matter of act, from ancient times until now, nobody has been able to do. The realization in life of the principle of mutual love is a completely different matter: Love is possible, people have shown it and show it now, they have always exchanged and continue to exchange mutual services and have done and continue to do good to each other.

So that, if only rulers really and sincerely wanted their people to prosper and not to live in poverty, if they really wanted to rule well and spare people horrible squabbles, and the disorders of life, then, they would let themselves be guided by the principle of mutual love. That is how it was in ancient times, when there were wise rulers.

Part 3

The task of wise men should be to elicit in people everything that brings about the spreading of goodness among them and which prevents that which is disastrous for people.

What are the main disasters for peoples? These disasters are, in the first place, attacks of states against other states; in the second place, they are violence and insults, which distinguished and powerful people inflict on those who are weak and insignificant. In the third place, they are robberies by the few of the many. In the fourth place there is the oppression of the weak because of the deception of simple people by clever cheats. In the fifth place, there is the cruelty and injustice of rulers. In the sixth place, there is a lack of goodness on the part of parents and disobedience on the part of children. In the seventh place there is all unpleasantness which people cause each other: arson, thievery, the draining off of water from irrigated fields, etc.

From where does it all come? Not because people love each other and wish to do good turns to each other? No. On the contrary, all this comes about because people hate and try to insult each other. But, why do people hate and try to insult each other? It is because people love some and don't love others—they make differences between people. When misery exists in a country it is only because people make differences between each other.

Only one thing can save people from the miseries which they inflict on each other: this is a love without differences, an equal love. In order for such a love to transform those who hold another view, it is necessary that rulers be ready to treat others as they treat themselves, that fathers or heads of families, relate to other families as they do to their own. And if rulers would not attack each other and fathers or heads of families would not insult other families, then, armies which are maintained to attack each other, would not be necessary and there would be no hostility between families. And if such a blessing were to occur, it would not arise from hatred, but from love for others, a love which does not make differences between people. And for this reason if prosperity can be established among people, then, it can be only as a result of a love for each other, which does not distinguish between people. Differences among people originate in the judgments we lend against them; we consider some good and others bad, but nobody has the right to judge.

The one who judges others should have the means of improving them. To judge people and not be able to change them is the same as saving a person from fire in order to drown him in water. If one does not know how to improve people, one should not judge them. When the principle of love spreads among people, they will listen and look at each other and really see and hear one another. The strong ones will, then, help the weak ones and the educated people will instruct the uneducated ones. Old men and those without relatives will find the people who will support them and help them live the remainder of their lives in security while young people and children without parents will also find people who will support them and give them an opportunity to stand firmly on their feet in life.

But, learned people, stubbornly, insist on their own opinion and say: "Perhaps love is a good thing, but it is impossible that all people would love each other."

Let us take the example of two persons: one believes that it is necessary to distinguish between people, the other believes that everybody should be loved. The first one says: "How can I take care of another person in the same way I do myself? How can I take care of someone else's parents in the same way I do my own?" Reasoning this way he may see another person hungry and not feed him, he may see another person cold and not clothe him, he may see a sick person without helping him and he may see a dead person and not bury him. Whatever the judgments of this person are his actions follow them. The other man says: "I heard that someone who wants to live happily among people will take care of others in the same way he takes care of himself and his own parents. Only acting this way, can a person live happily." And reasoning in this way, he, upon seeing another person hungry, will feed him, he will clothe the person who is cold, take care of the sick one and bury the dead one.

The reasoning as well as the actions of these two persons will be completely opposite. What kind of reasoning is considered correct by anybody who finds himself in a difficult situation, who needs help? And therefore it is quite incomprehensible how all these clever and learned people don't understand the importance of the idea that all people should be guided by the principle of love. But even if people recognize that this may be good and possible for subjects in relation to a ruler, they consider this impossible for a ruler in relation to his subjects. It is impossible, they say, for a ruler to love all his subjects in the same way he does himself.

But if we compare two rulers-one, who says: how can I love my people as I do myself? this is contrary to human nature," and another one who first takes care of people and then of himself which one of the two will people prefer when bad times come? Everybody, of course, will tell you that he would prefer the ruler who forgets about himself for the sake of the people's benefit.

But learned people nevertheless continue to assert their opinions. They say love for everybody is impossible because it will undermine the exclusive attachment of children to their parents, it will violate filial piety.

But if a son really loves his parents, then he will naturally try to secure their happiness. And if this is so, then he will strive naturally so that other people will love his parents and show goodness to them and in no way hate his parents and try to insult them. And if he wants his parents to be loved what should he do? It is obvious; he should relate lovingly to other people so that others will love his parents. One can also answer to this objection of learned men with one response: Only by loving all people is it possible to better show one's love and respect for one's parents.

Why doesn't mutual love spread among people? Only because rulers don't understand all of its meaning in the life of people. If rulers and other powerful men would understand the entire meaning of mutual love, which does not differentiate between anybody, and would encourage it among people, then all-embracing mutual love would spread among the people of the whole world so naturally, as naturally as fire rises upward and water flows downward.

Kunala's Eyes

The King Asoka had a son whose name was Kunala. This name was given to him because he had wonderfully beautiful eyes, as beautiful as the eyes of the Kunala bird. He lived far from the palace steeped in the contemplation of God and eternity. One of the queens fell in love with him but he rejected her love. The queen felt insulted and decided to take revenge on him. When he was sent to a faraway district, she with the help of some girls, enticed from the King his ivory seal and composed an order that the prince's eyes should be gouged. She sealed it with the king's masthead and sent it to the head of the district.

The head, having received the order, did not dare carry it out but the prince, himself, insisted on it. The man was found who agreed to gouge the prince's eyes. When he, with the sound of the crying and the screaming of the crowd, took out one of Kunala's eyes, the prince took the eye in his hands and said: "Why don't you see anymore these shapes, a while ago you saw that coarse flesh fall. How deceived and lost is that one, to whom you are precious and who says: this is I."

When they gouged him in the other eye, he said: "The fleshy eye, the envious treasure, it was gouged from me, but I obtained a perfect, unblemished eye of truth. The King does not allow me to be his son any longer but I have become a Son of the Supreme King. In truth, I lost the kingdom with all its connected griefs and sorrows, but I obtained the kingdom of truth which destroys griefs and sorrows."

When he was told that his eyes were gouged at the highest point of their green color, he said, "Let her who sent the order enjoy happiness and life. Thanks to it I received great treasure."

Having lost his sight, he traveled together with his wife through cities and villages, singing songs and playing the flute. When he arrived at his father's city and began to sing under the windows of his palace, the king recognized his voice and ordered that he be invited inside. Having found out that he was deprived of his eyes by an order from that queen, the King ordered her execution. But Kunala told him: "King, if she acted unnobly, you act nobly. The greatest virtue is compassion. I don't feel any anger. I wish only good to the mother or father that had my eyes gouged. If I speak the truth, let my eyes become the same as they were before."

And his eyes hone again with that beautiful and wonderful brightness.

A Buddhist Legend
Translated by **Dragan Milivojevic**
from the Reading Circle: Krug Chtenia
No. 6. Biblioteka L. N. Tolstoi, Moskva, 1912, pp. 125-127

SOURCES

1. **Dragan Milivojevic** – *Introduction*.
2. **Dragan Milivojevic** – "Tolstoy's Views on Buddhism"
(first published in *Tolstoy Studies Journal*, Vol. 3, 1990, 62-75).
3. **Vytas Dukas, Glenn A. Sandstrom** – "Taoistic Patterns
in War and Peace" (from *SEEJ*, Vol. XIV, No. 2, 1970, 182-193).
4. **Dragan Milivojevic** – "Some Buddhist Inklings in Prince Andrei
and Pierre Bezukhov in War and Peace".
5. **Harry Hill Walsh** – "A Buddhistic Leitmotif in Anna Karenina"
(from *Canadian-American Slavic Studies*, Vol. 11, No. 4
(Winter 1977), 561-67).
6. **Dragan Milivojevic** – "Tolstoy's Concept of Reason
as Applied to Buddhism" (from Wimal Dissanayake
and Steven Bradbury – *Literary History, Narrative and Culture*,
University of Hawaii, 1989, 104-113).
7. **Nathan T. Carr** – "Leo Tolstoy and Lao Tzu's Tao-Te Ching:
Tolstoy as a Taoist Sage".
8. **Dragan Milivojevic** – "Some Similarities
and Differences Between Tolstoy's Concept of Identity
and Vocation and Their Parallels in Hinduism"
(*Tolstoy Studies Journal*, Vol. 4, 1991, 97-103).
9. **A. Syrkin** – "The 'Indian' in Tolstoy"
Wiener Slawistischer Almanach, Vol. 23, 1989, 85-114.

Translations from Russian:

10. L. Tolstoy, in cooperation with P. Bulanzhe –
"Life and Teaching of Siddartha Gautama called the Buddha,
that is The Most Perfect One" from *Zhizn'Dl'a Vsekh*, No. 3,
March 1910, 110-127.

11. **L. Tolstoy**, editor, posthumously, with the cooperation
of Chertkov – "Siddartha Called Buddha, That is the Holy One,
His Life and Teaching" from *Yedinenie*, No. 2, 1916, 15-35.

12. **L. Tolstoy** – "Sunday Reading, the Buddha,"
Polnoe Sobranie Sochinenij, Vol. 41, 96-101.

13. **L. Tolstoy**, editor – "Kunala's Eyes" *Krug Chtenija*, No. 6,
Biblioteka L. N. Tolstoy, Moskva 1912, 125-127.

14. **L. Tolstoy** – "It is You" *Polnoe Sobranie Sochinenij*,
Vol. 34, 138-140.

15. **L. Tolstoy**, in cooperation with P. Bulanzhe –
"Mi-Ti, The Teaching of All-Embracing Love" *Posrednik*, No. 773.